OUR SEARCH TO
KNOW THE LORD

OUR SEARCH TO KNOW THE LORD

GEORGE W. PACE

Deseret Book Company
Salt Lake City, Utah

Library of Congress Cataloging-in-Publication Data

Pace, George W.
    Our search to know the Lord / George W. Pace.
      p. cm.
    Bibliography: p.
    Includes index.
    ISBN 0-87579-136-0
    1. Spiritual life — Mormon authors. I. Title.
BX8656.P27   1988
248.4'89332 — dc19   88-18862
                                           CIP

Printed in the United States of America

10   9   8   7   6   5   4   3   2

CONTENTS

Chapter 1

THE PEARL OF GREATEST PRICE

"The kingdom of heaven is like unto a merchant man, seeking goodly pearls: who, when he had found one pearl of great price, went and sold all that he had, and bought it." (Matthew 13:45–46.) In the church and kingdom of God, there are many pearls of great price, but one pearl is of greatest price and of greatest value. What is it?

The Savior told us: "And this is life eternal, that they might know thee the only true God, and Jesus Christ, whom thou hast sent." (John 17:3.) There simply isn't anything more important in heaven or on earth than to know, to really know, with a perfect knowledge, the Father and the Son.

The observations that follow are my attempt to explore why it is so important to know the Father and the Son and what that knowledge means in our individual lives. It is one thing to know by the power of the Spirit what the characteristics and attributes of God are, but to *apply* that knowledge is what effects a tremendous change in our lives.

For example, I'm convinced that most of us believe that it is a great thing to know that Joseph Smith was a prophet of God, but it is an even greater thing to experience, through the gospel he restored, the kinds of things he experienced. It's marvelous to know that the heavens have opened and that great powers are available to us in our day, but what will enable us to become true Saints is to become worthy to experience those powers ourselves.

If what changes our lives is experiencing the powers of the Father through his Son, Jesus Christ, then our relationship with them is of supreme importance. Joseph Smith learned that he could speak with the Father and the Son, that they knew him by name, and that they were anxious and pleased to answer his prayers and bless him with their powers. We too can gain a similar understanding of the Father and the Son and have a similar relationship with them.

As beautiful and meaningful as our relationships are with one another, our relationship with our Creator and Redeemer can be the most beautiful relationship we experience in mortality. Indeed, by coming to know the Father and the Son through the experience of feeling their love and influence in our lives, our relationships with others will take on a deeper, more godlike meaning. In fact, it seems fundamental in the gospel to believe that the kind of relationship we have with God will determine the kind of relationship we have with others.

A meaningful life, an abundant life, is made up of personal relationships with one another, and it seems natural to believe that eternal life will be made up of similar relationships. Perhaps that is what Joseph Smith meant when he said, "That same sociality which exists amongst us here will exist among us there only it will be coupled with eternal glory which we do not enjoy now." (*The Words of Joseph Smith*, p. 169.) The Prophet Joseph also said that no man's name will be sealed in the Lamb's book of life until he has a perfect love. (See *Teachings of the Prophet Joseph Smith*, p. 9.) A perfect love for whom? Surely he meant a perfect love for God and for all men. (See 2 Nephi 31:20.)

What marvelous relationships can we anticipate having here and in the hereafter with gods, angels, and one another if we are faithful in Christ! Paul the apostle seemed to glimpse the greatness of our future relationships when he said, "Eye hath not seen, nor ear heard, neither have entered into the heart of man, the things which God hath prepared for them that love him." (1 Corinthians 2:9.) Our experiences with the Father and the Son are most sacred and distill in us an ever-increasing sense of awe and respect for them, and yet we can feel a profound closeness to God, a closeness that is warm, comforting, constant, and marvelously fulfilling.

I want to testify of an association with a Heavenly Father and a divine Redeemer who love beyond comprehension all of the children of men and yet reserve for the obedient in Christ the designation of "friend" (John 15:14; D&C 84:63, 77) and give to such the promise of eternal life. With all the glory, honor, and majesty of the Father and the Son, their promise to us is that their infinite power and love can be translated into such personal and heart-touching experiences as "wip[ing] away all tears from our eyes" (Revelation 7:17), "heal[ing] the brokenhearted" (Luke 4:18), leading us by the hand, and giving us answer to our prayers (see D&C 112:10). We can be endowed with the very same love that Deity possesses (see Moroni 7:46–47), a love that at times will seem to consume our very flesh (see 2 Nephi 4:21).

The Father and the Son are so aware of all their creations that they are mindful when a sparrow falls. (See Matthew 10:29.) Will they not then be mindful of our heartaches, concerns, and hopes? It seems to me to be a valid proposition that our daily association with those we worship can become so meaningful that the time will come when we will know from them with a perfect knowledge that the path we are following—that is, the lives we are living and the sacrifices we have made—is totally acceptable to the Lord. (See *Lectures on Faith*, p. 38.)

How marvelous it is that we have been invited to increase our faith and our ability to communicate with God so that "we may converse with him as one man converses with another." (*Teachings of the Prophet Joseph Smith*, p. 345; see also Ether 12:39.)

One of the greatest teachings of the restored gospel is that the Lord has commanded us to prepare ourselves while we are yet in the flesh that we might see him. (See D&C 67:10.) Indeed, "thus saith the Lord: It shall come to pass that every soul who forsaketh his sins and cometh unto me, and calleth on my name, and obeyeth my voice, and keepeth my commandments, shall see my face and know that I am." (D&C 93:1.) Such an invitation from Deity speaks volumes about the potentially close, sacred association we can have with him. Further, the Lord on a few

3

occasions has not only invited faithful Saints to see him but also to "thrust their hands into his side, and . . . feel the prints of the nails in his hands and in his feet." (3 Nephi 11:15.)

In a marvelous way the Prophet Joseph is our great exemplar in this dispensation of what it means to know God and what feelings and hopes it will be most natural for us to have toward the Lord as we try to draw close to him. On one occasion, the Prophet declared, "Jesus Christ, the Son of God, is my Great Counselor." (*History of the Church*, 6:93.) On another occasion, Joseph Smith had been separated from his wife, Emma, for some time and had hoped to receive a letter from her. When he didn't, being very disappointed, he wrote: "I will try to be contented with my lot knowing that God is my friend. In him I shall find comfort. I have given my life into his hands. I am prepared to go at his call. I desire to be with Christ. I count not my life dear to me only to do his will." (Quoted in LaMar C. Berrett, in *BYU Studies*, Summer 1971, p. 520.)

Let me conclude my discussion of the importance of knowing God and knowing the kind of relationship we can have with the Father and the Son with an account of a vision that was given to Joseph Smith and recorded by Heber C. Kimball. The Prophet Joseph "saw the Twelve going forth, and they appeared to be in a far distant land. After some time they unexpectedly met together, apparently in great tribulation, their clothes all ragged, and their knees and feet sore. . . . He (Joseph) saw until they had accomplished their work, and arrived at the gate of the celestial city; there Father Adam stood and opened the gate to them, and as they entered he embraced them one by one and kissed them. He then led them to the throne of God, and then the Savior embraced each one of them and kissed them, and crowned each one of them in the presence of God." (Orson F. Whitney, *Life of Heber C. Kimball*, pp. 93–94.)

I believe we are well within the mark to assume that all relationships we have with others which are good and beautiful are but a shadow of the relationship we can acquire, through the restored gospel, with our Heavenly Father and his Son Jesus Christ by the power of the Holy Ghost.

Along with the recognition that our relationship with the

Father and the Son can be very real and very personal comes the recognition that because of our relationship with them, our experiences with others will improve and in time be perfected. It is crucial to obtain the pearl of greatest price — knowing the Father and the Son. The Savior said, "Neither knoweth any man the Father, save the Son, and he to whomsoever the Son will reveal him." (Matthew 11:27.) The Son came to the earth to reveal the Father to us. There really isn't any other way to know the Father than to come to know the Son. As we come to know the Son, we simultaneously come to know the Father. Indeed, the greatest revelation of God our Heavenly Father is Jesus Christ.

As we search the scriptures, which are so Savior-centered, and understand more fully the life and mission of the Lord and Savior, we are simultaneously coming to know the mind, will, glory, and reality of the Father. The Father is the Author of the plan of salvation; the Son, his life, and his mission are a perfect reflection of the plan — to testify of the greatness and glory of the Father. To honor the Son is to honor the Father. To know the Son is to know the Father.

Let me elaborate further on this theme. The Savior said, "I came down from heaven, not to do mine own will, but the will of him that sent me." (John 6:38.) Further, the Savior confirmed to the Israelites on the American continent this same truth when as a resurrected being he stated: "I came into the world to do the will of my Father, because my Father sent me. And my Father sent me that I might be lifted up upon the cross." (3 Nephi 27:13–14.) For us to glimpse the majestic power and feeling of the infinite atonement is to glimpse the mind, the feeling, and the power of God the Father, for it was he who sent his Son to fulfill its awesome requirements.

Paul the apostle acknowledged the Father as the author of the plan of redemption and His role through Christ in fulfilling that plan when he said: "All things are of God, who hath reconciled us to himself by Jesus Christ, and hath given to us the ministry of reconciliation; to wit, that God was in Christ, reconciling the world unto himself." (2 Corinthians 5:18–19.)

Perhaps one of the most powerful of many scriptures on this

subject is the following: "No man knoweth . . . who the Father is, but the Son, and he to whom the Son will reveal him." (Luke 10:22; see also Matthew 11:27.) Paul's statement to Timothy also confirms powerfully that the only way to the Father is through the Son: "There is one God, and one mediator between God and men, the man Christ Jesus." (1 Timothy 2:5.)

Christ, then, is the revealer of the Father. He is "the way, the truth, and the life." (John 14:6.) The Savior said that all men should honor him even as they honor the Father. (See John 5:23.) To become members of The Church of Jesus Christ of Latter-day Saints is to commence the journey of coming to know the Father through Christ.

As we seek for eternal life, we acknowledge the Savior's teaching that "no man cometh unto the Father, but by me." (John 14:6.) When we accept the Savior as the Son of God, we recognize that in his name and his name alone is salvation possible. (See 2 Nephi 25:20.)

It is my feeling, to emphasize again, that the greatest revelation of the Father is Jesus Christ; that for us to honor the Father we must acquire a mighty knowledge of his Son; that out of that knowledge will come adequate faith to become like our Redeemer; that he, Christ, will then introduce us to the Father so that we might return safely to him.

Is it any wonder that the first principle of the gospel is faith in Jesus Christ? And yet, again, because the Father and the Son are one, to have faith in Christ is also to have faith in the Father. Is it just a coincidence that the Book of Mormon, another testament of Christ, has 3,925 references to the Savior in 531 pages, or an average of one reference for approximately every 1.5 verses? (See Susan Easton Black, *Finding Christ through the Book of Mormon*, pp. 15–16.) Is it not most natural that Nephi testified that everything that has been given from God to man is the typifying of Christ? (See 2 Nephi 11:4.)

The Savior came to be the mediator between us and the Father. President Joseph Fielding Smith declared: "After Adam's transgression he was shut out of the presence of the Father who has remained hidden from his children to this day, with few exceptions wherein righteous men have been privileged with the glorious privilege of seeing him." (*Man: His Origin and Destiny,* p. 304.) The Father "hid" himself so that we might know that the only way we could "find" him was to acquire a mighty faith in his beloved Son and be obedient to him.

Therefore, because Jesus is the Savior and Redeemer of the world and the key to knowing the Father, my central theme is the tremendous importance of coming to know Jesus Christ. It involves not simply sensing the remarkable power that is available through the gospel of Jesus Christ but recognizing that he, Christ, is the source of that power. It involves not merely having a testimony of the divinity of the restored Church but also actually acquiring through that restored Church a profound knowledge of the very creator of heaven and earth and making a commitment to obey him. What I would like to explore with you has to do with placing the many pearls of the gospel, as it were, in perspective so as to accent that pearl of greatest price, recognizing that the full value of those pearls is achieved when you and I accept them and use them as a means of developing a full and complete relationship with the Father through his beloved Son.

Even to approach the topic of what it means to know the Father and the Son is an awesome undertaking and one that would be out of the question if I didn't know that Jesus is the Christ, the literal and eternal Son of God. I know that through faith in Christ we can be forgiven of our sins, have our fallen nature changed, and enjoy an abhorrence for sin. I know that our Lord is a God of power, for I have seen him make bare his mighty arm and enable the otherwise impossible to be accomplished. The promise has been burned into my soul by the whisperings of the Spirit that if we are faithful in keeping the commandments and honoring every word that proceeds from the mouth of God, we will come to know the Savior marvelously well. (See Mosiah 12:24; Jeremiah 9:23–24.) In time, the Lord will transform us into his image, and ultimately we may have the privilege, perhaps while yet in mortality, of seeing his face. The capstone of my testimony, the essence of what I have to say, is that we can come to know the Savior better than we know any other person on earth—that the Savior can have, and indeed must have, a greater effect on our lives than the combined effect of everyone else we know if we ever hope to fulfill the will of the Father and return to his presence.

Obtaining a Greater Faith

My own experience of gradually growing in awareness of the Father through the Savior and of the Savior's place as the center of all things has not been atypical. I was raised as an active member of a small country ward in southern Idaho. I sensed early in my life that the testimonies I heard in the small frame chapel each fast and testimony meeting were sincere and indeed true. I felt very positive about the teachings I heard and the concepts I learned in the many auxiliary meetings I attended. I observed also that the more diligently I tried to keep the commandments and to stay in close contact with the Church, although I often fell far short, the more peace I felt in my heart. And even though much of the motivation behind my activity in the Church was probably social (there were some really attractive girls in the ward), my involvement in the Church was uplifting and beneficial.

Nevertheless, had I been asked in my late teens how I felt about the Church — that is, did I know the doctrines of the Church were true? — my response would have been something like, "I really think there is a strong possibility that the Church just might be true," or "There is absolutely no question in my mind that a lot of people I know really know the Church is true," or "Oh, I sure hope the Church is true!" In any event, even though I felt very good about the Church — indeed, there was absolutely no question in my mind that the effect of the Church in my life was very positive — I knew there had to be much, much more to my membership. I sensed that I hadn't yet found that pearl of great price that would give greater meaning to my membership in the Church and enable me to obtain a greater power to enjoy life more abundantly.

Somewhere along the line, I came to the conclusion that I desperately needed to learn more fully for myself by personal revelation that Joseph Smith was a prophet of God and that the true Church of Jesus Christ was indeed restored to the earth. I determined that the quickest, surest way to do that was to read the Book of Mormon and pray mightily about it. Consequently, in my nineteenth year and while farming my father's farm, I decided to tuck a copy of the Book of Mormon in my back pocket and take it with me everywhere I went. I carried out my plan with some determination. Whenever I got a chance between changes of water while irrigating, while waiting for the final preparation of my meals, and during every other spare moment I could find, I read the Book of Mormon with genuine intensity for the first time. I had, of course, read portions of it before, both in the auxiliaries and in seminary, but not really of my own volition and not with real intent. Along with diligently reading the Book of Mormon every time I got a chance, for the first time in my life, I also lifted up my voice many times each day in mighty vocal prayer and pleaded for the witness of the Spirit that I might know that the Book of Mormon is true.

My experience that summer of reading the Book of Mormon and fervently pouring out my heart in prayer changed my life. Before the summer was half over, it seemed I had walked into a whole new dimension of life. The unseen things of the Spirit started to become more real than the things of the world. There gradually deepened in my heart the unquestionable assurance that what I was reading was true, and with that revealed assurance, Joseph Smith's divine calling as a prophet of God emerged as my great anchor in the reality of the restoration of the gospel. With those assurances, there seemed to come to me a desire to be more personally involved in the great unfolding drama of the redemption of man, a feeling that there was a preparation to be made, a mission to be fulfilled, a reason for being. Incidentally, I've noticed over the years that when anyone obtains a sure testimony of the divine origins of the Church, invariably that person will get excited about doing all he or she can do to effectively build the kingdom.

As beautiful and as great as those feelings were, however, I still hadn't glimpsed what the real pearl was. One experience I had that summer made a particularly deep impression on me and seemed to bring me a step closer to finding the pearl of greatest price. I had been irrigating alfalfa, a task that gave me several hours for reading interspersed with vocal prayer. About midmorning, I was sitting on a small bridge made of railroad ties that crossed the irrigation ditch. I was dangling my rubber boots in the water to keep my feet cool. As I sat there reading and reflecting, there came to me a quiet but particularly powerful witness of the Spirit that what I was reading was true. The feeling was so intense that I instinctively glanced heavenward. Although I didn't see anyone or hear anything, I seemed to feel strongly the presence of Nephi—so strongly, in fact, that I wouldn't have been at all surprised to have seen him standing there. It seemed to me that he spoke to my heart and said: "I want you to know that what you're reading is true, for I wrote it. I want you to know that I have seen the Lord and talked with him. I have been carried by his Spirit to the tops of high mountains and have been shown marvelous things. (See 2 Nephi 4:24–25.) And I want you to know he has endowed me with great power to fulfill all the commandments he has given me."

What a great assurance it was for me to feel so deeply and powerfully the truth of Nephi's words, and especially to know of his relationship with the Lord and of the great power the Lord had given him. As the summer continued and I persisted in reading and lifting up my voice in prayer, there came into my heart, by the power of the Spirit, an even greater and more exciting idea, an idea that helped me learn more fully what the gospel was really all about. It seemed to come from the Spirit and reflected the testimony of Nephi. The message was: "It's wonderful that you now know that what I have written is true, and that you know I have seen and talked with Christ and have received of his marvelous power in my life. But it is even more important for you to know that you, too, can see him as I have seen him; that you, too, can talk with him as I have; and that you, too, can obtain his mighty power to help you accomplish all he would have you do." (See 1 Nephi 10:17, 19.)

What an electrifying, soul-transforming thought that was to me! It has continued to be the mainspring of my spiritual motivation and the greatest idea planted in my heart through the restored gospel. I learned later that the Prophet Joseph Smith had taught this very principle. He said, "God hath not revealed anything to Joseph, but what He will make known unto the

Twelve, and even the least Saint may know all things as fast as he is able to bear them." He stated further that "reading the experience of others, or the revelations given to *them,* can never give *us* a comprehensive view of our condition and true relation to God. Knowledge of these things can only be obtained by experience through the ordinances of God set forth for that purpose." (*Teachings of the Prophet Joseph Smith,* pp. 149, 324.)

I began to see the connection between Nephi's knowledge of the Savior and the power of revelation he enjoyed. I began to realize that his ability to explain Isaiah so beautifully, to teach the doctrine of Christ so powerfully, to work such a mighty and everlasting work, came because he knew the Savior so well and was in such marvelous contact with him. But even more important was the realization that he was saying, in effect, "You can know him, even Christ, as well as I do, and in knowing him, you will not only enjoy his marvelous power even as I have done, but you will grow in a marvelous knowledge of the Father."

What a great appreciation I feel for Nephi and for all the prophets for having inspired me with such great ideas, for they have changed my life. Surely all of us are grateful for the tremendous testimonies of others that Jesus is the Christ, our advocate with the Father, that he is a God of power, a God of miracles. But unless each one of us experiences the reality of the Savior, comes to know him as the prophets have, and comes to enjoy the selfsame power, we have failed to take full advantage of their testimonies, and we have failed to receive the greatest blessing the church and kingdom of God can bestow upon us, and that blessing is the pearl of greatest price: to know the Father through Christ.

The gradual awakening in my heart of the truth that the only way to know the Father is by first coming to know the Son kindled within me a greater and greater desire to learn of him. I determined to try to use the Spirit more effectively, to try more diligently to magnify my callings in the priesthood, and to try to understand how all the programs and efforts of the church and kingdom of God could bring me to the marvelous knowledge I desperately desired. As the years slipped by, special experiences I had from time to time seemed to beckon me to strive more diligently to know the Lord more fully. These experiences reminded me powerfully that if I would center my life in Christ, if I would see him as the source of all blessings, if I would root the ordinances, the principles, and the priesthood in him, the divine Redeemer, if everything I did would be done to bring honor and glory to him and to the Father, then in time I would know both him and the Father better than I knew anyone else on earth.

One experience that has kept alive my hope that someday I might know the Savior as well as have the prophets, both ancient and modern, occurred while I was in the mission home in Salt Lake City just before leaving on my mission. There were approximately three hundred missionaries assembled in the old Barratt Hall on Temple Square (the hall has since been torn down) to be instructed by various brethren, most of whom were General Authorities. Don Colton, the mission home president, announced the next speaker, whose topic was the atonement of Christ. I had not heard of that particular man and had no idea what to expect, but as his talk on the Atonement unfolded, I felt the fire of the Spirit come into my heart with a greater intensity than I had ever felt before. I knew without question that the man speaking enjoyed a deep and profound knowledge of the Savior—an understanding of Christ and a commitment to him that went far beyond the words he used. I felt a strong assurance that someday I too could know the Lord as well as the good man who was speaking knew him. I say assurance, but in that most profound feeling I felt an invitation—a powerful invitation—to come to know the Lord, and with that assurance and invitation, I vowed with all the energy of my heart that someday I would! Of all the beautiful, meaningful talks I heard in the mission home, no other left such a lasting, motivating impression on my heart as did this one. I am sure I will forever hold in high esteem the first living mortal who successfully fired my entire being with the idea that I too could know Christ in a marvelous way and in so doing bring greater honor to the Father.

Other experiences since have encouraged me to continue my quest to really know the Savior. For example, on the opening day of April general conference one year, I had returned from a fifty-mile hike with thirty Boy Scouts. I gathered the family together in the family room to watch on television the conference proceedings. President Harold B. Lee announced the next speaker, and as he did, I felt unusually excited to hear that individual talk. When he commenced, he said that he wanted to talk about the Savior. The Spirit was so intense, so powerful, that I could hardly hear with my outer ears. I felt an even more intense desire to know the Savior with a perfect knowledge. I believe I shall never forget in time or eternity the effect of that Spirit-borne message. (See Boyd K. Packer, in Conference Report, Apr. 1971, pp. 122–25.)

It is important to remember that every principle of the gospel and every commandment are significant and play a vital role in our salvation and exaltation. We desperately need to know the entire gospel, to catch a vision of the width and depth of the entire plan of salvation, to know the mysteries as well as the practical day-by-day things. I would be remiss as a member of the Church if I did not declare with every fiber of my being that what has changed my life the most, what has caused me to want to serve others the most, what has revealed the Father to me more completely than anything else, is the idea that I can know the Savior myself and that I must come to him in order to fulfill the will of the Father. It isn't enough to know his gospel, his commandments, the doctrine of the priesthood; we must, in addition, know the Master himself.

All things — all creation and all of Heavenly Father's dealings with people on earth — point to Christ and center in him. Once this idea is embedded in our hearts, the marvelous idea of a Savior-centered universe will reveal the reality and majesty of the Father and the Son in such a way that with every breath and thought we will acknowledge them, and our every action will be to the honor and glory of God our Heavenly Father.

All Things Point to Christ

I once listened to a Sunday School lesson on Abraham's sacrifice of Isaac. I was somewhat intrigued that the lesson was presented, discussed, and summarized without any mention of the Savior's atoning sacrifice. The principles of faith and obedience were quite effectively explored, but the greater message of the imagery, or typology, foreshadowing the sacrifice of the Lord was completely missed. I was disappointed because I had been convinced from my scripture study that, as Nephi stated, "All things which have been given of God from the beginning of the world, unto man, are the typifying of him." (2 Nephi 11:4.) I felt that surely this was the case in a special way with Abraham's experience.

What a realization it is that everything given from God to man is given to typify Christ and direct our attention fully to him, that we might comprehend his atonement and his gospel. The very heavens and the earth were created to bear record of him. (See Moses 6:63.) Christ is the light of the sun, the moon, and the stars. (See D&C 88:7–9.) It is he who lights every person who comes into the world (see John 1:9), and it is he who enables us to live, move, and have our being (see Acts 17:28). To see the sun in its majesty, the heavenly planets moving in their courses, the light reflecting from the eyes of others, to enjoy life in its infinitely varied forms, indeed, to experience spiritual life moment by moment, is to see the Savior in and through all things.

In addition, the events in the scriptures are also in similitude of Christ. One is well within the mark to state that these events are veritable gold mines of revelation about the Father revealed through Christ. Consider the powerful message in the experience of Moses offering deliverance to the Israelites who were dying from the bites of the poisonous serpents. Moses lifted a brazen serpent high on a pole and promised that all who would look would live. This action was taken in similitude of the Savior's being lifted on the cross that "as many as should look upon the Son of God with faith, having a contrite spirit, might live, even unto that life which is eternal." (Helaman 8:15.) The Liahona given to the people of Lehi's colony to guide them to the promised land worked according to their faith in Christ. Each of us, as members of the Church, has his or her own Liahona in the gift of the Holy Ghost. If we will give heed, the Holy Ghost will teach us the words of Christ and guide us through this vale of sorrow into a far better land of promise. (See Alma 37:43–46.)

The experience in the scriptures that is seen as the classic test of faith, obedience to God, and love of him, but which is more especially in similitude of the sacrifice of Christ (see Jacob 4:5), is Abraham's call to offer his son, Isaac, as a sacrifice (see Genesis 22). Even though his father had turned away from righteousness and he himself was living in an idolatrous society, Abraham became a mighty man of faith. He knew the sanctity of life and loathed the practice of human sacrifice, which was prevalent in his day. In fact, Abraham had nearly been offered as a sacrifice on the altar of a heathen god but at the last moment was delivered by an angel. (See Abraham 1:12, 15.)

In time, Abraham was commanded by the Lord to leave the land of his fathers, Ur of the Chaldees, and travel to the land of Canaan. It was shortly after his arrival in this new land that Abraham became aware of his marvelous destiny. One night as the starry heavens shone forth in their resplendent glory, Jehovah told Abraham in a face-to-face conversation that he would become the father of nations and that his seed would be more numerous than the stars in the sky and the sands on the seashore. (See Abraham 3:11–14.) The Lord told Abraham that through him and the priesthood he bore, all nations of the earth would be blessed. Abraham had lived so close to the Lord, and now he had the privilege of seeing the face of the Lord, of hearing with his own ears the voice of truth that distilled such unbelievable peace and comfort into the very center of his soul, and of knowing in such a perfect way that he and Sarah would be blessed with innumerable posterity. How these heaven-sent assurances must have thrilled his entire being.

Yet Abraham may have been close to seventy-five years old when Jehovah appeared to him in Canaan, and the years quickly slipped by without Sarah's conceiving a child. When he was eighty-six, Abraham was blessed with a son, Ishmael, by Sarah's handmaiden, Hagar, whom Sarah had given to Abraham as a wife. When Ishmael was thirteen, however, the Lord spoke to Abraham, stressing that the promised covenant was not to be fulfilled through Ishmael. The Lord told Abraham, "But my covenant will I establish with Isaac, which Sarah shall bear unto thee at this set time in the next year." (Genesis 17:21.)

From this point on in the lives of Abraham and Sarah, the typology, or foreshadowing, of the life and mission of the Savior increases in its dramatic nature. Abraham was approaching his one-hundredth birthday and Sarah was nearly ninety when they learned that Sarah would conceive and bring forth a son whose name would be Isaac. The similitude of Isaac's birth to that of the Savior is initially seen in the incredulous reaction of both Sarah and Mary to the announcement that each would conceive and bear a son. Heavenly visitors offered to both the assurance of the Lord's power: the disbelieving Sarah was asked, "Is any thing too hard for the Lord?" (Genesis 18:14), and Mary was told, "With God nothing shall be impossible " (Luke 1:37). The miraculous conception by the aged Sarah was in similitude of the miraculous manner in which Mary, a virgin, would conceive. Sarah would give birth to her only son as Mary would give birth to the Only Begotten Son of God. Isaac would come forth as a child of promise through whom all generations of the earth would be blessed. The Savior would come forth as a child of promise through whom all generations of the earth would be blessed. Isaac was a man of faith in similitude of the faith and righteousness of the Savior. Abraham delighted in his son and loved him dearly, even as God the Father loved his Son. (See Matthew 3:17.)

I cannot imagine more ideal circumstances than those of Abraham and Isaac in which God could test the faith and obedience of one of his children. Yet not only would Abraham be proven a man of perfect faith but also, in the process of manifesting that faith, he would come to know in a deep and personal way to some extent what it would cost the Father to give his Son as a sacrifice for the sins of the world.

I'm sure there is no way the human tongue could describe the feelings that must have come into Abraham's heart when Jehovah appeared to Abraham and, without any explanation, commanded him to offer Isaac as a burnt offering. (See Genesis 22:2.) Can we even imagine the struggle that was Abraham's as he realized that this command seemingly would nullify the promises God had made? After having lived a life of obedience to God, how difficult it must have been for Abraham, in order to maintain that obedience, to follow the command to slay his precious son. For

Abraham, who loved life, whose own life had been preserved from the horrible death of a sacrificial victim, now even to contemplate thrusting a dagger into his own son's heart must have sent shudders into the depths of his soul. Yet in spite of his heartstrings being pulled to the very breaking point, Abraham immediately prepared to fulfill the terrifying command by traveling with Isaac and some servants to Mount Moriah.

Sacred writ is silent on Isaac's age when this experience occurred. He is called a "lad" (Genesis 22:12); however, the term *lad* is used in various places in the scriptures to mean a boy of about seventeen (see Genesis 37:2) and a married man (see Genesis 43:8). Enoch called himself a lad when he was at least sixty-five years old! (See Moses 6:25, 31.)

After arriving at the base of the small mount called Moriah, Abraham laid upon Isaac's shoulders the wood upon which Isaac would be placed (see Genesis 22:6), even as the Savior, approximately two thousand years later, would take upon his shoulders the wood, or cross, upon which he would be nailed. Abraham and Isaac ascended a small mount even as the Savior would ascend the small hill Golgotha. From all indications, Isaac, like the Son of God, was a willing sacrifice. According to the apocryphal book of Jasher, when Abraham explained why they were there, Isaac responded: "I will do all that the Lord spoke to thee with joy and cheerfulness of heart. . . . Blessed is the Lord who has this day chosen me to be a burnt offering before him." (Jasher 23:52, 56.)

As the last embrace was shared, the final parting words spoken, and the knife lifted to the zenith of Abraham's reach, how Abraham must have understood the love God would manifest for him and for all mankind in sending his Son as a sacrifice for the sins of the world. Surely Abraham comprehended the meaning of Gethsemane and Golgotha as few mortals have understood. In that comprehension Abraham obtained a faith that earned for him celestial powers while yet in mortality and the fulfillment of all the promises Jehovah made to him. Thus, Abraham's experience with Isaac, like all great foreshadowings, or typologies, in the scriptures, had as its purpose pointing to Christ and his atoning sacrifice.

The Purpose of the Church

Simply put, the purpose of the restored Church as the sole repository of the fulness of the gospel of Jesus Christ on earth (see D&C 1:30) is to teach the correct principles and administer the true ordinances so that the power of godliness might flow into our lives. The Church, it seems to me, fulfills its sacred trust and responsibility as it successfully helps people realize that God's redemption is because of Christ, that it centers in Christ, and that it flows from Christ through the ordinances of the gospel as we grasp, comprehend, and exercise the principle of faith in Christ. I don't think it can be said too strongly that redemption is not in the principles, ordinances, or programs of the Church themselves but rather in Christ. The ordinances and the principles and the programs of the Church are channels by which the power of Christ can flow into our lives if, again, we truly exercise faith in the Holy One of Israel.

The idea that the Savior is the source of the power of redemption, that we need desperately to know him and come to him, and that the Church and the gospel are the means to bring us to him is vividly portrayed in Lehi's dream of the tree of life. When Nephi sought for an interpretation of the tree of life, or the love of God (see 1 Nephi 11:22), he was shown the birth, life, and mission (the Atonement) of Christ. In other words, he understood that the tree of life, the central object of the dream, symbolizes Jesus Christ. Further, walking along the path symbolizes embracing the Church and gospel of Christ; holding on to the iron rod symbolizes living by every word that proceeds from God through the scriptures, the living prophets, and personal revelation; and partaking of the tree represents partaking fully of the love of God—the blessings and powers of the Savior's atonement. From all indications, coming to the Savior is the greatest experience that can occur to us during our mortal probation.

It is impossible, according to this great vision, to come to Christ fully, to partake of his atonement, to have the promise of eternal life, unless we get on the path, unless we go through baptism of the water and of the Spirit, and unless we move along the path, clinging to the iron rod. We all need to be careful to realize that getting on the path and moving along the path are two different things, and making it all the way to the tree and remaining faithful thereafter are additional, distinct accomplishments. It appears that it is not an unusual experience for us as members of the Church to be so thrilled and excited about finding and being on the path (belonging to the true church) that we take up homestead on the path! How awful it would be to come to Judgment Day as members of the Church, having been on the path for years, and discover that we had never made the journey all the way to the tree—all the way to the Savior! Indeed, the path, or membership in the Church, is exciting, and the association with many wonderful people who share a common commitment is a great blessing in itself. The benefits from Church programs are a great boon to all who involve themselves in them. But if we think the path is great, wait till we have followed the path to the tree! Then and only then will the central majesty of the Savior and his atonement be fully appreciated in our lives. Then and only then will the greater powers of heaven be ours to use in building the kingdom of God. Then and only then will the pure love of Christ be our personal gift and daily companion in the fullest sense. No wonder Lehi said that the fruit of the tree of life was desirable above all other fruit. (See 1 Nephi 8:12.)

A simple analogy here may be helpful. One summer evening a good friend of ours came to our home to take my wife and me to dinner. He drove up in a brand new Thunderbird, one of the most beautiful cars I had ever seen. It was white upon white—everything was white. I imagined that if I were to open the hood, the engine would be white—the car probably even used white oil! As my friend pulled up alongside my 1961 Falcon, the contrast between his car and my Falcon was almost more than I could bear. Even the tires on my Falcon suddenly seemed square in comparison!

The Thunderbird had a sunroof, and I immediately asked my friend if he would mind if I put a blanket on the front seat so I could stand in the seat with my body pushed up through the sunroof. Then I suggested he drive all around town honking his horn so everyone who had seen me in my Falcon could now see me in such a fancy, beautiful car.

Often members of the Church use their membership in the Church as they would a beautiful, powerful car—the most beautiful, powerful car on earth. They drive the car all around, showing it off, honking quite loudly, and telling everyone all about the car and how marvelous the car is and how absolutely necessary it is that everyone have a car exactly like it. Yet in all their frantic showoff efforts, they forget that a car has but one basic function: transportation. Likewise, our membership in the Church has essentially one great and grand function: to help us successfully journey all the way to the Savior and, in achieving that goal, be successful in bringing ourselves and others to the Father through Christ.

My own experiences with members of the Church have helped me realize that the challenge of using the gospel to come to Christ and of seeing the centrality of Christ in all things is a very real one, perhaps the greatest in the Church. Too many people, both in and out of the Church, are exposed to the message of the Restoration but see only the path and not the tree. Let me illustrate what I mean.

While serving as the director of the LDS institute of religion near Colorado State University in Fort Collins, Colorado, I was an active member of the University Religious Directors Association. At one of our monthly meetings, we brainstormed ideas that would stimulate more interest in religion on campus. The idea evolved that one approach might be to offer free seminars on various Old and New Testament topics. I thought the idea was a good one and indicated that I would be happy to support the effort. The next idea that immediately surfaced was that the seminars must be nondenominational. I'm not sure why everyone looked at me when that idea came up, but quickly I said, "Naturally, they must be nondenominational." Most of the other directors looked a little incredulous when I volunteered to teach a course on the life and teachings of Paul. They mumbled something again about the importance of a very broad, nondenominational approach to any seminar taught. I sensed, in fact, that they felt the possibility of a Mormon institute director teaching a nondenominational seminar was highly unlikely, and I certainly couldn't argue with them on that point! Nevertheless, my offer was accepted. A thorough advertising campaign ensued, and on the appointed Friday, much to my delight, I found a room full of people who had signed up for my seminar on the life and teachings of Paul.

Anyone who has spent much time reading about Paul's life and his teachings has been overwhelmed at the singularly powerful and Savior-centered testimony of that great apostle, who was one of the greatest missionaries of all time. His power was so great that irate Jewish rulers referred to him as having "turned the world upside down." (Acts 17:6.) His message was direct and to the point: "I determined not to know any thing among you, save Jesus Christ, and him crucified." (1 Corinthians 2:2.)

The course lasted five weeks and was an absolutely delightful teaching experience. I explained to the class that we wouldn't have time to explore the fascinating cultural peculiarities of the Greeks, Romans, or Jews, nor the geographical distances between the cities in which Paul preached. The emphasis was clearly to be on the doctrine of Christ.

As we discussed such topics as divine authority, church organization, and baptism for the dead, I will admit that some questions became pretty difficult to handle. For example, when we discussed baptism, one class member raised his hand and inquired why I insisted that baptism was not for infants but only for those who were, "as you would put it, Mr. Pace, accountable." I thought, Oh, how can I give a nondenominational answer to that question? Right at that moment, another class member abruptly spoke up and said, "I can tell you why Mr. Pace takes that position. Having studied a lot of psychology and sociology, I have become convinced that people aren't capable of really understanding what they are doing—in other words, aren't accountable—until somewhere between the ages of seven and nine!"

During the five weeks that the seminar was held, I taught the doctrine of Christ in some depth. I told the students that I knew that through the ordinances of the gospel, Christ's divine nature could flow into our beings and that if we would honor the Father by developing a meaningful relationship with the Savior, it would be possible, through the gifts of the Spirit, to have the image of Christ engraven upon our countenances.

I spent the entire hour of the last session simply bearing testimony that I knew that God lives and that Jesus is the Christ, the Son of God and the Savior and Redeemer of the world. In that concluding session I felt the Lord's Spirit in a special way. After I bore my testimony, and I did it in the name of Jesus Christ, the entire group seemed subdued, yet very warm and responsive. Although I dismissed the class, no one immediately got up and left. They all just sat there with a special kind of reverence. Finally, someone raised his hand and gently asked, "Mr. Pace, would you mind telling us what church you belong to?"

I replied, "I would be very happy to tell you. I'm a member of The Church of Jesus Christ of Latter-day Saints, more commonly called the Mormon Church."

There were audible gasps. I thought several students might even fall off their chairs. One person in his amazement blurted out, "Mr. Pace, you're a Mormon, and you've been teaching Jesus Christ to us the way you have?"

That comment hurt a great deal. It was disappointing to think that anyone would be surprised to learn that a Mormon would teach Jesus Christ in the way that I had. Into my mind came a response, which I refrained from saying aloud: "Young man, there is not anyone on the face of the earth who can teach Jesus Christ the way a Mormon can. Not only that, we've seen him since you have."

As the group began to leave, I hurriedly asked as many members of the class as I could if they, too, were surprised to learn that I was a Mormon. All those I spoke with responded that they were surprised. I then asked them if they personally were acquainted with any Latter-day Saints. It so happened that everyone I spoke with had lived next door to members of the Church.

As I walked home late that afternoon, I thought how unfortunate it was that any nonmember could be exposed to any active Latter-day Saint and not know that the whole point and purpose of Joseph Smith and the Restoration is to declare to a confused world that indeed God lives and Jesus is the Christ, that he has appeared and is appearing in our day, and that once again anyone who seeks with any kind of intensity can come to know him in a marvelous way.

Keeping Our Eye on the Savior

Having visited the Holy Land on many different occasions, I've crossed the Sea of Galilee quite a few times. Each time I do, numerous scriptural experiences in the life of the Savior come vividly to mind. One such experience, which illustrates our need to center our lives in Christ, is recorded in Matthew 14:26–32.

After feeding the five thousand, the Savior directed the Twelve to cross the Sea of Galilee and go to Capernaum; in due time he was to meet them in Bethsaida. But as they were crossing the sea, a storm arose. They were making little progress toward their destination when, much to their amazement, they saw Jesus walking toward them across the waves. At first the Twelve were frightened, but the Savior's speaking to them reassured them. Then, even though the Savior was coming to them, it seems that Peter just couldn't wait. He impetuously and boldly cried out, "Lord, if it be thou, bid me come unto thee on the water." (V. 28.)

Jesus replied, "Come." (V. 29.)

The simple frankness of the invitation and Peter's excitement at seeing the Lord so kindled his faith that he climbed out of the boat and started walking on the water to his beloved Master. But when Peter "saw the wind boisterous, he was afraid; and beginning to sink, he cried, saying, Lord, save me." (V. 30.)

I believe that Peter at first succeeded at walking on the water because he riveted his eye on the Savior, trusting implicitly in the Savior's admonition to come to him. As soon as Peter took his eyes off the Savior, however, and admitted such other considerations into his mind as the boisterous waves and the fact that he was doing something that was ordinarily impossible—he immediately began to sink!

So it is with us. If we really want to come all the way to the Lord and be found pleasing in his sight, if we really want to enjoy the greater power that can come from the ordinances and principles of the gospel, if we really want to overcome the boisterous waves of the lusts of the flesh and the cunning wisdom of man, then we must rivet our eyes on the Lord.

I personally thrill in the Savior-centered witness of the prophets. I hear in their witnesses a challenge to each of us to come to know the Lord so that in our living and teaching the gospel, in our serving and administering in the affairs of the kingdom, we will influence others to come into the kingdom of God and commit themselves wholeheartedly to know the Master, to come to him, and to build up his kingdom on the earth.

President Brigham Young expressed a beautiful invitation to know the Savior: "The greatest and most important of all requirements of our Father in heaven and of his Son, Jesus Christ, is . . . to believe in Jesus Christ, confess him, seek to know him, cling to him, make friends with him. Take a course to open and keep open a communication with your Elder Brother or file-leader — our Savior." (In *Journal of Discourses,* 8:339.)

A most beautiful scriptural testimony of Christ and a most powerful invitation to come to know him are found in the words of Moroni: "And then [at the judgment day] shall ye know that I have seen Jesus, and that he hath talked with me face to face, and that he told me in plain humility, even as a man telleth another in mine own language, concerning these things. . . . And now, I would commend you to seek this Jesus of whom the prophets and apostles have written, that the grace of God the Father, and also the Lord Jesus Christ, and the Holy Ghost, which beareth record of them, may be and abide in you forever." (Ether 12:39, 41.)

May we respond to Moroni's invitation to "seek this Jesus of whom the apostles and prophets have written." May we remember that the message of Joseph Smith to all of us is that we, like him, can know the God of Abraham, Isaac, and Jacob; that He, even Christ, can be known ever so well. May we believe with all of our hearts that we can know him, for only in so believing will we have faith and consequent determination great enough to achieve such a marvelous goal. And may the Lord bless each of us that we might be fully successful in finding, obtaining, and keeping the pearl of greatest price, to the honor and glory of the Father.

Chapter 2

MIGHTY PRAYER

On one occasion I received an invitation to speak in sacrament meeting to some combined wards of Brigham Young University students the sabbath before Christmas. Because Christmastime is my favorite time of the year, a time when a special spirit of brotherhood seems to pervade the earth, I especially desired to speak in a meaningful way about the Savior and what it really means to know him.

I had gradually been obtaining stronger and stronger feelings about the Savior's role as a mediator between God and man. But as I began to prepare my talk, I felt I wanted to obtain some additional, specific ideas that would help me and those to whom I was to speak come to a greater understanding of the reality and majesty of Christ.

I approached Heavenly Father in prayer. My question to him was simple and to the point: "How can I come to know thy Son more fully?" Almost immediately a question came into my mind: "Of all the people you know on earth, whom do you know the best?" As I reflected for just a moment, the person who came immediately to mind was my father. The thought came with considerable force, for indeed there was no question in my mind that I knew my earthly father very well.

Another thought seemed to form in my mind: "What kind of experiences did you have with your earthly father that enabled you to know him so well?" I honestly wondered for a moment what all of this had to do with knowing Christ; and then all of a sudden the idea flooded into my mind that the experiences I'd had in getting to know my dad were similar to the kinds of experiences I need to have to really come to know the Savior! What a simple and exciting idea that was to me! How marvelous it was to realize that experiences I'd had with my father were a pattern of the kinds of experiences I could have in coming to know my Redeemer. In fact, that particular idea did more to give me specific direction in seeking for a knowledge of the Son than any single idea I'd ever had previously.

Earthly Relationships: A Shadow, or Type, of Heavenly Relationships

On that occasion I continued praying and thinking about my relationship with my father and the experiences I'd had with him that might assist me in knowing the Son. Many aspects of my relationship with Dad came into focus — such things as how deeply I admired him and wanted to become like him; how much it meant to me when he openly expressed his love for me; how much it meant to have him embrace me warmly on occasion; how much it meant to learn how to work by working with him. Of all the beautiful and good experiences I had with my father, the ones that enabled me to come to really know him were those when we had occasion to talk with each other frequently and for extended periods of time. For example, even though milking cows night and morning was sometimes an exasperating ordeal for a teenager, the morning and evening routine was softened and even made enjoyable because of the opportunity it afforded to explore all kinds of subjects with Dad. Similarly, being perched beside him on top of a wagon of hay heading for the stack yard, which was nearly a mile away, afforded another chance for him to leisurely recall and share many of his exciting experiences as a boy in the Mormon colonies in Mexico or as a sheriff when the west was still a place that hadn't totally been won. There were other such times during the hours we spent going up and down rows of sugar beets or rows of pinto beans facing the stark reality that thorns and weeds are indeed the opposition in all things in the world of farming. Both of us, while leaning on shovels, waiting for water to slake the thirst of growing crops, capitalized on the opportunity to turn many a hot summer day into priceless memories of comradery, fellowship, and meaningful communication.

The key, then, to coming to know my father was spending the time and putting forth the effort to open real lines of communication with each other. So it is with our Heavenly Father and our Savior. If we really want to open and keep open lines of communication with our Heavenly Father through Christ, we must be willing to invest daily the time and energy to talk with him.

As the years slipped by and my conversations with Dad continued, I arrived at a point where I enjoyed talking to him more than I enjoyed talking with anyone else I knew. What a goal to seek in our communication with our Heavenly Father through Christ, to actually enjoy talking with him more than we enjoy talking with anyone else! Further, I came to the point where I hated to have my conversations with Dad end, and oh, how true that can be in our prayers to God. How wonderful it is to arrive at a point where the feelings, the information gleaned, the motivation that comes, and the peace that is felt are so real that it's difficult to conclude one's prayer.

Incidentally, I came to appreciate even more fully the blessings of our conversations with each other because of what was to be my last conversation with him.

I had traveled to Provo, Utah, to attend a workshop for institute directors, and afterwards I drove to southern Idaho to visit my parents before driving back to Colorado.

My mother had died when I was nine years old, leaving ten living children, three of whom were married. Dad later married a remarkable woman who was willing to assume the awesome care and responsibility of a large family. As their new marriage unfolded, I grew to love and appreciate my stepmother deeply and to appreciate all she did in taking care of the family.

Before leaving for Colorado, after visiting with Dad and my "second mom" for a couple of days, I walked with Dad out to the corrals where we talked very seriously with each other for some time. Dad seemed somewhat discouraged. Out of a desire to give him some word of encouragement, I expressed the hope that he would be very patient and do all he could to be Christlike in what he said and did. Then, almost before I realized what I was saying, I boldly said to him, "Dad, before you know it, this life will be over, and you'll be back with Mother, and all will be well." I'll not forget the look on his face as he responded, "Yes, yes, I know what you mean." Then he said, "George, let me share with you a beautiful experience I had with your mother many years after she passed away." He went on to relate in some detail a marvelous spiritual experience that had given him great comfort over the years. As he shared it with me I was, to say the least, grateful, and I comforted myself to know he had received such a strengthening experience.

We embraced and kissed each other, and I left. As I drove away, I felt without question that I had been especially honored to have Dad share with me such a sacred experience, and I knew he never would have done so had we not built a close relationship by spending a great deal of time communicating with each other.

Little did I realize that in just a week's time, I would come to appreciate the special significance of our last conversation together. I had set out on a trip to Wyoming and Nebraska to coordinate some early-morning seminaries. After taking care of some business in Cheyenne, I got back into my little Volkswagen and headed west toward Scottsbluff, Nebraska. It was a beautiful night—a few low clouds were scooting along, and the moon was almost full. I had made it a practice while driving alone over such long distances to pray vocally—it was a great way to spend my time, and it was always spiritually stimulating. In fact, some of the greatest spiritual experiences I've had have occurred while I was pouring out my heart in prayer as I drove alone.

This particular evening when I lifted my voice in prayer, my mind flooded with feelings about my dad. It seemed I was not only reviewing but also reliving many of the choicest experiences I had had with him. I seemed to feel his presence, and I sensed deeply the love he had for me and the hope that we could be together again. I basked in a love for my father that was deeper than anything I had previously felt. The tears flowed freely as I realized more completely how much my father meant to me and that the bonds of love that linked our hearts were indeed eternal.

I arrived in Scottsbluff quite late and stayed in the bishop's home. The following morning while I was preparing for breakfast, the phone rang. It was a long distance call for me, and I learned that during the night my father had very unexpectedly passed away.

As I hung up the phone, there immediately came into my mind the beautiful experience I had had in talking to Dad just one week before. How grateful I was that we had opened our hearts so totally to each other and had shared so deeply our love for each other.

The experience the night before took on even greater meaning now. I felt that the Lord had prepared me for my father's passing by allowing me to feel so deeply of his presence and so deeply of the love that bound us together. I count that evening as one of the sweetest experiences of my life. How profoundly grateful I am for the principle of prayer and for the reality of the love, comfort, and strength of the Savior.

But of necessity, I have to conclude that I don't believe I ever would have had those experiences with Dad had we not spent a great deal of time talking with each other and had I not been so motivated by the prophets to pray mightily and persistently to my Heavenly Father in the name of Christ.

Knowing Christ through Prayer to the Father

We acknowledge that it is the Father, even Elohim, who provided for us a redeemer in Christ. It is the Father's plan of redemption, not Christ's; however, we call upon the Father in the name of the Son because the Son provided the possibility of our actual redemption from the Fall. He, the Son, suffered for us, died for us, and broke the bands of death for us, thereby earning the right and title of advocate with the Father (see D&C 45:3) and the only mediator between God and man (see 1 Timothy 2:5). Because the Savior is our mediator, we always pray to the Father in the name of Christ, and the Father answers our prayers through his Son. (See Bruce R. McConkie, *Promised Messiah*, pp. 335, 557.)

I think a classic example of this idea is found in the First Vision. As Joseph Smith read the promise of the apostle James (see James 1:5–6), the Spirit bore such a powerful witness to him that the promise of James was true that Joseph immediately went out into the grove and lifted his voice in prayer to Heavenly Father. In answer to his prayer, both the Father and the Son appeared to him, but all the Father did was introduce his Son and invite Joseph to "hear him." (Joseph Smith–History 1:17.) Joseph's prayer was actually answered by the Savior.

Consider a second example that has to do with our receiving any spiritual endowment or blessing. Suppose we seek mightily for a remission of sins, acknowledging that it is the Savior who made available the means by which we might be freed from our sins. It is Heavenly Father whom we ask explicitly and in the name of Christ that we might through our faith in Christ obtain that blessed gift. If our faith is sufficient and our repentance complete, the Father responds to our prayers by having his Son cleanse and sanctify us. By the time we are sanctified and made clean, we, like thousands of others, can testify of the reality and goodness of God through Christ, and we feel a profound kinship with him for the blessing he has given us.

As we, like the prophets, call upon the Father in the name of Christ and receive more and more personal revelation, we will come out of our private chambers, off the mountains, or out of the deserts testifying of the living reality of Christ and of his marvelous intervention in our lives. Initially it may seem difficult to understand how it is that as we call upon the Father in the name of Christ, we will come to know the Savior in a marvelous way. But it is a true principle, and one that we will understand more fully when we experience it.

Letting the Spirit Teach You How to Pray

Moroni testified that when we are "wrought upon and cleansed by the power of the Holy Ghost" and "nourished by the good word of God," we are "relying alone upon the merits of

Christ, who was the author and the finisher of their faith." (Moroni 6:4.) Indeed, without the grace of God through Christ, we could not commence, let alone finish, a faith in our hearts that would bring us to salvation. The truth of this statement is especially evident when it comes to calling upon the Father in the name of Christ and receiving answers to our prayers. We may try hard to pray effectively, but if the Lord doesn't send his Spirit upon us, we will never learn to communicate with God in the manner that we should. We must rely on the merits of Christ.

Through Joseph Smith the Lord promised us that he would "gather his people even as a hen gathereth her chickens under her wings, even as many as will hearken to my voice and humble themselves before me, and call upon me in mighty prayer." (D&C 29:2.) How do we pray mightily? What is it that enables us to persist and plead at the throne of God's grace? What is it that causes us to hunger and thirst so deeply that we desire the things of the Spirit more than we desire food and drink? It is the quickening, guiding power of the Savior through the Spirit.

The Nephite disciples, we are told, so desired the endowment of the Spirit when the resurrected Christ was with them that they continued to pray for an extended period of time. Mormon recorded, "They did still continue, without ceasing, to pray unto him; and they did not multiply many words, for it was given unto them what they should pray, and they were filled with desire." (3 Nephi 19:24.)

Paul the apostle expressed the same idea when he said, "Likewise the Spirit also helpeth our infirmities: for we know not what we should pray for as we ought: but the Spirit itself maketh intercession for us with groanings which cannot be uttered." (Romans 8:26.)

I'm convinced that if we will pray mightily in the best way we know how, persisting from day to day, the time will gradually come when we are aware that the Spirit is prompting us about what we should pray for. With that gentle prompting comes a great desire to receive what we know the Lord wants us to have. It is phenomenal how much faith you can exercise when the things you are seeking are the things you know the Lord wants you to have!

The Labor of Prayer

I was once having lunch with some friends whose young son was quite a gifted pianist. I asked him, "John, how much time do you spend each day practicing the piano?"

He responded without hesitation, "About five hours a day."

I thought, What a price to pay to develop a musical talent!

I have observed over the years the tremendous price students will pay to obtain their degrees, to excel in debate or athletics, or to achieve anything else they really desire. There is no question that the law of the harvest is real and applies to everything we do in life. If we want to reap a bounteous harvest, we must plant and cultivate a bounteous crop. So it is with prayer. If we really want to obtain the powers of heaven, I believe we've got to put a great deal of time and effort into prayer.

When I returned home from my mission, my spiritual appetite had been whetted, and I was determined to keep the spiritual generators humming. But what a challenge it was to switch from missionary work to farm work! It was hard to feel that I was growing spiritually, even though I was attending my meetings, doing my church work, and searching the scriptures. I felt that there was surely something else I could do and must do—a greater price I needed to pay—that would assure me of continued spiritual growth and development.

While I looked desperately for a practical formula that, if applied regularly, would assure me of the growth and development I desired, I commenced rereading the Book of Mormon. As I read, I was especially impressed by the experience of Enos, son of Jacob. It seemed as if Enos were speaking directly to me. It seemed, in fact, that I received a personal challenge to go into the mountains and pray all day and into the night.

I determined that that was what I would do. I made arrangements for my chores to be done by someone else, and I set aside a whole day and a night for that experience.

It was a beautiful summer day, and as I drove as high as I could on the highest mountain around and then hiked way above the timberline to the very top, I was about as excited as I'd ever been. I anticipated that surely I would rend the veil and receive a remission of my sins.

I found a place right on the very top of the mountain where I could kneel by a flat rock and support part of my weight by leaning on it. (I wanted to be reasonably comfortable because I was going to be there a long time!) Knowing that I was alone, that no one was around for miles, that everything was in readiness, I tilted back my head and really lifted my voice to the heavens. As I did, the image of Enos and Nephi and other prophets in the attitude of prayer came into my mind, and I was quite pleased with what I was doing.

Much to my amazement, however, after roughly twenty minutes I completely ran out of things to say. Even at that, I had been a little repetitious. I felt totally chagrined that I was through so soon and couldn't think of one more thing to say. After a few more minutes of just staring blankly into space, I got up off my knees, hiked down to the car, and drove home. On the way, I guess because I was so shocked and disappointed at not having been able to pray for more than twenty minutes, I started rationalizing (to rationalize is to bring one's ideals down to one's conduct). The first thing I thought was, "Enos, you must have really been a sinner. It took you all day and into the night and after twenty minutes I feel fine. Not only that, but do you know how many widows you could have visited in a day and a night, and how much scripture you could have read in that much time, and how many potatoes you could have picked on the welfare farm?" But the real clincher was this thought: "Enos, do you know how many ward and stake leaders I know who have never prayed for more than a few minutes at a time?"

Despite my rationalization, by the time I drove into the farm and turned the key off in the car, I was exhausted from disappointment. I sat in the car for some time, convinced that there must be a way to develop sufficient spiritual starch in our spine to pay the kind of price that not only Enos paid, but, in my estimation, all the truly righteous Saints have paid, a price that would enable us to say with Joseph Smith, "We may converse with him [God] as one man converses with another." (*Teachings of the Prophet Joseph Smith*, p. 345.)

That day (and this is what made the whole experience so worthwhile) I determined to set aside time each day for praying aloud, a period of time sufficient to require the real exercise of faith, enough time to demand some real reaching and struggling so that the spiritual fibers of my being would be exercised and become strong. I determined that fifteen or twenty minutes a day would accomplish that exercise, so I made a commitment that I would spend at least that much time in praying aloud each day.

In the ensuing days and weeks as I tried to stick with my commitment, I found it was very hard. The fifteen or twenty minutes a day really stretched my spiritual faculties. In fact, I was stunned at how hard it was to pray consistently for that much time each day. It was hard emotionally as well as physically. It was much easier to read the scriptures regularly and to do my church work consistently (both of which I continued doing) but so very hard to subdue my body and lift my voice in vocal prayer for just fifteen or twenty minutes a day. I would stay with my commitment for a time, but then because of the many pressures of family responsibilities, church callings, earning a living, and so forth, I'd quit doing it for a while. As I reflected on what I honestly wanted to achieve in life, however, invariably my desire to communicate more fully in prayer would return with increased intensity, and I would pick up my challenge again.

Even though I was inconsistent in my efforts, I realized that something was beginning to happen. I sensed that my appetite for the things of the Spirit was increasing. I had a deeper feeling of optimism about life. I felt a closer affinity for the Lord. Little bits of inspiration started coming that really made a difference in my life. It was hard to put my finger right on it, but some exciting feelings were coming. Although many times I still had to push myself to keep my commitment to pray for fifteen to twenty minutes a day, over several months it started to become an important part of my life. It still took some pushing and struggling to maintain a consistent pattern, but by now the benefits were so obvious, the blessings so much greater, that my devotion to prayer became an integral part of my daily life and, in fact, the very highlight of each day.

I have become convinced that when we persist in prayer, our

spirits are actually exercising their muscles, becoming strong, becoming prepared, so that as the gates of revelation gradually start opening, we will have the strength and the courage to implement the ideas and directions that come to us. The Lord is so kind and gracious that he generally won't give us more light and knowledge than we can handle, but when he sees the sincerity of our hearts as evidenced by our determination to knock and knock and knock, we will know that our prayers are not in vain.

Persistence, effort, and determination to really make contact with the powers of heaven in order to communicate with God as one man converses with another will pay off in dividends and blessings greater than we can imagine.

I invite you to accept the challenge to pray vocally for fifteen or twenty minutes in uninterrupted prayer each day for a month. The suggestion of fifteen or twenty minutes is simply to push you to enable you to break the prayer barrier that keeps so many precious Saints from enjoying the greater blessings and powers of heaven.

After years of struggling in mighty prayer, I felt a confirmation of my convictions when I read the following by President Spencer W. Kimball. Speaking of Enos, he wrote:

"Could the Redeemer resist such determined imploring? How many have thus persisted? How many, with or without transgressions, have ever prayed all day and into the night? How many have ever wept and prayed for ten hours? for five hours? for one? for thirty minutes? for ten? Our praying is usually measured in seconds and yet with a heavy debt to pay we still expect forgiveness of our sins. We offer pennies to pay the debt of thousands of dollars.

"How much do you pray, my friends? How often? How earnestly? If you have errors in your life, have you really wrestled before the Lord? Have you yet found your deep forest of solitude? How much has your soul hungered? How deeply have your needs impressed your heart? When did you kneel before your Maker in total quiet? For what did you pray—your own soul? How long did you thus plead for recognition—all day long? And when the shadows fell, did you still raise your voice in mighty prayer, or

did you satisfy yourself with some hackneyed word and phrase?"
(*Faith Precedes the Miracle,* p. 211.)

Becoming Filled with Desire

I stood one spring on Mars Hill in Athens, Greece, and as I
looked across a small valley to the Acropolis where the remains
of the famous Parthenon stood, I remembered a story told about
Socrates, the famous Greek philosopher. It appears that a young
man went to Socrates and inquired how he could obtain the
knowledge Socrates possessed. The great philosopher invited the
young man to follow him, and they walked until they came to a
river. Without pausing, Socrates walked out until the water was
chest high, and the young man followed. Socrates grabbed the
inquirer, plunged him under the water, and held him there until
he passed out. He then dragged him to land and let him lie on
the shore.

When the young man came to and his strength returned, he
sought out Socrates again and asked, "Why did you do that? I
almost lost my life!"

Socrates replied, "While you were under the water, what did
you want more than anything else?"

The young man answered, "Air."

Socrates said, "As soon as you want knowledge as much as
you wanted air, nothing on the face of the earth can keep you
from getting it!"

A similar point was brought home to me once when I was
lecturing in San Fernando, California. I was really pleading with
the Saints to take the time and effort to pray when this thought
entered my mind: George, had you been willing to spend one-
fifth of the time reaching for the things of the Spirit that you
spent practicing and playing high school football, you could have
been translated by the time you were nineteen!

At that moment there flooded into my memory the intense
desire I had had while in high school to play football. It had been
an obsession with me: I was willing to run great distances, scrim-
mage for hours, do calisthenics—I ate, drank, and slept football,

so to speak, and it paid off. I got to be on the team all through high school.

It is true that our desires determine the course and destiny of our lives. We can tell easily enough how much we wanted something by whether or not we got it. If we really desire righteousness, we will receive it. In quite a real sense, on Judgment Day, we will receive exactly what we lived and worked for. If the verdict given us is less than celestial glory, the Lord won't send an unusually strong angel to carry us screaming and protesting wildly to the terrestrial or telestial kingdom. We will be pleased to accept quietly the verdict and go to our assigned place because we will have received exactly what we desired.

The ability to persist in our prayers is actually a gift of God. Only the Lord finally can endow us with the strength to pay a consistent price in mighty prayer, and he does it by giving us the desire. In no other place is this idea more effectively taught than in the experience of the twelve Nephite disciples when "they did still continue, without ceasing, to pray unto him; and they did not multiply many words, for it was given unto them what they should pray, and they were filled with desire." (3 Nephi 19:24; see also Romans 8:26; Jude 1:20; D&C 50:29-30.)

Why were they placed in a position to persist as they did? Because, I believe, the Spirit took over and gave them the desire.

The Lord is so gracious. Knowing our fallen nature, he sends mighty men of God in our midst (see Moroni 7:31-32) to testify in power of the greater blessings that are available. Their witness causes righteous desires to be planted in our hearts. But it is important to realize that although we are influenced by the testimonies of others, we remain agents unto ourselves. If we don't have the desire to pray, we have to ask to have the desire! We have enough control over our minds and bodies to dictate to ourselves, to tell our bodies to kneel and our tongue to ask for righteous desires. When we do that, lo and behold, the Lord will give those desires to us. Again, if we ask, if we persist, our desires in righteousness will grow and grow and become the wellspring of eternal life.

The following experience might be helpful in showing how

37

the Lord will give us the ability to pray with fervor by filling us with desire.

One morning in the early hours, I was going where I like to go for my private devotionals. It was quite cold, and because the night's rest had been far too brief, I felt extremely tired. I wondered if I just ought to collapse into a ball and roll back down the mountain into bed. In fact, about the only thing that kept coming into my mind as I walked along so dreary-eyed was "retire to thy bed early, that ye may not be weary." (D&C 88:124.) Nevertheless, I pushed on to where I like to go and knelt in prayer for ten or fifteen minutes. The words were hard to come by, and when they did come, they seemed listless and without power. But I persisted, and then it came—the quiet assurance that I was being heard—and I felt such a strong desire to pray, to make contact, to come alive in the Lord's Spirit and power. Ideas started coming. I became so excited about the new day dawning and the opportunities it presented that I was physically rejuvenated. After a half an hour or so had passed, I jumped up off my knees and ran all the way down to the house. I was now ready for the day, knowing I had really conversed with my Maker.

When the Heavens Seem Like Brass

One reason we may find it hard to persist in mighty prayer is that perhaps most of the time our prayers are not answered while we are asking them. A General Authority once told how, when faced with a particular challenge, he fasted one day a week and sought help in fervent prayer each day for a year before the answer came. Often decisions must be made, presented to the Lord, and the process of carrying them out commenced before the full confirmation comes that the decision was correct. In these instances and many more that could be cited, evidence is ample that our faith is really tested when answers do not come quickly and the heavens seem like brass, although the prayers continue to ascend to heaven.

Perhaps another reason the heavens might seem like brass is that we often do not recognize answers when they come. We might be looking for the spectacular and miss the quiet increase of peace, confidence, and optimism that is coming into our hearts.

Another reason persistence may be hard is that some of the time while we are praying, the Spirit may actually withdraw from us. How difficult it is to continue to cry unto God when the Spirit is not there! But there has to be a compelling reason why this happens. Is there a greater challenge to our faith than to pray persistently when the Spirit is withdrawn? I think not. To show what I mean, let me describe an experience that particularly illustrates this point.

Eleven years after my attempt to imitate Enos, I was in the little hamlet of Rye, Colorado, which sits quite high on the eastern slope of the Rocky Mountains, twenty or thirty miles south of Pueblo. I visited an early-morning seminary class and thrilled with the spirit of a great teacher who had every Latter-day Saint high school youth in class, as well as several nonmembers. When the class concluded, I drove up the valley to the end of the road and obtained permission from a rancher to hike up the mountains above his ranch. It was wintertime, and although there was quite a bit of snow on the ground, it was warm and comfortable on the sunny side of the mountain. As I climbed higher and higher, I felt a very strong desire to obtain more power from the Lord that I might be a better husband and a better father. I wanted to be much more effective in magnifying my callings in the priesthood. I desired a greater ability to teach the gospel with the Spirit, to have the convincing power of God, that I might particularly be able to touch the lives of the inactive Latter-day Saint youth at Colorado State University.

Finally, I located the place I wanted to spend the day—it was next to a large, fallen tree. I knelt and prayed for an hour and was surprised that the Spirit didn't come as I was used to feeling it. I continued another hour and another, but still no quiet assurance came that my Heavenly Father was there and listening. Despite what appeared to be a lack of the Spirit, with some determination I persisted in vocal prayer throughout the entire day. Much to my distress, the heavens were indeed like brass. To persist that day in vocal prayer ended up being the hardest, most difficult, challenging experience of my entire life—emotionally, physically, and spiritually. I knew what it was to work hard on the farm. I had had the experience of bucking sacks of potatoes for twenty hours straight; I had wondered if my back would allow me ever to walk upright again. But even that experience did not tax my endurance as did praying all day long high on a mountain above Rye, Colorado.

About evening I concluded my prayers, worked my way down the mountain, and drove back to Fort Collins. I felt exhausted and discouraged, and I honestly wondered if I had wasted the whole day. I also wondered if I were a fanatic to desire so intently the greater blessings that seemed so consistently promised in the scriptures.

Over the next few weeks, however, interesting things began to occur. The day after my experience on the mountain, when I put my arms around my wife and held her close, and then held my children one by one, I felt a greater intensity of love for them than I had ever felt before. Throughout the next several weeks as I knocked on fraternity and sorority doors and invited inactive young men and women to participate in the Lord's program, I felt the convincing power of God more strongly than I had ever felt it. It seemed to me that when I opened the scriptures, everywhere I looked I saw the majesty of the Savior and his infinite atonement. For weeks I felt a greater outpouring of the Spirit than during any previous period in my life. What a blessing that day of prayer was to me. How grateful I was that even though throughout the entire day I did not feel his Spirit, I persisted in prayer.

Repetitious Prayers

Obviously, the Lord doesn't want us to use vain repetitions. (See Matthew 6:7.) But by "vain repetition" does the Lord mean prayers in which we ask for the same thing again and again? Does he mean prayers that are uttered too often or are too lengthy? I don't think so. I think the Lord means prayers that are not uttered sincerely or with real intent.

The Lord's parable of the importunate widow (see Luke 18:1–7) is an excellent case in point, illustrating how we should be willing to persist and persist in prayer. The parable tells of a certain widow who kept approaching a judge to avenge her of her adversary. The widow kept persisting until her continued requests wearied the judge. Finally the judge, although he "feared not God, neither regarded man" (v. 2), responded to the widow's request. Having a loving Father as we do, how much more willing is he to respond to our persistent requests.

The following analogy further illustrates. Suppose you are swimming in a river with a friend. After a while you climb out on the bank to rest. While you are watching your friend, you become alarmed when you suddenly hear him frantically calling, "Help! Help!" He disappears beneath the water for a few moments, but upon reappearing again yells, "Help! Help!" When you hear him cry for help the second time, I doubt very much that you would say, "I'm sorry, dear friend, but you requested help the second time in exactly the same way that you requested help the first time. Now, when you go under and come up again, if you request help in a clever, novel way, I just might consider rendering assistance!"

We might on different occasions ask again and again and again for particular blessings; however, we will not be guilty of vain repetitions if we really desire what we are praying for.

What to Pray For and About

I believe the Lord expects us to become mindful of the many blessings and endowments that he wants us to have. Then, as we wrestle in mighty prayer and we feel impressed to ask for particular blessings, we can do so with great confidence and faith. A partial list of those things we surely should always pray about follows. We need to —

• Give appreciation for the marvelous atonement of Christ.
• Give appreciation for Joseph Smith and the Restoration.
• Give appreciation for the Lord's anointed and for all who labor in the building of Zion.
• Give appreciation for our loved ones.
• Recognize our sins and weaknesses.

• Seek with all of our energy for the baptism of the Spirit and the constant companionship of the Spirit.

• Pray with all of our hearts for charity, the pure love of Christ.

Let me elaborate on some things we should pray about that represent some special challenges.

Pray to acquire faith. I think it is obvious that the purpose of prayer is to increase our faith in the Savior. The more we learn about him, the more experiences we have with him, and the more we understand his mind and will, the greater is our faith in him. President Marion G. Romney taught that "prayer is the key that unlocks your heart and lets Christ in."

I would like to stress that in my estimation the quickest way to acquire a mighty faith is through prayer. To illustrate, let's return to the experience of Enos. Enos had gone to hunt animals, but he began to reflect on his relationship with the Lord and determined to obtain a remission of his sins. He testified, "All the day long did I cry unto him; yea, and when the night came I did still raise my voice high that it reached the heavens." (Enos 1:4.)

Let's imagine, for the purpose of making our point, that Enos started praying sometime in the early morning. By noon he hadn't received a remission of his sins, nor had he by the late afternoon. (Incidentally, it is my opinion that Enos surely must have prayed many times before this experience to have had the spiritual stamina to persist as he did.) But Enos continued with great determination, and sometime late that night, let's say at 10 P.M., Enos heard the voice of the Lord and received a remission of sins. In other words, after a day and into the night, Enos, through his struggle in mighty prayer, obtained enough faith to hear the voice of the Lord and receive a remission of sins. What a correlation between his persistence in prayer and the faith he enjoyed!

Pray for loved ones. How important it is to pray for our loved ones. "Pray one for another," counseled the apostle James, for "the effectual fervent prayer of a righteous man availeth much."

(James 5:16.) And even though we ourselves are weak and in many ways fall short of being the individuals we should be, the Lord nevertheless hears our prayers in behalf of our loved ones.

One New Year's day, I determined to commence the New Year by putting forth a special effort in early-morning prayer. It was several hours before dawn, and the ground was heavily blanketed with snow. The lights from the city reflected off the snow, and as I looked down from my position high on the mountain, I found it was indeed a beautiful sight.

I persisted for a period of time in prayer, and while mentioning those things I generally pray about, my attention turned with great intensity to my beloved brothers and sisters. I was caught up in unusually powerful feelings of love for each of them, and I lifted my voice in their behalf. Words are inadequate to express the feelings for my brothers and sisters that came on that occasion, and for quite a length of time I continued to pray for their welfare.

After concluding my prayers, I returned home to awaken the family, and we began to prepare for a New Year's dinner to which we had invited one of my brothers and his family.

Later that day, after dinner and when most of the children had left the table, I felt strongly impressed to ask my brother if I could give him a priesthood blessing. I felt bold in asking, but his instant response removed any apprehension I had. He, his wife, their daughter, and I went into another room where we would have more privacy.

The blessing given came from above and was a special experience between two brothers. At the conclusion of that blessing, it seemed natural to ask if his wife wanted a blessing. She too responded yes, and again the kindness of the Lord was manifest. Then, at the daughter's request, I gave her a blessing.

At the end of that most beautiful day, I felt in my heart a special appreciation for the prophets, who encourage us to make effective prayer for others an important part of our lives.

Some months later my brother called long distance to tell me about some progress he had made because of the blessing he had received. How I thrilled at this report, and I knew again that the Lord blesses our loved ones in response to our prayers for them.

Pray for comfort. We are assured that we can have peace in this world in spite of the challenges and difficulties that come our way. The Lord has promised us the Comforter to help us though sorrows, grief, and heartaches, but prayer is the key to that peace and comfort.

At one time in my life, I was unusually discouraged. It seemed too difficult to do all the things that I felt were expected of me, and, furthermore, I really wondered if it was all worth it. I went to the place where I like to pray, wondering if I even wanted to ask for encouragement and comfort. I knelt and for some time prayed specifically about the heavy burdens that seemed to be mine. I then enjoyed the following delightful experience. (I might add that the Lord works with all of us according to our particular needs and experiences. He also draws from our experiences to teach us great lessons. Such was the case that day with me.)

After I had pleaded for a while in prayer, it seemed to me that I was on a football field, and all the feelings I had had as a high school football player seemed to return — the crisp fall air of southern Idaho, the sound of the high school band, the excitement of having my parents watching, and the thrill that comes in anticipation of the kickoff. It was all there and seemed so real.

Finally, the whistle blew, the ball was kicked, and I caught it. I immediately started running down the field to make a touchdown. Then discouragement number one set in. When I looked for the goal posts, they appeared to be about a mile away. I had never seen such a long football field. I wondered if I could even run that far, let alone fight my way through the opposing team. My discouragement turned to hope as I remembered the fired-up talk of the coach.

Then I became aware of the opposing team. It looked like there were at least eighteen men! I thought, "Wait a minute. This isn't right. There are supposed to be only eleven — and not only that, they don't all have to weigh three hundred pounds!" That was discouragement number two. But when competition gets the adrenaline working, anything seems possible, and in spite of the odds, I kept running as fast as I could.

As I ran, the comforting thought came that my team would surely run interference for me. So while continuing to run, I looked to the right and to the left. Discouragement number three: I was the only one on my team!

Oh, I'll never forget the feeling of utter hopelessness that came then. I just knew there was no way I could make a touchdown. In fact, I felt that if I were smart, I would throw the ball away and just lie down—do anything to stop what was an impossible situation!

But right at that moment of greatest discouragement, I became aware that there seemed to be individuals lined up on both sides of the field—it seemed they were the prophets from Adam to Spencer W. Kimball, who was then president of the Church. They were speaking words of great encouragement, telling me to keep going, to give it all I had, not to let down, that everything I had been asked to do the Lord would give me the power to do if I would look to him.

Then the experience was over, but I felt a profound sense of comfort and an assurance that even though greater trials would yet come, in Christ I could find the strength to endure. The apostle Paul's words to the Philippians seemed so meaningful: "I can do all things through Christ which strengtheneth me." (Philippians 4:13.)

One day in class, after I had shared the foregoing experience, a student shared with the class a similar experience of his own. He had dreamed one night that he was crossing a desert. It was hot, and he was carrying on his shoulders a very heavy cross. After a while, he become so tired of carrying the cross that he laid it down and sawed off part of the upright. Having done so, he lifted the cross back on his shoulders and continued his journey. Soon the cross again became too heavy, so he laid it down and sawed off another portion. After stopping and sawing off several portions of the cross, he came to a narrow but very deep ravine. He stood at the edge and looked across. There, standing on the other side with outstretched arms, was the Savior. As their eyes met, the Savior beckoned him to come to Him. He indicated to the Savior that he couldn't because, narrow as it was, the ravine was too wide for him to jump across. The Savior told him to lay the cross he was carrying over the ravine and use it as a bridge to walk upon. He quickly took up the cross, but as he attempted to span the ravine with it, he discovered that the cross was too short! At that moment he awakened.

The Challenge

What if we were to discover that of all the important things we need to do to qualify ourselves for exaltation, the one thing that will do the most to enable us to do everything else is mighty prayer? And further, that the one thing that will enable our prayers to be truly mighty is praying long enough each day to demand a real effort, a real exercise of faith? And finally, that fifteen or twenty minutes a day in vocal prayer, if persisted in, will connect us with the powers we need to be connected with in order to become all the Lord would like us to become? Surely, if we discovered such truths, would we not be pleased to take advantage of them?

But it seems as though there exists an invisible barrier that keeps us from achieving various goals that are really challenging. For example, to break into a consistent pattern of running and jogging at first requires us to make some strenuous effort, but once our bodies are conditioned, how enjoyable we find running can be. To develop our ability to do difficult gymnastics routines demands overcoming fear and developing muscles never used before, but once we have broken through those barriers, we find that the thrilling satisfaction of successfully doing challenging routines is difficult to describe. To learn how to fast effectively requires a cleansing of the body that for the first several fasts is somewhat uncomfortable, if not painful. But once the body is cleansed, a barrier is cleared, and fasting can be a beautiful experience for us and remarkably rewarding spiritually.

It is no different with prayer. In order to arrive at a point where "mighty prayer" (D&C 29:1–2) is an integral part of our daily life, it seems as though there is a barrier to break, that at first a struggle is required, but once the barrier is broken, the blessings of mighty prayer are inestimable.

It is possible to know a great deal about religion and not necessarily live our lives in harmony with what we know. It isn't too difficult to be "hearers of the word," but it is a great challenge to be "doers of the word" as well. (James 1:22.) Something that has caused me to stress the importance of prayer is the discovery that not very many of the students I have taught had ever invested very much time in prayer! It was uncommon to discover individuals who had reached beyond the perfunctory saying of their prayers. It was very rare to discover one who had ever prayed for thirty minutes, let alone an hour. Again, these discoveries caused me to stress mighty prayer, to plead with the students to set aside sufficient time to lift up their voices in mighty prayer in the same way they set aside so many minutes to search the scriptures or to do other things. As a result, I have challenged my students over the years to pray for fifteen or twenty minutes a day for a month in order to break the "prayer barrier" and begin to see what mighty prayer is all about.

The challenge to pray for fifteen or twenty minutes a day has produced more spiritual growth in the lives of those who seriously implemented the challenge than any other challenge I have given. Something happens when we struggle and plead for that long. There is a stretching of our spiritual fibers that causes them to grow; there is a concentration demanded that pulls on the stuff real faith is made of; there is a gradual infusion into our spine of spiritual starch that really strengthens us to seek, hunger, thirst, and strive for righteousness. We can't pray for fifteen or twenty minutes a day without pushing ourselves beyond the mechanical aspects of prayer into the prayer of real faith, which invariably brings ever greater knowledge and power from the Lord.

I encourage you with all my heart to accept the challenge to pray for fifteen or twenty minutes a day. If you will do it diligently, I believe that you will begin to taste of some powers that will give you the confidence not only that life is worthwhile but also that you can ultimately receive everything the Father and the Son have. It is hard to break the prayer barrier, but you can do it, and once you do break that barrier, mighty prayer will be such an integral part of your life that it will be a daily experience as natural and spontaneous as breathing.

I believe there is an advantage in having a special place and a special time for our individual prayers. To keep a period of the day hallowed and to have a place that has become especially sacred is to build a tradition that will itself become a great source of strength. We may choose to set aside the early hours of the day, or noon, or late at night; we may go to a bedroom, a furnace room, a grove of trees, or a mountain—just so we have a time and a place to turn our attention to the sacred experience of prayer.

Prayer Unlocks the Doors of Heaven

Is it any wonder that prayer is the very key to a knowledge of God? The first step to eternal life? The connecting link between God and ourselves? The message of the prophets of all ages is that we can converse with God and obtain from him the knowledge and ability to live by faith. How powerfully and beautifully the Prophet Joseph Smith said it: "It is the first principle of the Gospel to know for a certainty the Character of God, and to know that we may converse with him as one man converses with another." (*Teachings of the Prophet Joseph Smith,* p. 345.)

What a beautiful principle. As with the development of any Christlike quality, it takes a great deal of determination and persistence to have our prayers be meaningful every day. But as the truth of the principle is burned into your soul by the witness of the Spirit as you grow and persist in mighty prayer, your experiences in prayer will be a great source of spiritual motivation in your life, and, if sanctioned by the Father, you will be permitted in time come to converse with the Father in the name of Christ "as one man converses with another."

I know that God hears and answers prayers and that through the quiet whisperings of the Holy Ghost and through other means, he can and will bless us with whatever we need. Conversing with God is the means by which we develop a personal relationship with him. As we grow in the spirit and power of prayer, the reality of the Savior, his atonement, and his revelations through mighty prophets of God will become the anchor and the strength of our lives. A statement by the Prophet Joseph Smith sums up the concept of mighty prayer: "Come to God [and] weary him until he blesses you." (*The Words of Joseph Smith,* p. 15.)

Chapter 3

JESUS CHRIST, THE SON OF GOD

The essential doctrine of true Christianity — the doctrine that upholds, supports, and sustains the entire structure of the plan of salvation — is that Jesus Christ is literally divine, the offspring of Deity. Without that doctrine, which is taught abundantly in the scriptures and through the words of living prophets, there is little to distinguish Christianity from other religions and from the vain philosophies of man's wisdom. It becomes nothing more than a mere system of ethics.

The scriptures contain many beautiful testimonies of the literal sonship of Christ. In the Book of Mormon, Nephi, after having been shown the vision of the tree of life that his father had seen, asked for an interpretation of that vision. Nephi then was shown "a virgin, most beautiful and fair above all other virgins," and he was told by an angel that she was "the mother of the Son of God, after the manner of the flesh." (1 Nephi 11:15, 18.) This virgin whom Nephi saw was "carried away in the Spirit for the space of a time" and then appeared again, "bearing a child in her arms." (Vv. 19–20.) The angel declared, "Behold the Lamb of God, yea, even the Son of the Eternal Father!" (V. 21.)

The New Testament accounts that Jesus was begotten of the Father are equally clear and should leave no question in the minds of those filled with the Spirit that Jesus is the literal offspring of God our Heavenly Father.

Modern scripture contains perhaps the most powerful declaration of the divine Sonship of Christ in the Prophet Joseph Smith's inspired witness: "And now, after the many testimonies which have been given of him, this is the testimony, last of all, which we give of him: That he lives! For we saw him, even on the right hand of God; and we heard the voice bearing record that he is the Only Begotten of the Father." (D&C 76:22–23.)

Another beautiful account that portrays the sanctity, beauty, and reality of the Savior's divine birth is the following by Elder S. Dilworth Young:

"What I am about to say and the manner of its saying is in response to a request made by those who planned this program. Some of the things I shall mention are based on the accepted accounts; some are imaginary. You will recognize each of these without further comment from me. What liberties I have taken with established texts are also easily recognized and need no explanation. However, I should like to tell you that I shall take liberty with two proper names in the sense that I have chosen to use these names in English as derived from the Aramaic tongue, the language spoken by the Jews at the time of Christ, rather than from the Greek from which these names usually come down to you. I shall have to make myself somebody else. You will forgive me for that.

"Let me introduce myself as being named James. I have four brothers. Jeshua is the oldest — my elder brother. Joses, Simon, Judas are my younger brothers. I have three sisters.

"We lived quite simply in a little town called Nazareth. We had to live simply. My father was a carpenter. The carpenter's trade was dull business in our town. We made furniture as needed by the townspeople; we repaired furniture; we built houses; and we built stables and other shelter.

"As small boys we often sat upon the roof of our house in the cool of the evening, and we would ask mother and father for stories. One story we liked especially well was how the angel came to each house in Mizraim and spared the first-born of those whose houses were marked with the blood of the sacrificial lamb. Then we liked, too, how when our people were in the wilderness, they were fed manna.

"I asked my mother, 'What is manna?'

50

"She said, 'I do not know, only that they were told that they must gather only enough for the day, for if they took more, it would spoil.'

"And the story of how the quails miraculously became food for them when they were desperately hungry. Those stories brought the ancient customs of our people to my mind.

"But our favorite story was the one about the time when Father and Mother and Jeshua went to live in Mizraim shortly after Jeshua was born; how when they had no money, some men from the East had visited them and had given them gold and frankincense and myrrh as a birth gift to Jeshua. She told how they had said that they had followed a star to our door.

"We would ask, 'Was Jeshua born in a stable?'

"Mother would say, 'Yes, but when these men came, we had moved from the stable into a house. It had been several days before we could obtain the lodgings, but your father searched and finally found a place.'

" 'Was there a star?'

"Mother said, 'I did not see it, but the men said that a star showed them which way to go and indicated where to find us.'

" 'Why did you go to Mizraim?'

" 'An angel came and warned us,' said my father, 'to leave and not come back until we were told, so we felt we needed to obey. It was fortunate for us that the men gave us gifts, for with the gold, we purchased asses to go to Mizraim—four of them, and with the money from the sale of the frankincense and the myrrh, we lived in Mizraim until it was safe to come home.'

"And how excited I became when my mother told me about the great sandstorm which they met on the way, which so suddenly came up that they could not pitch their little tent. How they were enveloped in the terrible wind and darkness of blowing and drifting sand. They struggled on and fortunately fell into, literally, a caravan with tents pitched and safe. The caravan leaders took them in, preserved them; and, from then on, they accompanied the caravan to Mizraim. Those were our favorite stories as we would sit on the roof of our house looking up at the stars.

"Daily we learned our trade. Father was a hard taskmaster

51

in the sense that he insisted that we learn—that is, all but Jeshua. He had liberty. He used to take long walks alone. Sometimes, as we grew older, He would be gone two or three nights; and Mother would worry about Him. Father, upon His return, never rebuked Him.

"I would hear him say, 'Jeshua, was your trip fruitful?'

" 'Yes, Father.'

" 'Did you find what you sought?'

" 'I found fourfold,' He would reply.

"It is easy now, looking back, to see what He meant. I think our friend Matthew, who wrote so extensively of His life, truly said He "grew up with his brethren, and waxed strong, and waited upon the Lord for the time of his ministry to come. And he served under his father, and he spake not as other men, neither could he be taught; for he needed not that any man should teach him." [JST, Matthew 3:24–25.]

"It was on THAT day—that day when Mother prepared a special feast for us. She had procured a lamb and cooked it with vegetables into a most tasty dish. When we were through eating, Jeshua arose, kissed his sisters, embraced Father and each of us, and gave honor especially to Mother and said good-by.

" 'The time has come, Mother. I am thankful to you for being my mother—and to you, Father, for your care of me.'

"Later we asked Mother why He must leave, and she said: 'He is going to His work. God, His Father, has called Him.'

" 'What work?'

" 'I cannot tell you. I am not quite sure myself. I know only that He is to save the people. I have not told you before, but now you should know that when He was born, an angel commanded your father to name Him "Jeshua," "The Anointed One." The angel told your father that He was born to save the people from their sins. How He will do it, I do not know; but He is leaving us now to begin that work.'

" 'Is He a prophet?'

"She nodded and said, 'He is a prophet.'

"I never forgot that.

"Then Jeshua came home. We had news of His work in nearby towns—how He healed the sick, and was teaching a new kingdom, a different kingdom than one we knew. We hardly had expected Him back so soon, but we were glad to see Him. Many friends called, and a feast was had in His honor. The Rabbi invited Him to read on the Sabbath. So we went—Father, Jeshua, I, Joses, Simon, and Judas—sitting on the little cushions on the men's side of the synagogue. Then the Rabbi invited Jeshua up to read. He asked the Rabbi for the roll from Esaias, and when it was procured, He opened it and then He read. I can still remember the words:

" 'The Spirit of the Lord God is upon *Me*; because the Lord hath anointed *Me* to preach good tidings unto the meek; he hath sent *Me* to bind up the brokenhearted, to proclaim liberty to the captives, and the opening of the prison to them that are bound; To proclaim the acceptable year of the Lord. . . . ' Here He stopped. There was something in His manner which held everybody in close attention. My father was leaning forward slightly, hardly breathing.

"Then, 'This day this scripture is fulfilled in your hearing.' [See Luke 4:16–30.]

"There was an indrawn gasp of the assembled people. I turned to Father.

" 'What is He saying?'

"My father turned and whispered to me, 'Don't forget this, for this is true. He is saying that He is the person of whom Esaias was speaking.'

" 'Is He the Messiah?'

" 'He is the Messiah.'

"There were accusations; and someone shouted, 'Blasphemy!'

"Another yelled, 'If you are that prophet, let us see you do the works they say you do in Capernaum. You look to me like Jeshua, the son of old Joseph there.'

"Jeshua replied, 'No prophet is accepted in his own country.'

"The whole audience seemed to be pulled by an intense anger. They arose to take Him, shouting that they would throw Him over a cliff nearby; but He stepped down and walked to the door and out, they appearing not to see Him.

"My father smiled, 'He will come to no harm. He has His work to do.'

"There is no need of my telling you all that He taught or all that He did. These things have been written, and well written, by my friends and associates.

"I regret only one thing. One of our later associates, Dr. Luke, wrote an account of His life to the Greek people. I wish that He had not translated the name of my brother into that language. Proper names need not be translated, but the Doctor did it. Sometimes when I hear people now speak of Jesus Christ, I have to stop and catch myself before I realize that they are talking about my elder brother, Jeshua, the Anointed One.

"The writings tell well enough of the accusations, the death — and of His resurrection. It was not until after that — when the excited Mary had told Peter and John, and they had seen the empty tomb — that we began to have clear in our minds what He meant when He so often had said He would rise the third day.

"Sometime after this we were sitting on the roof of our old house in Nazareth. Peter and the apostles had organized the Church. I was appointed to be president of the Nazareth Branch. As the stars shone that night on us with all the glory of their clear beauty, I felt impelled to ask,

" 'Mother, was Jeshua the Son of God?'

" 'Yes, my son.'

" 'But Joseph was His father.'

" 'No, Joseph was *not* His father. Joseph was *your* father, but not His father.'

" 'Then who was His father?'

" 'I have told you. He was the Son of God.'

"She continued:

" 'Years ago I was visited by an angel who told me that I should bear a son who would be called Jeshua, the Anointed One, the Son of God. Your father had intended to break the engagement when he discovered that I was expecting a baby. The angel commanded him to marry me and raise the child. These things, my sons, we have carried in our hearts all through the years: The joy of rearing, the pride of His accomplishments, the puzzlement in our souls when He did what we least expected and when He taught new doctrine. Yet we waited, knowing God's will would be done: The agony of frustration at His death and the sight of His glorious resurrection have at last each one been put in its proper place. Remember always, my sons and daughters, He is the Son of God, literally and finally. Your mother gave Him His earthly tabernacle. Your father was privileged to act as His foster father.'

"I can see my mother now as she sat there in the dignity of her old age, silver-haired, as she bore witness that their Jeshua, Jesus Christ to the Greeks, was the Son of God, the Redeemer. As Esaias said, " . . . Wonderful, Counseller, The mighty God, The everlasting Father, The Prince of Peace." [Isaiah 9:6.]

"She said to us, 'Let us never forget it.'

"Well, let you and me never forget it either. He is the Son of God. He is the Prince of Peace. He is your Saviour; He is my Saviour. He was resurrected; He did establish this Church. Let us all be united in that testimony, in His holy name, Amen." ("Jesus Christ, the Son of God," *Instructor*, Dec. 1961, pp. 402-3, 405.)

A Divine Birth for an Infinite Atonement

The major theme of the scriptures and the living prophets is the reality that Christ, even Jehovah, the firstborn in the spirit, would take upon himself a tabernacle of flesh as the literal offspring of God our Heavenly Father in order to redeem all mankind. That theme is inextricably connected with the theme that it was his miraculous conception and birth that enabled him to perform this great mission. The divine birth had to precede the divine redemption.

Had the Savior not been the Son of God the Father in the flesh, he would not have been endowed with the ability to live a sinless life, nor could he have taken upon his shoulders the sins of the world, nor could he have broken the bands of death to enable all mankind to be resurrected. Had the Savior not also been the son of a mortal woman, he would not have been tempted in all things and thus would not be able to succor us in all things. In addition, having a mortal mother, Jesus inherited the seeds of physical death, enabling him to give up his life to effect his infinite atonement.

In spite of the enormous evidence that Jesus is the Son of God and that his being the Son of God is what breathes the redemptive power into the gospel of Christ, many so-called Christian denominations reject that great message by rejecting the ordinances and principles that are the lifeblood of the gospel or by rejecting outright the doctrine that Christ is the Son of God or by rejecting both.

"Who Knows But What Another Man Will Come Along . . . "

As an institute of religion director on various college campuses in the West, I have had several experiences that enabled me to feel the pulse of many people who represent a broad spectrum of commitments to so-called Christianity. Many people outside the Church—people who live lives of honor and service—evidence a solid belief in Christ's divinity. I have been greatly disappointed, however, at the number of individuals in ecclesiastical positions in the Christian world who outwardly accept Christ as the Son of God but who in reality do not believe in his divinity. Invariably these individuals do not openly voice rejection of Christ's divinity until they are challenged by those who sincerely want to know where their leaders stand on that most crucial issue in Christianity. Then they declare emphatically that the Savior is not divine and thus reject the very cornerstone of the religion they profess.

One such experience occurred while I was director of the institute of religion near Colorado State University. Each year the University Religious Directors Association sponsored a Religious Emphasis Week. A prominent person who had made significant contributions in the area of religion would be invited to campus. During his stay, he would give several formal addresses as well as meet with small groups of students in the dorms and other places for informal discussion. This particular year, the invited guest was a very prominent minister of a large Protestant denomination. He had served as a missionary to China for many years and was also heavily involved in civic and political activities.

Eager to support the week-long activity, I attended almost all of his formal lectures. I was very impressed with his understanding of both the Old and the New Testaments. He showed real insight into how the scriptures could be applied to help solve difficult national and international problems. And he spoke often and reverently about the Lord. As I listened to him, I felt respect for this good man and admired his sensitive teachings.

To encourage academic excellence, the university arranged for an "I Disagree" session to be held at the end of Religious Emphasis Week. Everyone was invited to the session, and it was arranged and advertised to encourage a free, open atmosphere where individuals would be willing to say what they really thought and felt. Part of the "I Disagree" session was a discussion by a panel selected to defend Christianity. The panel was composed of the distinguished guest, some university officials, and representatives of the major churches on campus, including me.

After our guest's last formal sermon, those on the panel and all others who were interested filed out of the large ballroom and down into a sizable basement room known as "the cave." As I observed the loud talk and the spirit of resistance to the things that had been taught all week long, it seemed the battle lines were indeed drawn.

After preliminary introductions, questions and comments were invited from the audience. The response was quick in coming and was in general extremely critical. One individual said he was sick and tired of religion because more blood had been shed under the flag of Christianity than under any other banner. (As I reflected on the Inquisition and the Crusades, I concluded that was probably true.) Others were incensed with those who teach that there are absolute truths, particularly in the area of sexual morality. They emphasized "situational ethics": the idea that one's ethics should be determined by the particular situation one might find himself in. Much was said about the "social gospel," which suggests that churches should be more involved in social action than they are. The historicity of the Old Testament prophets was strongly challenged, many saying that men like Abraham and Moses never really lived and that the stories about them in the scriptures are mythical, fabricated simply to teach moral principles. The divinity of Christ was particularly challenged: Christ, many felt, was a great teacher, but not divine—not the literal Son of God.

What really shocked me was that members of the panel who were supposed to be defending Christianity were essentially as critical of Christianity as the audience was. In fact, they were using their training to confirm the criticisms leveled at the basic premises of Christianity. What a disappointing experience to hear professed Christians saying that the Old Testament prophets probably never really existed, implying so boldly that there are no absolute truths, and making observations that took away from the idea that Jesus Christ is indeed the Son of God and the Redeemer of the world.

While all this was happening, my disappointment grew into disgust and then into good old, pure, righteous indignation. Several times I formulated responses to what was being said only to have those responses overpowered by a heart that was pounding uncontrollably. I so wanted to defend the gospel, the scriptures, and especially the Savior, but considering how unusually perturbed I was, I hesitated to stand up and say anything for fear my anxiety would keep me from making any sense. Finally, and with some excitement and enthusiasm, I jumped up. It was immediately recognized that I wanted to say something and say it very quickly. Somehow both roving microphones gravitated to me, so I had a microphone in each hand.

I will admit that for a few moments I felt some real fear. I knew that I would have to at least strongly imply that most of the criticism leveled that evening at Christianity was really criticism of an apostate form of Christianity. After a few moments, I felt a real peace, and I knew what I needed to say.

I testified, probably with a greater power than I had felt before, that Jesus is the Christ, the Son of the living God. I bore witness that the scriptures contain absolute truths, which, if we live them, will assure us of happiness and well-being.

I declared that I knew the Old Testament prophets were historical individuals who had lived and held communion with

God. I further testified that the Savior was coming again to judge the world and that all of us would be accountable to him for the lives we lived. I knew I was coming on very strong, and yet the audience was quiet and very respectful. In fact, for the first time that night, there was no laughing, talking, or heckling.

I emphasized again that I knew Jesus Christ is the divine Son of God and that we would be accountable to him for the lives we lived. When I said, "And I bear testimony of these things in the name of Jesus Christ," much to my surprise there was an immediate burst of applause that continued for some time.

The applause caught me off guard. I was surprised and puzzled. I thought almost everyone there wanted to throw Christianity out the window, and yet here they are applauding with such fervor! Finally, it dawned on me what was happening—they were saying, in effect, Thank God someone knows he lives, that someone knows Jesus is indeed the Christ, that there are absolute truths in a terrible sea of relativity.

When the applause ended, a student stood up and, pointing to our distinguished guest, asked quite bluntly: "Sir, do you believe Jesus Christ is divine—the Son of God?" A hush came over the entire audience. Everyone looked toward the guest. He paused for several moments and then, almost with a full smile, he said, "I would rather not believe Jesus Christ is divine, for if I did, that would give him a head start over me!" He continued, "Who knows but what in the next twenty years another man will come along who will live a better life than Christ did, and I will revere him as my Redeemer!"

I was stunned. Most of the people in the audience were stunned. We had listened for a week to a man who quoted the Master constantly, who claimed great respect for the Savior's teachings, who gave the distinct impression that he accepted Christ as the Son of God; but now, challenged to declare where he actually stood, he unhesitantly denied Christ's divinity. In denying Christ's divinity, the speaker negated most, if not all, of what he had taught during the week.

There is a postscript to that experience. Shortly after the featured guest denied the Savior's divinity, the "I Disagree" session ended. Immediately a half dozen or so students surrounded me and began asking me questions. Not one of them questioned whether or not I really knew God lived and Jesus was the Christ; rather, almost all of them asked how I was able to find out or learn those great truths. I was impressed that if testimonies are borne under the influence of the Spirit, people, even those living lives seriously counter to the gospel, will know that what is being said is true.

I learned later that my wife, Diane, who had also attended the session, had been asked point blank by a fellow how he could learn that what I had said was true. Her reply was simple and to the point: "If you'll get a copy of the Book of Mormon and read it and pray about it, you'll learn that God lives and that Jesus is the Christ." Another fellow blurted out, "I know about you Mormons and the Book of Mormon. I got a copy of the Book of Mormon, and I read it, and I prayed about it, but I didn't learn it was true!"

What do you do when you give someone the formula to learn that the restored gospel is true, and then the formula doesn't seem to work? Do you come up with another formula? Well, I'm glad Diane was answering the question because I might not have had the courage necessary to do what she did. She looked him in the eye and asked, "What kind of a life were you living when you read the Book of Mormon?"

He said, "What do you mean?"

She said, "Were you living in fornication?"

He said, "Yes, whenever I could."

She replied, "Young man, don't you ever think that God will reveal to you the sacred truths my husband testified of when you are living in violation of such a sacred law."

After it was all over and we were walking home, both my wife and I spoke of how surprised we had been to discover that one who had given his life to the ministry denied the divinity of Christ, and we marveled together at the privilege it was to bear testimony of the divinity of the Savior.

Denying the More Parts of the Gospel

There is an unmistakably clear profile of apostasy written time and again across the pages of holy writ. The pattern found in 4 Nephi is not atypical. Two hundred years after the visit of the glorified, resurrected Christ, the Saints became lifted up in the pride of their hearts and manifested that pride by wearing costly apparel. They then refused to have all things in common — that is, they refused to have the welfare of every individual at heart. They next divided into classes and built up churches unto themselves. Finally they began to "deny the more parts of his gospel," and they actually created a church that denied the Christ. (4 Nephi 1:27.)

The final manifestation of apostasy is complete rejection of the Savior, his gospel, and his church. But there is an earlier manifestation of apostasy that crops up which, although not denying directly the divinity of Christ and his kingdom on earth, tends to take away almost as effectively from the effect of the Savior's power in their lives. I speak of the tendency for some in the Church to become so enamored with their academic achievements and learning that they give more credence to the wisdom of men than they do to the revelations of God.

President J. Reuben Clark, Jr., taught that "there are for the Church and for each and all of its members, two prime things which may not be overlooked, forgotten, shaded, or discarded:

"First: That Jesus Christ is the Son of God, the Only Begotten of the Father in the flesh. . . .

"The second of the two things to which we must all give full faith is: That the Father and the Son actually and in truth and very deed appeared to the Prophet Joseph in a vision in the woods." (*The Charted Course of the Church in Education* [address to seminary, institute, and Church school teachers, Aspen Grove, Utah, 8 Aug. 1938], in *Charge to Religious Educators,* p. 3.)

President Clark reminded us that it isn't too difficult even in the Church to take away from the significance of the great truth that Jesus Christ is literally the Son of God. In a day and age when so many of the traditional doctrines and values of Christianity have been changed or rejected, we can readily acknowledge that most of Christendom has lost the significant meaning of the literal Sonship of Christ. But how could rank-and-file Latter-day Saint professional teachers, auxiliary teachers, and lay members of the Church find themselves in a similar situation?

Let me suggest that there are several ways that the importance of the divine Sonship of Christ could be weakened in the lives of members of the Church. First, I have observed that there is often a disparity between what is taught by members of the Church about the nature of fallen man and what the scriptures and the prophets of the Church seem to teach about that important subject. Second, I have found that, intentionally or unintentionally, many teachers have substituted for the doctrine of Christ—that is, first principles—the moral and ethical teaching of the gospel.

The Nature of Fallen Man

Few questions in or out of the Church elicit more excited discussion than this one: What is the nature of man?

The Church teaches clearly that Adam and Eve lived, that they partook of the forbidden fruit, and, consequently, that they brought physical death and spiritual death upon all mankind. The Church and the prophets confirm powerfully that we all suffer from spiritual death, but Church members often seem confused about what that actually means. Perhaps one of the best elaborations about what the scriptures mean when they speak of man's fallen nature is the following by the late Sidney B. Sperry, a former dean of the College of Religious Instruction at Brigham Young University:

"All men, whether 'incorrigible sinners' or so-called 'good men' who are ethical and just, 'the honorable men of the earth,' (D. & C. 76:75) are carnal and fallen as long as they fail to become 'new creatures' by yielding to 'the enticings of the Holy Spirit' and by laying aside the 'natural man' and becoming saints through the atonement of our Lord. (Mosiah 3:19) In other words, men must be spiritually reborn, even as the Lord taught Nicodemus, or they cannot see the kingdom of God. (John 3:3) Now we suppose that Nicodemus was an ethical, just, and honorable man in his relationships to others; nevertheless, the Savior made it perfectly clear that he had to have a spiritual rebirth or he would remain, as Book of Mormon language has it, a 'fallen' or 'natural' man.

"When the Nephite record refers to fallen man as 'carnal, sensual, and devilish,' it seems to shock some people—and it should. But let us here introduce the following explanation by Dr. David Yarn of Brigham Young University:

" 'An explanation . . . suggests . . . that the words *carnal, sensual,* and *devilish,* must not be limited to their more narrow and specific connotations, but that they are accurately, though more broadly, interpreted by the scriptural phrase "enemy to God." That is to say, not all men who have not made the covenants with the Christ are given to indulging in degrading practices which are appropriately designated carnal, sensual, and devilish in a dictionary sense. Yet all men, regardless of how moral and how pure they may be with reference to such practices, are enemies to God, until they yield to the enticings of the Holy Spirit, accept the Atonement of the Lord, and are submissive to His will. A significant point here is that what we conventionally call basic personal and social morality is not enough. . . . for one not to be an enemy to God he must endeavor to do all things whatsoever the Lord his God shall command him. (See Abraham 3:25)

" 'Summarily put, the natural man (he who is carnal, sensual, and devilish, he who is an enemy to God) is the man who has not humbled himself before God and made covenants with God by receiving the revealed ordinances at the hands of God's authorized servants; or the man who, having done these things, has failed to live according to the covenants made in baptism and to the injunction given when he was confirmed a member of the Church—"Receive the Holy Ghost." ' [*Gospel Living in the Home,* p. 51, Deseret Sunday School Union, 1962.]" (*Answers to Book of Mormon Questions,* pp. 5–6.)

It is important, when the nature of fallen man is discussed, to emphasize that because of the atonement of Christ, we are not born with original guilt—we are not born in a depraved condition. In fact, the effects of the Fall are so totally lifted from all of us by the Atonement that Lehi declared, "And because that they are redeemed from the fall they have become free forever, knowing good from evil." (2 Nephi 2:26.) We are born pure, holy, and innocent, and enjoy the marvelous light of Christ.

In spite of our being born free, of our having the light of

Christ, when we reach the age of accountability, we all (except Christ) suffer from spiritual death, for we are all sinners. (See Romans 3:23.) Adam was told, "When [children] begin to grow up, sin conceiveth in their hearts, and they taste the bitter, that they may know to prize the good." (Moses 6:55.)

In addition, it is important to realize that there is a difference between the nature of fallen man and the potential of fallen man. Because all of us suffer from spiritual death doesn't mean we do not have marvelous potential. In fact, the Psalmist's declaration, "Ye are gods" (Psalm 82:6), confirms that our potential is such that someday through faithfulness we can become as God.

When the prophets speak of the nature of "natural man," they are describing those attitudes and actions that are "natural" as a result of having become fallen. As an example, when it comes to mankind as a whole, is it "natural" for them, of themselves, to know God and Christ? Is it "natural" for them to respond to and accept the message of the Restoration? Is it "natural" for most people to take care of the poor? Is it "natural" for mankind in general to live in peace?

And how about members of the Church: is it "natural" for most members to pay an honest tithe, give generous fast offerings, marry in the temple, do their home teaching and visiting teaching? Statistics indicate and my own experience confirms that it takes a tremendous effort on the part of the Lord, his Holy Spirit, his anointed prophets, and those who labor in the Church to get a reasonable number of people to the point where it is natural for them to keep the commandments.

I believe with all my heart that *if* we become truly converted to the restored gospel of Christ (and only *if!*), we *can* arrive at a point where it will be "natural" for us to pay an honest tithe and a generous fast offering, to marry in the temple, and give our energy, time, and talents to build the kingdom of God. I'm fully convinced, however, that if it were not for the restoration of the gospel, for the holy priesthood, for the gift and power of the Holy Ghost, for the inspired pleading of living prophets in our midst, and if it were not for a decided effort on our part to humble ourselves, to hunger and thirst and strive and seek for righteousness, we would forever remain subject to the flesh, taking our cues constantly from the flesh instead of from the Spirit. We would forever be spiritually dead, incapable of comprehending our godlike potential, and we would remain candidates for the terrestrial or telestial kingdom.

Personally, I'm quite overwhelmed at what a challenge it is to subdue the flesh and to yield to the Spirit. I'm both fascinated and appalled at how hard it is to keep hold of the iron rod. (See 1 Nephi 8:24.) It isn't terribly difficult to be basically good, but how hard it is to pull down the revelations of heaven, to be filled with the love of God and obtain the power to make a difference in the lives of others. We can appreciate why President David O. McKay said:

"Man has a dual nature; one, related to the earthly or animal life; the other, akin to the Divine. Whether a man remains satisfied within what we designate the animal world, satisfied with what the animal world will give him, yielding without effort to the whim of his appetites and passions and slipping farther and farther into the realm of indulgence, or whether, through self-mastery, he rises toward intellectual, moral, and spiritual enjoyments depends upon the kind of choice he makes every day, nay, every hour of his life." (*Gospel Ideals*, pp. 347–48.)

The achievement of the self-mastery President McKay spoke of is only through the gospel, for, he declared, "the whole purpose of life is to bring under subjection the animal passions, proclivities, and tendencies that we might realize the companionship always of God's Holy Spirit." ("The Influence of the Temples," *Improvement Era*, May 1964, p. 349.)

This question about the nature of fallen man is crucial in our search to know Christ. If we as Latter-day Saints reject the seriousness of man's fallen condition and teach that natural man — that is, man who has not yet "yield[ed] to the enticings of the Holy Spirit" (Mosiah 3:19) — is basically good instead of teaching the correct concept that man has a dual nature and is under the bondage of sin until he comes to the Savior (see D&C 84:51), then we take away from the awesome necessity for Christ to be the Son of God. Christ was sired by God that he might obtain the power to enable men and women to "know good from evil" as plainly as they know daylight from dark. (Moroni 7:15.) Millions have responded to the light of Christ and have benefited immeasurably from the divine sonship of Christ, which enabled him, even Jesus, to offer a power of redemption beyond that of the light of Christ. This greater power can enable people, as Moroni put it, to "lay hold upon every good thing" (Moroni 7:20), and it is this greater power that enables us and the world to be "cleanse[d] from all unrighteousness" (D&C 76:41).

The Lord has provided the way, the means, the power through his restored gospel whereby men and women, by exercising great faith in Christ, can arrive at the point where it is natural to abhor sin, natural to keep the commandments, natural to love all mankind with a perfect love, natural to go on a mission, natural to marry in the house of the Lord, and so on. It will never be "natural" to keep the high standards of the gospel of Jesus Christ until our hearts, our natures, are changed by the power of the Lord through the marvelous workings of the Holy Ghost.

When we realize that even the most basic problems confronting mankind cannot be solved unaided by the power and direction of the Master, when we realize that war is more predominant on earth than peace, selfishness more predominant than generosity, then we can begin to see how desperately we need to look to the Savior and his gospel if we ever hope to attain consistent peace and prosperity.

I'm convinced that nothing in the gospel of Christ will cause us to be more determined to obtain the power of godliness than to glimpse by revelation the seriousness of our fallen condition. On the other hand, in my estimation, nothing does more to keep the Saints from enjoying the greater powers of the gospel more than does putting the wisdom of man in the place of the gospel.

Perhaps an analogy would be helpful. The man of whom I speak in this analogy is someone who sees himself as quite bright, well educated, and emotionally stable, is doing well in a chosen vocation or profession, and, in general, feels he has "prospered according to his genius." (Alma 30:17.) Our friend is challenged by an associate to run a thirty-mile marathon, and, if he runs it successfully between sunrise and sunset, he will receive many prestigious honors. This is no ordinary marathon, however, for it must be run over many different types of terrain — gently rolling plain, a large and steep mountain, and swampland. Although he is mindful that it will be a tremendous challenge, our friend doesn't know that it is impossible for any human being to cover the distance prescribed within a day, and he has accepted the challenge on good faith that it can be done. His situation is somewhat akin to Adam and Eve's predicament in the Garden of Eden where they were given the commandment to multiply and replenish the earth and at the same time were forbidden to partake of the tree of knowledge of good and evil—two commandments which simply could not be kept simultaneously. Having great confidence in his own ability and enjoying a lot of spunk and determination (two ingredients that are good in and of themselves and so necessary to survive the challenges of mortality), he is ready the following morning at the crack of dawn for his great adventure.

As the sun slips up over the eastern horizon, the starting gun is fired, and he is on his way. His optimism is high as he runs swiftly over the gently rolling landscape—he's convinced, in fact, because of the miles he covers in the first hour, that it will be quite easy to achieve his goal. But the terrain steepens, his pace slackens, and he finds himself climbing a mountain. As he climbs higher on the mountain itself, he no longer is running but can only struggle in a slow, laborious way to negotiate the steep cliffs.

Eventually, after great effort, he reaches the summit and commences his descent down into the valley, but he is deeply disturbed to realize that it took him much longer to get to the summit than he had hoped it would. Nevertheless, he makes good time going down the mountain and once again feels confident that he can still reach his goal. As he enters the valley, however, he is troubled because he must now work his way across a sizable swampland. He glances toward the sky and sees that the sun is well past the midpoint of its journey. Now, more than ever, he must take great care to stay on solid ground and not step where there very well could be treacherous quicksand.

After spending some time carefully crossing the swamp, he again checks the position of the sun and is startled to realize he has only a little time left to reach his goal. Becoming a little careless, even reckless, he hurries faster and faster. Almost before he realizes what he has done, he finds himself on ground that had appeared safe but is now quivering under his feet. He frantically reverses his direction to seek more stable footing, but the ground gives way, and he is caught in quicksand.

Although he realizes his predicament is quite serious, he is somewhat angry to have used poor judgment in allowing himself to be trapped. He has always been a man of great confidence and self-assurance; he is convinced that he can remove himself from his predicament by his own power. He calmly attempts to move his feet forward but to no avail. He then vigorously attempts to thrash his legs, but the faster and harder he tries to extricate himself, the quicker he sinks into the quicksand. Sensing for the first time the awful seriousness of his predicament and in a fit of irrationality, he reaches down into the quicksand, takes hold of his bootstraps, and proceeds to pull and pull for all he's worth! He then realizes how foolish it is to try to free himself by pulling on his own bootstraps! His embarrassment is heightened as he remembers his extensive academic training and his remarkable ability in times past to be calm and controlled at all times.

Finally, our friend admits that he simply cannot free himself by his own ability. He knows he must have help from some other source and that the help must be found quickly. For the first time he becomes aware that just a few feet ahead and above his head, a strong branch of a tree is within reach. (In our analogy the branch and the tree represent the combined wisdom and strength of mankind.) With tremendous effort, he inches forward and finally grasps the thick branch with both hands. Oh, what a relief it is to him, what an assurance to have hold of something that seems so solid and so sure! After resting for a few moments, he begins to pull himself up on the branch. It takes a great deal of effort, but the farther he pulls his body onto the branch, the more confidence he has that surely the branch will be the means of his salvation from the quicksand. In fact, even before he has managed to lift himself out of the mire of the quicksand, his feelings of independence and self-confidence, even a pride that is akin to arrogance, return. Finally, with a great lurch, he pulls himself completely onto the limb—but as he does, he hears a sickening crack and the limb snaps off, plunging him back into the quicksand. Having expended so much energy and effort, having placed so much confidence in what he was sure was his sole source of redemption, our friend is intellectually, emotionally, and physically wiped out. He continues to struggle, but he now knows in a way he has never known before that his predicament is completely hopeless. There is no way that his own strength or the strength of the combined wisdom of men can free him from imminent death.

As he sinks deeper into the quicksand, the panorama of his entire life passes before him. Things that had once seemed so important now seem so childish. His lifelong ambition to obtain the honors of men, to own the finest home and the most expensive car—all of these ambitions fade into utter insignificance. He begins to realize that his relationships with others, especially with his wife and family, are of utmost importance. He is utterly humiliated by the clear realization that he has allowed his appetites to be aroused and debauched by relentless unethical advertising campaigns that artificially stimulated his appetites. He begins to sense the eternal verity of God and Christ and the hereafter. He is very uneasy about the prospect of death, for he is only now appreciating the significance of life—and oh, how he wants to live! The hills in the distance, the trees, the sky, the sun—all things seem to take on a greater beauty and significance.

During what appear to be the closing moments of his life, the realization deepens in his heart that much of his predicament was caused by his pride and vanity, his unwillingness to seek for a deeper meaning in life. He is broken-hearted, and he so desperately wants to live! He finally concludes that if he is going to be saved, it will have to be through a superhuman power.

The sand has covered his shoulders and is oozing up around his neck. He is reaching, still reaching upward, hoping against hope that somehow, something will happen. His face is turned upward that he might breathe as long as possible, when much to his astonishment, an arm and a hand appear and extend toward him—an arm and a hand actually within reach!

He recognizes immediately that the arm and hand are powerful. "Thou hast a mighty arm: strong is thy hand." (Psalm

89:13.) Because of his predicament, our friend doesn't rationalize for a moment. He doesn't intellectualize about how an arm and a hand can appear in midair. He simply realizes that any hope for redemption will be in that hand and arm. He reaches upward and clasps the extended hand. As soon as he does so, he feels a kind of power like no other power he's ever felt before. He feels a power coming into his hand and his whole being that generates a confidence, a trust, a faith, a marvelous assurance that in this new power he can and will be freed from his predicament. He hangs on with all the strength and determination he can muster. He feels himself being lifted out of the mire, but with a great struggle because of his having trusted so long "in the arm of flesh" (2 Nephi 4:34), his having built so deeply into his very nature an attitude of complete self-reliance and self-sufficiency, his having become convinced that the development of moral character comes strictly from within an individual—a process of self-determination rather than of yielding one's heart to God.

As he struggles to hold on, he feels his hand slipping out of the proffered hand. His hand is slipping, not because of the lack of power in the other hand, but because of a lack of strength in his own. Try as hard as he can, he isn't able to hold on, his hand slips out, and he falls back into the quicksand. But (and this is the great message of the gospel of Jesus Christ) our friend quickly looks up to where the hand was and sees that the hand is still there! He quickly reaches up and takes hold again. The struggle again ensues, and in time, using all the persistence, determination, strength, and faith he can muster, he is able to avail himself fully of the means of redemption that is afforded him. His own strength grows as he struggles, and, ultimately, he is raised out of the quicksand that almost became his tomb and is placed on solid rock.

He soon realizes that not only has he been delivered from the awful possibility of death but he is a different person. He is totally clean from the effects of swamp water, mud, and sand. As the full realization of his deliverance and the tremendous change that has come over him sinks into his heart, he spontaneously falls upon his knees and with profound expressions of gratitude acknowledges that it was a power greater than any and all powers on earth that enabled him to be delivered. Oh, the joy, the ecstasy that fills his being as he contemplates the loving kindness and tender goodness of his God and his Redeemer! The Psalmist wrote, "He brought me up also out of an horrible pit, out of the miry clay, and set my feet upon a rock, and established my goings." (Psalm 40:2.)

Even though we as fallen men are capable of doing many things, our efforts to obtain freedom from the effects of the Fall (sin, ignorance, and death) are completely wasted without the Savior's lifting us by his power. Having made available his atonement, the Savior cannot redeem us unless we reach and struggle with all our power to grasp his hand and to hold on until we are safely placed "upon the rock of our Redeemer, who is Christ, the Son of God." (Helaman 5:12.)

We are, then, totally dependent upon the Lord to be reclaimed from our fallen condition. All the combined wisdom and learning of man cannot change our nature and free us from our predicament. Rather than stressing mere self-sufficiency, it seems to me that we should be stressing self-sufficiency in Christ. We need to reach with all the energy we possess to make contact with the Lord, but it is his power that changes our lives.

Another way people deliberately or otherwise take away from the central truth that Jesus Christ is the Son of God is by confusing what the gospel is and what it is not. Strictly speaking, the gospel is the "glad tidings," or good news, that the Son of God, tabernacled in the flesh, suffered, died, and rose again to "sanctify the world, and to cleanse it from all unrighteousness." (D&C 76:40–41.)

I'm genuinely concerned that there are those among us who are convinced that the world will be sanctified and cleansed from all unrighteousness if the inhabitants will familiarize themselves with all the known moral and ethical principles, and then, through sheer will power, make those virtues part of themselves, thinking, I suppose, that in time their sins would be remitted and their nature changed, and that they would then possess the nature of Christ. If that is true, why be concerned with the Restoration, angels, visions, ordinances, priesthood authority, and innumerable meetings? We don't need a Joseph Smith or a First Vision or a new set of scriptures to set out on a five-year, goal-setting spree to blossom into well-rounded advocates of the power of positive thinking!

But I really don't think that is the message of the Restoration. In our covenant with Christ, he has said that if we remember his blood that was shed and keep his commandments, he will in a marvelous way abide with us and we will become new creatures in and of the Holy One of Israel. (See 2 Corinthians 5:17.) As the apostle Paul put it, then Christ will be formed in us. (See Galatians 4:19.)

I've talked again and again with active Latter-day Saints who are not convinced that there is a peculiar power embedded in the fulness of the gospel that is not found in any good religion, be it Christian or otherwise, which to me negates the very heart of what the Restoration is all about. In fact, it very well could be true that the teaching of and commitment to good moral and ethical qualities has actually replaced, in the lives of many, the teaching of and commitment to the doctrine of Christ (that is, the first principles of the gospel). They fail to realize that the power to change lives is in the doctrine of Christ. If we truly implement the doctrine of Christ, we will not only be moral and ethical in the fullest sense of the words but we will also be holy, we will have the nature and character of Christ. The power to change our lives is in Christ and comes to us through the doctrine of Christ. The fruit, or blessing, of that power is a celestial level of morality and ethicalness. Men and women can become remarkably good by practicing the virtues of the good life, but it takes a divine Redeemer and his ordinances and principles to infuse in us his qualities and divine nature. Someone once said, "There is a righteousness of man and a righteousness of God, and it takes revelation to tell the difference between the two."

I'm convinced that the reason the Book of Mormon is so crucial in the development of the man and woman of Christ (see Helaman 3:29) is that it is centered on the reality and power that is available through a dynamic faith in Christ. The Book of Mormon is so crucial because the necessity of changing our lives through the workings, blessing, and endowment of the Holy

Ghost pulses through the pages of that great book. (See 1 Nephi 10:17–19; 3 Nephi 19:8–14.)

This problem reminds me of an article I saw once printed in a ward newspaper. The article was entitled, "What's Happened to the Scriptures?" The gist of the article was that there must be a new set of standard works in the ward, for observation had shown that such popular writers as Kahlil Gibran, Erich Fromm, and others were quoted much, much more than were Moses or Paul or Peter or Moroni or Joseph Smith or the current prophet. While obviously there is great wisdom in the writings of good people outside the Church, it seems ironic that sometimes Latter-day Saints seem more interested in quoting popular writers than they are in quoting the prophets both ancient and modern.

President J. Reuben Clark said: "Students fully sense the hollowness of teachings which would make the Gospel plan a mere system of ethics, they know that Christ's teachings are in the highest degree ethical, but they also know they are more than this. They will see that ethics relate primarily to the doings of this life, and that to make of the Gospel a mere system of ethics is to confess a lack of faith, if not a disbelief, in the here-after." (*Charted Course*, p. 5.) It is important to realize that the moral and ethical teachings of Christ's gospel are contained in every major religion of mankind; even a cursory study of Buddhism, Muhammadanism, or Zoroastrianism reveals powerful commitments to such ideals as love, kindness, patience, integrity, respect for life, and so forth. It is important also to realize that an understanding of moral and ethical teachings and an effort to live them will bless all who do so, but never, worlds without end, will such an approach by itself change the fallen nature of man and prepare a person for exaltation in the kingdom of God.

The power of redemption centers in the Savior's great atonement. Growing out of that atonement are peculiar principles and ordinances that are necessary means to focus our faith in Christ and to act as channels for the power of Christ to flow into our lives. As we receive from the Lord his power through obedience to the ordinances and the principles of his gospel, as we are transformed in his image and we become like him, we are moral

73

and ethical in all we do, but we are much, much more than that. In addition, we know the Savior, we understand the reality of his redemption, and we enjoy a character and a love that are immeasurably greater than the character and the love that are available outside the fulness of the gospel.

If we keep this distinction in mind, we will always recognize the Holy One of Israel as the source of power and see that everything else in the gospel (ordinances, principles, and programs) is a means to obtain that power. If we see the Savior as the source of redemptive power, I believe we will stress the necessity of knowing him ever so well and the importance of obtaining the companionship of the Holy Ghost to change our lives instead of vesting our time, energy, and money in intricate systems of behavioral change that have a measure of lifting power but are bereft of godly power to change human nature.

President John Taylor pinpointed the problem. He declared in power that the Savior came, not to renew or emphasize a system of ethics, but to bring a way of life that includes all that is ethical and goes infinitely beyond a mere system of ethics. Speaking of man's innate limitations, President Taylor said: "As a man through the powers of his body he could attain to the dignity and completeness of manhood, but could go no further; as a man he is born, as a man he lives, and as a man he dies; but through the essence and power of the Godhead, which is in him, which descended to him as the gift of God from his heavenly Father, he is capable of rising from the contracted limits of manhood to the dignity of a God." (*The Mediation and Atonement,* p. 141.)

We cannot enjoy the greater powers available in the restored gospel unless we sense in a profound way our total dependence on the Son of God and realize that only in and through him can our nature be changed and our character become like his. To know that Jesus is literally the Son of God is to acknowledge that because of that divine sonship he was able to come to the earth, break the bands of sin and death, and offer through his divine gospel the power to become like him and in so doing add to the honor and glory of the Father.

Chapter 4

THE SAVIOR'S ATONING SACRIFICE

The atonement of Christ is the most important event that has transpired or ever will transpire among all of God's creations. It is the very source of all life, light, power, truth, and love, and the center and object of all redemptive faith. To have faith in Jesus Christ is to have faith in his atonement, for the purpose of his life was to come forth to suffer, die, and rise again: "And this is the gospel, the glad tidings, which the voice out of the heavens bore record unto us—that he came into the world, even Jesus, to be crucified for the world, and to bear the sins of the world, and to sanctify the world, and to cleanse it from all unrighteousness." (D&C 76:40–41.) The Prophet Joseph Smith, after testifying of the central truth of the Savior's atonement, declared that "all other things which pertain to our religion are only appendages to it." (*Teachings of the Prophet Joseph Smith*, p. 121.)

In other words, the Atonement is the very heart of the gospel of Jesus Christ. Even as the human heart pumps life-giving blood to all parts of the body, so will the Atonement, if understood properly, act as a great spiritual heart, pumping life-giving blood through the ordinances and principles of the gospel to the life and soul of every member of the Church. Is it any wonder that every ordinance and principle, as indicated in the first chapter, is given from God to man to typify, or foreshadow, the Savior and his atonement? Is it any wonder that all the precious testimonies of men and women who have felt the redeeming power of the Savior in their lives have as their central theme the majesty and grandeur of that great act?

Even though the Atonement was wrought nearly two thousand years ago, its reality to us and its effect on us can be as great as though we had been contemporaries of the Savior living in Jerusalem. Indeed, under the quiet workings of the Holy Ghost, we can stand, as it were, in the Garden of Gethsemane, a witness of the Savior's agony; we can stand, as it were, at the foot of Golgotha and obtain an overwhelming awareness of the pain of the cross; we can receive in our hearts a measure, and only as the Spirit can reveal it, of the tremendous pain, sorrow, and humiliation he suffered. We can, in other words, experience in part the majesty of the Atonement and make it the greatest event in our lives.

The following experience of Elder Orson F. Whitney shows how real the Atonement became in his life:

"It was in a dream, or in a vision in a dream, as I lay upon my bed in the little town of Columbia, Lancaster County, Pennsylvania [while on a mission]. I seemed to be in the Garden of Gethsemane, a witness of the Savior's agony. I saw Him plainly as I have seen anyone. Standing behind a tree in the foreground, I beheld Jesus with Peter, James and John, as they came through a little wicket gate at my right. Leaving the three Apostles there, after telling them to kneel and pray, the Son of God passed over to the other side, where He also knelt and prayed. It was the same prayer with which all Bible readers are familiar: 'Oh, my Father, if it be possible, let this cup pass from me; nevertheless, not as I will but as Thou wilt.'

"As he prayed, the tears streamed down His face, which was toward me. I was so moved at the sight that I also wept, out of pure sympathy. My whole heart went out to Him; I loved Him with all my soul, and longed to be with Him as I longed for nothing else.

"Presently, He arose and walked to where those Apostles were kneeling—fast asleep! He shook them gently, awoke them, and in a tone of tender reproach, untinctured by the least show of anger or impatience, asked them plaintively if they could not

76

watch with Him one hour. There He was, with the awful weight of the world's sins upon His shoulders, with the pangs of every man, woman and child shooting through His sensitive soul—and they would not watch with Him one poor hour!

"Returning to His place, He offered up the same prayer as before; then went back and again found them sleeping. Again he awoke them, readmonished them, and once more returned and prayed. Three times this occurred, until I was perfectly familiar with His appearance—face, form and movements. He was of noble stature and majestic mien—not at all the weak, effeminate being that some painters have portrayed; but the very God that He was and is, as meek and humble as a little child.

"All at once the circumstance seemed to change, the scene remaining just the same. Instead of before, it was after the crucifixion, and the Savior, with the three Apostles, now stood together in a group at my left. They were about to depart and ascend to Heaven. I could endure it no longer. I ran from behind the tree, fell at his feet, clasped Him around the knees, and begged Him to take me with Him.

"I shall never forget the kind and gentle manner in which he stooped, raised me up and embraced me. It was so vivid, so real. I felt the very warmth of His body, as He held me in His arms and said in tenderest tones: 'No my son; these have finished their work; they can go with me; but you must stay and finish yours.' Still I clung to Him. Gazing up into His face—for He was taller than I—I besought Him fervently; 'Well, promise me that I will come to you at the last.' Smiling sweetly, He said, 'That will depend entirely upon yourself!' I awoke with a sob in my throat, and it was morning." (Quoted in Bryant S. Hinckley, *Faith of Our Pioneer Fathers*, pp. 211–12.)

Elder Harold B. Lee once spoke of his own similar experience:

"As one of the humblest among you, and occupying the station I do, I want to bear you my humble testimony that I have received by the voice and the power of revelation, the knowledge and an understanding that God is.

"It was a week following the conference, when I was preparing myself for a radio talk on the life of the Savior, when I read again the story of the life, the crucifixion and the resurrection of the Master—there came to me as I read that, a reality of that story, more than just what was on the written page. For in truth, I found myself viewing the scenes with a certainty as though I had been there in person. I know that these things come by the revelations of the living God." (*Divine Revelation*, Brigham Young University Speeches of the Year [Provo, Utah, 15 Oct. 1952], p. 12.)

When we are endowed with the kind of understanding that came to Elder Whitney and Elder Lee, we can offer the required sacrifice of a broken heart and a contrite spirit. The Savior in turn can offer us the promise of redemption from our sins, of freedom from ignorance, and of a glorious resurrection. I testify from my experience that we can understand the gospel fully, live life abundantly, help others to reach their godly potential, and achieve the promise of eternal life only by experiencing profoundly for ourselves the significance and actuality of the Atonement.

I believe that the Lord is aware, as we should be also, that the very course of our lives is determined not so much by what we know about a particular thing but rather by how we feel about it. Therefore, the Lord wants us to feel more deeply and profoundly about his atonement than we feel about anything else in life. He is eager to endow us, if we will seek for it, with an intensity of feeling about the Atonement so great that it will motivate us to forsake our sins, keep his commandments, and honor, love, and serve him forever.

The Doctrine of the Atonement

To prepare ourselves for the "feeling dimension" of the Atonement, we must strive to comprehend the seriousness of personal sin, the demands of justice, and the role of mercy.

Because of the fall of Adam, the circumstances of earth are such that all of us commit sins after we become accountable at eight years of age. The sins we commit cause us to become unclean and consequently unfit to return to the presence of God. When we sin, we actually contaminate both our body and our spirit. The contamination, or uncleanness, occurs because each time we sin, the spirit and power of the adversary are present with us.

Justice demands that for every broken law (sin), there be a penalty exacted, and the penalty is suffering. Somehow the demands of justice are so great that if we must pay them, we will have to suffer even as Christ suffered. (See D&C 19:16–18.) The Savior's infinite atonement, however, meets the demands of justice in our behalf and, in the process, not only are we forgiven of our sins but we become like the Savior. This change occurs because in the process of repenting and then living the gospel, we avail ourselves of the Savior's power and his divine nature enables us to become like him. People who resist the fulness of the gospel, refusing to repent and accept Christ's atonement, will satisfy the demands of justice by suffering for their own sins. Because they do not avail themselves of the Savior's power in the process of repentance, they do not become like him and consequently receive only some degree of the blessings of the Atonement, becoming heirs of either the terrestrial or the telestial degree of glory.

This brief elaboration of the doctrine of the Atonement can help us better appreciate that the Atonement is very personal. The Savior came to free individuals from sin. He assumed upon his shoulders the sins of each one of us, not simply the sins of "mankind." Viewing the Atonement as an experience that the Savior went through for each of us, individually, will make a great deal of difference in its effect in our lives.

Personal Testimony

After completing my junior year at Brigham Young University and while yet in our first year of marriage, my wife and I left school and moved to the farm to help my ailing father. Four days before high school started that fall, I received an appointment to teach seminary full time. My first assignment was to teach the life of Christ.

What a challenging and exciting year that first year of teaching was for me! I sensed deeply my lack of training, and I was amazed at the amount of reading and studying each day's teaching required. I didn't have the problem of teaching over the students' heads, because I wasn't knowledgeable enough. In fact, most of what I taught each day I had learned the night before, so at least it was fresh! It was a heavy burden to farm a hundred acres, milk twenty cows, and teach seminary. Nevertheless, that year was one of the most thrilling teaching years of my life.

I struggled valiantly for several weeks with all the supplementary material I had been given, but still I felt a deeper and deeper sense of frustration. I finally pulled the New Testament front and center and dived into it with all the energy I could muster. Oh, the excitement that came! I could hardly wait to walk into the classroom each day to share the new insights that had been unfolded. The students felt my excitement, and they responded. Together, we followed the scriptural account of the Savior's premortal existence, birth, youth, and ministry. As I studied the Savior's life more deeply than I ever had before, every phase of my life seemed to take on a greater meaning. It was a profound spiritual awakening for me.

By the time the class and I had progressed into the latter part of the Savior's ministry, winter had come and gone and a new spring was upon us. I had always felt a physical rejuvenation with the coming of another spring. My spirits were always lifted, and I had an overwhelming awareness of God's goodness in bringing a newness of life to the earth once again. After the snow melted under the warmth of the spring sun and the buds began bursting forth in another cycle of life, I felt pleasure in plowing the moist soil amidst circling sea gulls, planting crops once again in anticipation of another harvest.

And what a glorious privilege to teach the life of Christ at that time of year! I felt an inner radiance increasing from new understandings and new appreciations, and I sensed as never before the symbolism of the Atonement in the unfolding of a new spring. With these feelings and the approach of the Easter season, I desired more than anything else to plant in the hearts of my precious students a special understanding of the Atonement, that they might harvest a profound newness of life through the mercy, merits, and grace of Christ.

As I finished my classes the day before I was to teach the

atonement of Christ, I gathered together several books of my own and some from the seminary library that I thought would be helpful—the scriptures, Elder James E. Talmage's *Jesus the Christ*, and several historical works about the Savior. I carried them out to the car and dumped them in the back seat, drove home, changed my clothes, and went out into the fields to plow and harrow. About sundown I came in, had supper, and then went out to the barn to milk the cows. It was after ten that evening when I finished milking and returned to the house. I felt real excitement as I cleaned up a bit and carried my books to the kitchen table.

Everything about the evening is yet vivid. Diane and a baby daughter were asleep in the bedroom. I can still see in my mind's eye the white muslin curtains at the window and even the design of the wallpaper on the kitchen walls. I laid my books out on the little pinewood table, and then I knelt in prayer and asked my Heavenly Father to help me understand more fully what the Atonement was all about, so that somehow, on the morrow, I might help my precious students also understand more fully. I then sat down and began to review the scriptural account of the last week of the Savior's mortal life.

I had no open visions that night, I heard no audible voices, but as I read and pondered the scriptures, it seemed as though I was in Jerusalem, witnessing the scenes as they unfolded. For the first time in my life, I felt so deeply the sorrow and pain the Savior went through that I thought my heart would break. For the first time in my life, while reading the scriptures, I wept openly. Somehow, previous to that evening, I hadn't felt a really deep commitment on my part to the Savior, and perhaps that was because never before had I felt such a deep and profound commitment on his part to me! Before that evening, I had always viewed his suffering and sorrow in almost a detached way—almost as a spectator. I had felt, to a degree, how marvelous it was that he was the Savior of mankind, that he had suffered for everyone, but that night, I was overwhelmed at the atonement he performed in my behalf, the suffering he went through for me—not only the suffering he went through *for* me, but the suffering he went through *because* of me. That evening, the reality of the Savior's atonement, the sorrow, the humiliation, and the pain sank deeper into my heart than the reality of anything else in life. Especially this was so of Gethsemane. Again, although I saw no visions and heard no voices, it was as though I were actually there.

On that spring night, in the tiny farmhouse, something else that brought extremely deep feelings was reading about the Roman scourging the Savior suffered. The Romans referred to their scourging as a "halfway death": if administered beyond a prescribed time, it could be fatal. Historical evidence suggests that convicted criminals were either scourged or crucified but rarely subjected to both forms of punishment, as was Christ. The scriptural account implies that Pilate ordered Christ to be scourged, not because he felt Christ was guilty of any crime, but because he hoped it would satisfy the Jews. Pilate hoped not to have the terrible responsibility of approving Christ's crucifixion. As I studied, I visualized in my mind's eye a typical Roman scourging, but in my heart, with the help of the Spirit, I felt deeply the awfulness of that terrible ordeal.

I pictured the individual who was to be scourged being led by the Roman soldiers into a small courtyard, in the center of which were several stone pillars about three feet high. Steel rings were embedded on either side of the pillars, close to the ground. The clothes would be stripped from the victim's back, and he would be forced to bend over, resting his chest on the top of the pillar, his hands having been securely tied to the rings. A Roman soldier would stand to the side, holding in his hand a flagellum, or whip, which was made of a short, curved piece of wood to which were attached several strips of leather. Sewn into the end of each piece of leather was a jagged piece of bone or metal.

At a signal, the soldier would bring the flagellum in a powerful swing from over his shoulder onto the exposed back of the victim. With one stroke of the whip, the flesh would be laid bare to the bone. The scourging probably went on for several minutes. That night I sensed, as never before, the brutality of the scourging and the pain it brought the Savior.

I continued to follow the scriptural account of the last hours of the Savior's life. After the scourging, the Roman soldiers placed a robe of purple on the Savior and a platted crown of thorns on his head, and mocked him, crying "Hail, King of the Jews!" They led him out of the city to a small hill called Golgotha, or the Place of the Skull. (See Matthew 27; Mark 15; Luke 23; John 19.)

Though the Savior undoubtedly possessed a strong body, his suffering in Gethsemane, his spending the entire night in abusive treatment before Annas, Caiaphas, Herod, and Pilate, and his scourging left him without the strength to carry the cross upon which he would be crucified. Because the uprights were often left intact between crucifixions, especially in such prominent places of crucifixion as Golgotha, some historians believe that the Savior attempted to carry only the crosspiece and not the entire cross. If this was so, the crosspiece was probably not more than six feet long and perhaps five inches square, weighing about sixty or seventy pounds. However heavy it was, the Savior could not carry it, and Simon the Cyrene was pressed into service to carry the cross.

By the time the Savior arrived at the top of the small hill, his mother, several other women, and the apostle John were already there. I imagined that John the Beloved, after learning of the impending crucifixion, had hurried to the little village of Bethany to tell the Savior's mother of the fateful event. The terrible experience would be all the more difficult for the Savior, knowing his mother would be a witness to his agony; and yet it had been prophetically foretold to Mary that "a sword shall pierce through thy own soul also." (Luke 2:35.) That wounding of Mary's soul would take place that day. Again, I felt quite overwhelmed that the Savior would be willing to go through such humiliation for me.

The Romans had tried many different methods of putting people to death: boiling in oil, beheading, impaling with a spear, suffocating, and others. But none was so terrible as crucifixion, for that method, devised by the Phoenicians, extended the pain and suffering over a period of days. The Romans were skilled in crucifying: when they finally subdued the slave rebellion led by Spartacus, they crucified six thousand captives in a single day.

Having read all I could find about the history of Roman crucifixion and then studying the accounts of that event in the New

Testament, I sensed vividly the cruelty of the manner of the Savior's death. After he had reached Golgotha, the crosspiece was laid on the ground behind the Savior (I assumed that the uprights were already in position). Then a Roman soldier drove a five- to seven-inch, square-ended nail through Jesus' palm. To assure that the hand would not pull free from the nail, another nail was driven through the wrist. The same was done to the other hand. Two centurions next took hold of the ends of the crosspiece, dragging the Savior over to the upright. Lifting the crosspiece, the soldiers fit it into the top of the upright and nailed it in place. Then, bending his legs in order to put the soles of his feet flat on the upright, they drove large nails through the thick part of his feet.

His body hanging in that unnatural position, the muscles along the sides of his chest soon knotted, making it almost impossible to breathe. The only way the Lord could have continued to breathe would have been to put all the weight of his body on the nails in his feet and push up, relieving the arm and chest muscles so that normal breathing could be restored. But the pain in his feet would soon have become so severe that he would have to drop back down. The Savior, like others who were victims of the cross, would have been constantly writhing in pain.

The Jews, eager to honor their own sabbath, demanded that Jesus and the thieves be killed and their bodies removed before the Sabbath commenced at sundown Friday. The soldiers assigned to that detail arrived at the scene carrying a large cudgel (a stick or club) and a two- or three-foot-long, one-inch-thick board. Walking up to a thief on one side, a soldier held the board behind the big bone in the upper part of the leg while another soldier hit the bone and snapped it in two. After the same was done to the other leg, death would follow quickly.

Once the legs of both thieves were broken, a soldier stood in front of the Redeemer. Because it appeared that Jesus was dead, the soldier refrained from breaking the Savior's legs and instead used his sword to pierce the Savior's side. (All this was in fulfillment of prophecy; see Psalm 22:16–17; Zechariah 12:10.) The Gospel of John records that water and blood came forth from the wound. (See John 19:34.) Elder James E. Talmage indicated that the watery serum separated from the blood because the Savior died of a ruptured cardiac, or in more common terms, a broken heart. His great heart literally burst as he offered himself, fully, a sacrifice for fallen man. (See *Jesus the Christ,* p. 620, n. 8.)

Having already felt such a deep sorrow for what happened to the Savior in Gethsemane and while he was scourged, the additional feelings that came as I pondered the Crucifixion were almost more than I could bear. I thought—and again, this seems to be the key to understanding the Atonement—that my own heart would break because of the sorrow I felt.

Because of the intensity of my feelings that night—which came through a new awareness of the sorrow and suffering the Savior experienced and a new realization that my sins and inadequacies added immeasurably to his suffering—there came into my mind the following analogy. Bear in mind that it is only an analogy, yet perhaps it will help you sense the reality and significance of what the Savior went through. Before commencing it, let me add that it is not necessary to see the Lord or hear his voice to receive a remission of sins; however, obviously, that can and does happen. In my analogy, the idea of seeing and conversing with the Lord is used simply to emphasize the fact that as we become clean through his blood, we become overwhelmed by the realization that the Savior did suffer for each one of us, individually and personally. Because of that awareness on our part, we will feel a powerful, one-to-one relationship with him.

Assume that although you have been a member of the Church and very active for a number of years, something has happened that causes you to take a fresh look at your relationship with the Savior and his gospel. You find yourself acquiring a much deeper hunger and thirst for the things of the Spirit, which results in your searching the scriptures a great deal, fasting as you have never fasted before, praying mightily many times a day, and increasing your fervor in your church callings.

Pursuing your quest, you become aware that there are innumerable promises in the scriptures that you can receive great power from the Lord, that marvelous knowledge and understanding can be yours, that daily revelation can be yours, and that indeed the veil can become thin and even nonexistent. But as you continue to seek with all the energy of your soul for the greater things of God, you find that the many promises of the Lord are not being realized in your life, and you wonder why. Again, the more you search the scriptures and fast and pray and give yourself in service, the greater is your desire to receive "all mysteries, yea, all the hidden mysteries of my kingdom from days of old, and for ages to come." (D&C 76:7.)

Continuing to seek and desiring profoundly to know why you aren't enjoying greater revelation, there comes into your mind the realization that perhaps the reason you don't have the greater power you'd like to have is that you are not totally clean. Oh, perhaps you have never sinned grossly (although if you had, that would not negate the possibility of complete forgiveness), but you are mindful that you have been quite unkind on occasion, jealous, short-tempered, not always filled with complete commitment in building the kingdom. Perhaps you have been proud or haven't as yet really had a "broken heart and a contrite spirit." (3 Nephi 9:20.)

You have learned from your scripture study and from solid practical experience that the Lord is willing to work with us where we are. Perhaps the last part of the following promise has meant a great deal to you as you have sought the gifts of the Spirit: "They are given for the benefit of those who love me and keep all my commandments, *and him that seeketh so to do.*" (D&C 46:9; italics added.) You have further realized that "no man is possessor of all things except he be purified and cleansed from all sin." (D&C 50:28.)

You determine, then, to seek with all your heart for a remission of sins. You realize that on top of keeping the commandments and carrying a heavy load of responsibility in church work, the key to receiving a remission of sins will indeed be "mighty prayer." (D&C 29:2; Enos 1:4.)

You see more clearly than ever before that the reason the prophets talk of Christ, rejoice in Christ, preach of Christ, prophesy of Christ, and write according to their prophecies is so that "our children may know to what source they may look for a remission of their sins." (2 Nephi 25:26.) As you persist in your quest, your hunger and thirst for righteousness become even more intense. You begin to want to know if you are clean more than you want anything else.

Late one evening (remember this is an analogy) after a particularly great day and after perhaps weeks and maybe even months of diligently praying and searching the scriptures, you find yourself concluding the day by calling upon your heavenly Father in the name of Christ in mighty, vocal prayer, seeking specifically and pointedly for a remission of your sins. (See D&C 19:28.) After pouring out your heart for an extended period of time, you become suddenly aware of a bright light in front of you. You open your eyes, and there stands the Lord! What a glorious experience it is just to see him. He speaks, and as he does, each word seems to distill an intensity of pure love and peace to every cell of your body. "I have come to give you a remission of your sins," he says.

Your initial reaction is one of complete surprise. You are, in fact, startled to learn that a remission of sins comes directly from the Lord—that is, it is the Lord Jesus Christ who grants a remission of sins. You reflect on the scriptural accounts of men and women who have truly received a remission of sins and indeed they acknowledge that it was the Savior who cleansed them. (See, for example, Mosiah 2–5, the account of the people of King Benjamin and their acknowledgment of the role the Savior played in their becoming clean.)

Maybe until this moment, you saw your life becoming clean (through repentance and baptism of water and of the Spirit) as something happening quite mechanically—something that just occurred somewhere along the way. Perhaps you even imagined that an audiovisual disk of your life was being prepared for Judgment Day and, at the moment your judgment comes, your social security number is read and your disk is plucked from the celestial files, placed on the judgment machine, and played. If you have more good than evil in your life, the necessary wheels turn, levers go up and down, the pearly gate is opened, and you march through not knowing for sure how it happened but grateful that it did happen.

But such simply isn't the case. People who become cleansed

by the blood of the Lamb are most mindful of him who cleansed them and how it was that they were so privileged. (See Revelation 7:9–17.)

To return to the analogy, the Savior speaks again: "In order for you to receive a remission of your sins, you and I must walk back through the corridors of your life so that together we may review the sins you have committed."

You are shocked at his invitation. You do not want to review your sins with him. You had felt it was adequate to turn away from them and that should be sufficient. Now, however, just being in his presence has quickened your conscience and has already caused you to wince over some sins you thought you had pretty well forgotten. If it were not for the fact that you had sought so diligently over an extended period of time to receive a remission of your sins, you never would have had the courage to accept the Savior's invitation, but you have the courage, and so you reach out your hand to his. (See D&C 112:10.)

May I pause before continuing this analogy to urge you to have the courage to pay whatever price you have to pay to confess your sins and take all the steps necessary to receive the cleansing power of the Savior.

To return again to the analogy, you find you have sufficient courage as you start down the corridor of your life. You are mindful of what to expect, and, sure enough, you see yourself down the corridor, yet some distance away, in an act of deliberate transgression. You gently tug on the Savior's hand and suggest that you feel you are close enough, that you can see fine from where you are. The Lord reminds you that it is necessary to walk all the way up and face squarely the sins you have committed. In fact, with his reminder there flood into your mind the many declarations of the prophets, both ancient and modern, about the necessity of confessing all sins to the Lord.

So there you are, a witness with the Lord of your own transgressions. Seeing yourself in the act of sin and standing so close to the Lord cause an unbelievable sorrow to come over your entire being—a sorrow for your sins that indeed can be called a godly sorrow. (See 2 Corinthians 7:9–10.) As the reality and the seriousness of your sins increase in your heart, you honestly wonder if your heart will not literally break. For the first time in your life, you understand what Nephi must have meant when he said of the Savior, "Behold, he offereth himself a sacrifice for sin, to answer the ends of the law, unto all those who have a broken heart and a contrite spirit; and unto none else can the ends of the law be answered." (2 Nephi 2:7.)

When the sorrow becomes almost more than you can bear, into your mind come the many scriptures you have read that promise that you can be forgiven of your sins — such promises as "there shall be no other name given nor any other way nor means whereby salvation can come unto the children of men, only in and through the name of Christ, the Lord Omnipotent" (Mosiah 3:17) and "there is no other way nor means whereby man can be saved, only through the atoning blood of Jesus Christ" (Helaman 5:9). With these scriptures and others pounding through your mind, you feel hope coming into your heart. With that hope comes a resurgence of faith, and with great feeling you cry out, "Heavenly Father, I sense deeply the seriousness of my sins. I'm profoundly sorrowful for all that I have done that was wrong and sinful. I know thy Son is the Savior and Redeemer of the world, and I pray with all my heart that I might be forgiven of my sins and cleansed by his atoning blood."

As you continue with a broken heart to cry for forgiveness, gradually the pain you have been feeling lessens. Your sorrow is replaced with peace and joy. Every cell of your body is quickened with a newfound aliveness, and your entire being tingles with a wonderful sense of innocence and cleanliness. Perhaps the best way to describe the joy, the peace, the aliveness, and especially the newfound feeling of incredible love is to exclaim with great joy, "Behold I am born of the Spirit." (Mosiah 27:24.)

In this analogy, you have been so intently pleading for mercy and have been so involved in what is happening to you, that you haven't noticed the Savior for several minutes. You become aware that whereas his countenance had been one of joy and peace, his face is now deeply etched with pain and sorrow. As you watch, it seems that he begins to sweat profusely and to tremble in great agony. The pain becomes so great that the creator of heaven and earth falls to the ground. (See Mark 14:35.) You notice as he is writhing in agony that his sweat changes to a reddish hue, and you become aware that he is sweating "great drops of blood" from every pore. (Luke 22:44.) Then you realize that he has just assumed the terrible effects of your sins, that he is suffering not only *for* you but also *because* of you. As you realize the magnitude of what he has done for you, you feel again that your heart will break for the sorrow he is experiencing.

The reality of the Lord's own testimony in the Doctrine and Covenants of the price he paid as a ransom for the sins of the world is quite overwhelming: "For behold, I, God, have suffered these things for all, that they might not suffer if they would repent; but if they would not repent they must suffer even as I; which suffering caused myself, even God, the greatest of all, to tremble because of pain, and to bleed at every pore, and to suffer both body and spirit—and would that I might not drink the bitter cup, and shrink—nevertheless, glory be to the Father, and I partook and finished my preparations unto the children of men." (D&C 19:16–19.)

Your dream is now over, and you return to the regular activities of life. But now you are constantly aware of the significance of the Savior's atonement; it has become the greatest reality of your life, as well as the central theme of all you say and do. You find great motivation and ability to keep the commandments because you have been endowed with a marvelous increase of his love. You treat everyone in a Christlike way. You have a passion to do all in your power to bring others to the Father through Christ. You try to do all in your power to build the kingdom of God. And again, the central theme of your life is the graciousness of a loving God named Jehovah, who loved you so much that he was willing to pay the utmost price that you might be free from sin.

I believe that herein lies the great message of the restored gospel: to feel deeply the implications for each one of us of the Savior's sorrow, suffering, and death. We grasp the message as we recognize the seriousness of the fallen condition we are in and the unbending demands of justice, and yet we realize too that we can partake of the mercy and love of a divine Redeemer who is our advocate with the Father. (See D&C 45:3–5.)

How vital it is to seek with all of our hearts for a revealed understanding of the Atonement. As we search the scriptures, fast and pray, and give ourselves in untiring service in blessing the lives of others, we will be blessed and endowed with mighty power only as we come to a heartfelt, revealed understanding of the atonement of Christ.

The following experience of President Joseph Fielding Smith as told by his son sums up what I'm trying to say about the feelings we can have when we learn by revelation the importance of the Savior's sorrow and suffering:

"As children, so frequently we would hear him say, 'If only the people in the world would understand the trials, the tribulations, the sins our Lord took upon himself for our benefit.' Whenever he would refer to this, tears would come into his eyes.

"A few years ago, as I sat alone with my father in his study, I observed that he had been in deep meditation. I hesitated to break the silence, but finally he spoke. 'Oh my son, I wish you could have been with me last Thursday as I met with my Brethren in the temple. Oh, if you could have heard them testify of their love for their Lord and Savior, Jesus Christ!' And then he lowered his head, and tears streamed from his face and dropped to his shirt. Then, after many seconds, without as much as raising his head, but moving his head back and forth, he said, 'Oh how I love my Lord and Savior Jesus Christ!' " (Quoted in "President Joseph Fielding Smith: Student of the Gospel," *New Era*, Jan. 1972, p. 63.)

Chapter 5

BEING BORN AGAIN

"Adam fell that men might be; and men are, that they might have joy." (2 Nephi 2:25.) I haven't found any experience in the scriptures where joy bursts forth so fully in the lives of men and women as when they are truly born again. Nephi expressed his feelings about those who were baptized of fire and of the Holy Ghost by saying they would "shout praises unto the Holy One of Israel." (2 Nephi 31:13.) Alma, after his spiritual second birth, cried out, "Oh, what joy, and what marvelous light I did behold; yea, my soul was filled with joy as exceeding as was my pain!" (Alma 36:20.) The three hundred Lamanites who took seriously the admonition to "cry unto the voice, even until [they had] faith in Christ" were "filled with that joy which is unspeakable and full of glory." (Helaman 5:44.) The people of King Benjamin, who were already at a high level of righteousness, when they fully experienced the spiritual second birth, declared, "Whereby we do rejoice with such exceedingly great joy." (Mosiah 5:4.) The Prophet Joseph Smith, at the very first conference of the Church, witnessed with others the outpouring of the Spirit upon many who had just received the gift of the Holy Ghost: "Such scenes as these were calculated to inspire our hearts with joy unspeakable, and fill us with awe and reverence for that Almighty Being, by whose grace we had been called to be instrumental in bringing about, for the children of men, the enjoyment of such glorious blessings as were now at this time poured out upon us." (*History of the Church,* 1:85.)

Is it any wonder the gospel is called the "good news," the

"glad tidings," through which men and women can know that they can be forgiven of all their sins, that their very nature can be changed, that they can then look upon sin with abhorrence, that their bodies can be sanctified by the blood of the Lamb, and that they can be filled with indescribable love. Oh, should we not rejoice as did Ammon when he witnessed the mighty change that occurred to so many Lamanites? Should we be the slightest bit' hesitant to echo with him that "there never were men that had so great reason to rejoice as we, since the world began; yea, and my joy is carried away, even unto boasting in my God; for he has all power, all wisdom, and all understanding; he comprehendeth all things, and he is a merciful Being, even unto salvation, to those who will repent and believe on his name." (Alma 26:35.)

The scriptural emphasis on the spiritual second birth is interwoven with the doctrine of the Atonement. The Atonement is what opened the doors to redemption. The Atonement made available an infinite power by which we all can be freed from sin, ignorance, and death. Atonement is the means by which a God, even Christ, can reach down and lift us out of our fallen condition, out of carnality, out of sin, into cleanliness and righteousness. But how? How is the Savior able to transform us into his likeness through faith on his name? How are we actually cleansed when we truly obtain a broken heart and a contrite spirit? How are a body and spirit tainted with sin made clean by repentance? What changes our nature and gives us an abhorrence for sin? How do we actually acquire the "mind of Christ" (1 Corinthians 2:16) and "obtain his image in our countenances" (Alma 5:14)? Finally, how do we acquire the qualities and characteristics of the Savior so completely that we become the sons and daughters of Christ?

First, from what I have read in the scriptures and in the writings of the living prophet, everyone has to be born again. Every accountable person sins, becomes subject to the demands of justice, and can only satisfy the demands of justice and be changed from that fallen condition by being born again. (See Alma 42:22–23.) This seems to be true regardless of whether a person was raised in a saintly home or came from some of the further reaches of disbelief and transgression. Everyone sins. Every ac-

93

countable person becomes unclean. Each accountable person becomes fallen and spiritually dead. The following statement by
Elder Spencer W. Kimball is cause for all active members of the
Church to engage in serious introspection about our own condition: "There are many people in this Church today who think
they live, but they are dead to the spiritual things. And I believe
even many who are making pretenses of being active are also
spiritually dead. Their service is much of the letter and less of
the spirit." (In Conference Report, Apr. 1951, p. 105.)

The scriptures make no exception: everyone needs to be born
again. Nevertheless, if a person has been tutored to live a good
life and to respond to the light of Christ, "as the Holy Ghost falls
upon one of the Literal Seed of Abraham it is calm & serene."
(*Words of Joseph Smith*, p. 4.)

To me, one of the most helpful ways to see how the Savior
literally changes us through the spiritual second birth is to remember that everything reproduces after its kind, that like begets
like, or, as the Prophet Joseph Smith put it: "God set many signs
in the earth as well as in heaven, for instance, the oaks of the
forest, the fruit of the tree, the herb of the field — all bear a sign
that seed hath been planted there, for it is a decree of the Lord
that every tree, fruit, or herb bearing seed should bring forth
after its kind. . . . upon the same principle do I contend that baptism is a sign ordained of God for the believer in Christ to take
upon himself in order to enter into the Kingdom of God." (*Words
of Joseph Smith* [spelling and punctuation modernized], p. 107.)

What a marvelous eternal truth: as the oak tree is, so will
the acorn be; as the parent is, so will the child be. If the Savior
gives us a spiritual second birth and we maintain our commitment
to him, we will someday be like him.

On a beautiful spring day in Palo Alto, California, my wife
was about to give birth to our fourth child. It was a special experience to me because, for the first time, I was actually to
witness the birth of one of our children. After the birth of each
of our first three children, my wife had wept and wept for joy as
she tried to share with me the marvel of giving birth. How could
she describe to me the effort, pain, and labor, and then the joy?
Now that I finally had the opportunity to witness the birth of one

of our children, I was so excited I thought I would disintegrate, and I learned that the joy that came as I shared with my wife the first moments of mortality with a precious child has to be experienced to be believed.

Should not our own spiritual second birth be as joyous, as real, and as veil thinning? Should not the change from a selfish, egotistical, self-sufficient person to one who is really alive in Christ be as great as coming from another sphere into mortality? Should we expect less of a spiritual second birth, where the Savior and his gospel are so involved, than we would of a first, physical, birth?

Remembering then "that every seed will bring after its own kind," consider that we received our spirit bodies from our heavenly parents, thus becoming the literal sons and daughters of God. Through the eternal law of like begets like, we received into our newly formed spirit bodies the very seeds of God: a literal, tangible portion of our heavenly parents became a part of us. We received in embryonic form their attributes and characteristics, which would enable us, under certain circumstances, to someday become like them. In other words, we were born to be Gods! Paul the apostle put it beautifully when he said, "The Spirit itself beareth witness with our spirit, that we are the children of God: ... heirs of God, and joint-heirs with Christ." (Romans 8:16–17.)

If we can grasp the profound reality of that truth, then I'm convinced we will never be the same. In gaining that understanding, we will gain a hope, a confidence, an optimism about our godly potential that will carry us through the challenges and vicissitudes of life. Knowing by revelation that we have the seeds of godhood in us—that is, the very potential to become like God— will give us the determination to refrain from any conduct that is beneath the dignity of our potential.

Oh, how true the principle of like begets like is in human parentage. All of us readily acknowledge that our earthly parents have imprinted themselves upon us. We have received into our beings a portion of our earthly parents, physically, intellectually, socially, and spiritually. A brief example will illustrate my point. One day I entered a library room with some gusto and surprised the two men in the room. One of the men was a former junior high football coach of mine, and we hadn't seen each other for years. My sudden entrance caught him by surprise and, nearly falling off his chair, he exclaimed, "My goodness, George, I thought you were your father. Oh, how you look like him!" No one questions the infusion of our parents' qualities and characteristics into our bodies.

Yet, surprisingly enough, when it comes to the great doctrine of the spiritual second birth, which is supposed to be analogous to our mortal birth, many people fail to understand the greater significance of that analogy because they do not realize that we become "partakers of the divine nature" of Christ (2 Peter 1:4), partakers of his qualities and characteristics, when we are truly born again through him.

Next to our relationship with the Father and the Son, what is the greatest relationship on earth? Surely the answer is the marriage relationship. Nowhere in human relations is there the possibility for greater joy than in holy matrimony. The Lord himself likens his relationship with his church to a marriage relationship. (See Isaiah 50; Matthew 25.) Who is the husband in that relationship? Why, it is the Lord. Who is the bride in that relationship? Why, it is the church.

If you or I will be most respectful of the "bride," even the Church, we will acknowledge the prophet thereof as anointed and inspired of the Lord and we will submit to the sacred ordinances therein and remain true to those ordinances. And if, at the same time, we balance that commitment to the Church with a profound respect for and faith in the "husband," even Christ, then he, the Holy One of Israel, will allow his spirit, his power, his divine nature to flow through the ordinances into our lives, enabling us in time to become so much like him that it can be said of us, "this day he hath spiritually begotten you; ... therefore, ye are born of him and have become his sons and his daughters." (Mosiah 5:7.)

Oh, how important it is to realize that the genius of the gospel is that through the power of faith the Spirit can endow us with the qualities and characteristics of the Savior. No wonder Peter encouraged us to be "partakers of the divine nature" (2 Peter

1:4) that we might acquire virtue, knowledge, temperance, patience, godliness, brotherly kindness, and charity. (See 2 Peter 1:5–7.) The Savior spoke of giving his glory to those who believe on him. Why? That they might be one with the Father even as he is. (See John 17:22–24.)

We then acquire, in the process of the second birth, three fathers, as it were: our Heavenly Father, who begets our spirit body; our earthly father, who begets our physical body; and the Savior, who begets our spiritual body, which is our cleansed, sanctified, mortal body. In the process of the second birth, we receive a remission of sins (see 2 Nephi 31:17), we are "sanctified from all sin" (Moses 6:59), we become "new creatures" (Mosiah 27:26), our nature is changed and "we have no more disposition to do evil" (Mosiah 5:2), and we have the "image of God engraven upon [our] countenances" (Alma 5:19).

When does the second birth occur? Does it occur following baptism and confirmation, or does it occur later? Generally speaking, it seems to me that it requires some extended time after we are baptized of the water and have received the gift of the Holy Ghost. Before physical birth, there is a period of gestation between conception and birth, that is, a period of time when the child grows and develops preparatory to birth. It seems that such is usually the case with the spiritual second birth. At baptism and confirmation, we become members of the Church, we take upon ourselves the name of Christ and receive the gift of the Holy Ghost. If we will seek for the Spirit with all our hearts, repenting of our sins and keeping the commandments, we will grow and become prepared for the greater endowment of the second birth.

The Lord told Adam, as recorded in Moses 6:60, that "by the water ye keep the commandment; by the Spirit ye are justified, and by the blood ye are sanctified." It seems to me that when we are immersed in the water, we are simply fulfilling the commandment. We are participating in a physical ordinance that symbolizes the spiritual changes that can occur in our lives. As Paul explained baptism by water, "For if we have been planted together in the likeness of his death, we shall be also in the likeness of his resurrection." (Romans 6:5.) If, when we receive the gift of the Holy Ghost, we really exercise faith in Christ, then we are "justified," and our righteous acts are approved of the Lord. Then, if we persist in righteousness, we will be sanctified (made pure and holy), and thus enjoy the blessings of the second birth. How crucial to realize that the actual remission of sins, the cleansing of our bodies and the healing of our spirits, comes by and through the marvelous power of the Spirit. (See Alma 13:11–12.)

Elder Marion G. Romney emphasized the role of the Spirit and how it works in changing our lives:

"Conversion is effected by divine forgiveness, which remits sins. The sequence is something like this. An honest seeker hears the message. He asks the Lord in prayer if it is true. The Holy Spirit gives him a witness. This is a testimony. If one's testimony is strong enough, he repents and obeys the commandments. By such obedience he receives divine forgiveness which remits sins. Thus he is converted to a newness of life. His spirit is healed. . . .

"Getting people's spirits healed through conversion is the only way they can be healed. I know this is an unpopular doctrine and a slow way to solve the problems of men and nations. As a matter of fact, I am convinced that relatively few among the earth's inhabitants will be converted. Nevertheless, I know and solemnly witness that there is no other means by which the sin-sick souls of men can be healed or for a troubled world to find peace. I know that the unbelieving will reject this divine way. But this is nothing new." (In Conference Report, Oct. 1963, pp. 24–26.)

Although it is possible to be born again when we are baptized of water and receive the gift of the Holy Ghost, most of the time it seems to require much more effort and labor. Baptism of the Spirit has acquired for me much greater theological significance than it held in the first decades of my life. I've concluded that the spiritual second birth is the most important thing that can happen in our lives to facilitate our becoming true Saints.

We differ considerably from many in the Christian world who teach that once you are born again, you are always born again. Such a position seems untenable in light of the doctrine of enduring to the end, of Peter's reminder that we, after having escaped the pollution of the world, can be entangled again (see

2 Peter 2:20) and Alma's confirming witness that we can sing the song of redeeming love and then lose it (see Alma 5:26).

Is it possible to be born again before the laying on of hands? The answer is yes, but it is the exception to the rule, and if it does happen before baptism, those to whom it occurs are baptized immediately thereafter. (See Alma 19:33–35; Helaman 5:44–52; Acts 10.)

Is the baptism of the Spirit always accompanied by a spectacular experience? It is true that the New Testament has record of spectacular spiritual second births, such as that of Peter and the Saints on the day of Pentecost (see Acts 2) and of Saul on the road to Damascus (see Acts 9). The Book of Mormon has record of many similar spectacular experiences, such as that which occurred to King Benjamin's people (see Mosiah 2–5), Alma the Younger (see Mosiah 27; Alma 36), King Lamoni and his wife (see Alma 19:23–35), and the twelve Nephite disciples (see 3 Nephi 19).

Because so many such experiences have happened, it is natural to conclude that all people who are born again experience such dramatic experiences. Nevertheless, I think we would make a serious mistake to say that we must have a spectacular experience to be truly born again. Probably in most instances the preparation for the experience occurs over an extended period of time, but the actual experience — the remission of sins, the change of nature, the mighty change — can occur without the experience being a spectacular one.

It seems to me that the effort required and the blessing received from the spiritual second birth are essentially the same whether the experience occurs spectacularly or as "the wind bloweth . . . , and thou hearest the sound thereof, but canst not tell whence it cometh." (John 3:8.)

May I suggest a caution? Possibly because we may not be aware of dramatic experiences relative to the second birth occurring today as they did in the scriptures and in the early Church, we might assume that such experiences are not happening and therefore are not necessary. Or if we have been very faithful in keeping the commandments and laboring in the kingdom and haven't had any "veil-thinning" experiences, then we might conclude they surely aren't necessary. Or it may be that we have drawn the conclusion that "dramatic" experiences are reserved only for the leaders of the Church and are of a very private nature, and consequently we are not aware of them. Whatever the reason might be, we need to be very careful not to rule out the possibility that you and I and others can have experiences as marvelous as those had by Saul or by King Lamoni and his wife.

To appreciate the effort required to be born again, we need to remember that even the original Twelve Apostles of our dispensation, after having served in that holy calling for three years, were promised that "if they harden not their hearts, and stiffen not their necks against me, they shall be converted, and I will heal them." (D&C 112:13.) If such was the case with the members of the first Quorum of the Twelve Apostles of this dispensation, we, then, as members of the Church, should expect to make a very great effort to achieve the blessing of the second birth in our lives.

The Mighty Change

Obviously we can learn a lot from carefully studying the experiences of those who are truly born again. Perhaps the greatest value is in learning the "fruits" of the spiritual second birth. Consider the following quiet but powerful experience Joseph F. Smith had after his baptism:

"The feeling that came upon me was that of pure peace, of love and of light. I felt in my soul that if I had sinned — and surely I was not without sin — that it had been forgiven me; that I was indeed cleansed from sin; my heart was touched, and I felt that I would not injure the smallest insect beneath my feet. I felt as if I wanted to do good everywhere to everybody and to everything. I felt a newness of life, a newness of desire to do that which was right." (*Gospel Doctrine,* p. 96.)

Heber C. Kimball recorded that "under the ordinances of baptism and the laying on of hands, I received the Holy Ghost, as the disciples did in ancient days, which was like a consuming fire. I felt as though I sat at the feet of Jesus." (Quoted in Orson F. Whitney, *Life of Heber C. Kimball,* p. 22.)

President Lorenzo Snow related a beautiful experience some-what more dramatic in nature:

"Some two or three weeks after I was baptized, one day while engaged in my studies, I began to reflect upon the fact that I had not obtained a *knowledge* of the truth of the work . . . and I began to feel very uneasy. I laid aside my books, left the house, and wandered around through the fields under the oppressive influ-ence of a gloomy, disconsolate spirit, while an indescribable cloud of darkness seemed to envelop me. I had been accustomed, at the close of the day, to retire for secret prayer, to a grove a short distance from my lodgings, but at this time I felt no inclination to do so. The spirit of prayer had departed and the heavens seemed like brass over my head. At length, realizing that the usual time had come for secret prayer, I concluded I would not forego my evening service, and, as a matter of formality, knelt as I was in the habit of doing, and in my accustomed retired place, but not feeling as I was wont to feel.

"I had no sooner opened my lips in an effort to pray, than I heard a sound, just above my head, like the rustling of silken robes, and immediately the Spirit of God descended upon me, completely enveloping my whole person, filling me, from the crown of my head to the soles of my feet, and O, the joy and happiness I felt! No language can describe the almost instanta-neous transition from a dense cloud of mental and spiritual dark-ness into a refulgence of light and knowledge, as it was at that time imparted to my understanding. I then received a perfect knowledge that God lives, that Jesus Christ is the Son of God, and of the restoration of the holy Priesthood, and the fulness of the Gospel. It was a complete baptism—a tangible immersion in the heavenly principle or element, the Holy Ghost; and even more real and physical in its effects upon every part of my system than the immersion by water; dispelling forever, so long as reason and memory last, all possibility of doubt or fear in relation to the fact handed down to us historically, that the 'Babe of Bethlehem' is truly the Son of God. . . .

"I cannot tell how long I remained in the full flow of the blissful enjoyment and divine enlightenment, but it was several minutes before the celestial element which filled and surrounded me began gradually to withdraw. On arising from my kneeling posture, . . . I *knew* that He had conferred on me what only an omnipotent being can confer — that which is of greater value than all the wealth and honors worlds can bestow. That night, as I retired to rest, the same wonderful manifestations were repeated, and continued to be for several successive nights. The sweet remembrance of those glorious experiences, from that time to the present, bring them fresh before me, imparting an inspiring influence which pervades my whole being, and I trust will to the close of my earthly existence." (Eliza R. Snow, comp., *Biography and Family Record of Lorenzo Snow*, pp. 7–9.)

The Book of Mormon is a veritable gold mine of understanding when it comes to the spiritual second birth. As an example, let's look closely at the experience of King Benjamin and his people. They appear in many ways to have been similar to the good, active members of the Church today. They had achieved, through the gospel, freedom from dissension and war, they kept the commandments, they prospered economically, and they loved, respected, and adored their prophet.

These Nephites lived in a general condition of goodness. As King Benjamin began to speak to them, however, one of the first things he said was that he wanted to call them together "that I might be found blameless, and that your blood should not come upon me, when I shall stand to be judged of God of the things whereof he hath commanded me concerning you." (Mosiah 2:27.) He also said that he wanted to give the people a new name. (See Mosiah 1:11.) It seems that while the people of King Benjamin were very responsive to the gospel, they hadn't yet experienced the greater change of the second birth.

King Benjamin, by the power of the spoken word, went on to lead his people to new heights in achieving Christlike character. He opened a whole new world to a precious group of people who were already remarkably good in their obedience to God. How did he do it? How was he able to get the people to realize there was so much more to their membership in the Church than that which they were enjoying?

First, he stressed the tremendous importance of service:

"When ye are in the service of your fellow beings ye are only in the service of your God." (Mosiah 2:17.)

Second, he acknowledged in a kind way his appreciation for the reverence and love his subjects manifested so visibly for him. At the same time, however, he cautioned them in their adoration of him and lifted their sights measurably toward God by teaching them that if he as their earthly king merited any thanks, "O how you ought to thank your heavenly King!" (Mosiah 2:19.)

Third, and he did this delicately and yet powerfully, King Benjamin set about to bring his people to a deep humility so that they might be lifted to much greater heights. He did this by stressing that they, for all their goodness, for all their diligence in keeping the commandments, for all their determination to be of service to one another, were "not even as much as the dust of the earth; yet ye were created of the dust of the earth; but behold, it belongeth to him who created you." (Mosiah 2:25.)

Fourth, King Benjamin was apparently given a marvelous ability to help his subjects understand the majesty of the atonement of Christ. Somehow, even though the people were very active in the Church and were performing many good works, they hadn't yet comprehended that it would take the power of God to put off the "natural man." (Mosiah 3:19.) The Savior as their Redeemer hadn't yet become the very center of their lives; his power hadn't yet transformed their fallen nature. Consequently, speaking words given him by an angel the night before, the prophet-king delivered a remarkably powerful sermon that centered in the necessity of the atonement of Christ:

"For behold, the time cometh, and is not far distant, that with power, the Lord Omnipotent who reigneth, who was, and is from all eternity to all eternity, shall come down from heaven among the children of men, and shall dwell in a tabernacle of clay, and shall go forth amongst men, working mighty miracles, such as healing the sick, raising the dead, causing the lame to walk, the blind to receive their sight, and the deaf to hear, and curing all manner of diseases.

"And he shall cast out devils, or the evil spirits which dwell in the hearts of the children of men.

"And lo, he shall suffer temptations, and pain of body, hunger, thirst, and fatigue, even more than man can suffer, except it be unto death; for behold, blood cometh from every pore, so great shall be his anguish for the wickedness and the abominations of his people.

"And he shall be called Jesus Christ, the Son of God, the Father of heaven and earth, the Creator of all things from the beginning; and his mother shall be called Mary.

" And lo, he cometh unto his own, that salvation might come unto the children of men even through faith on his name; and even after all this they shall consider him a man, and say that he hath a devil, and shall scourge him, and shall crucify him.

"And he shall rise the third day from the dead; and behold, he standeth to judge the world; and behold, all these things are done that a righteous judgment might come upon the children of men.

"For behold, and also his blood atoneth for the sins of those who have fallen by the transgression of Adam, who have died not knowing the will of God concerning them, or who have ignorantly sinned. . . .

"And moreover, I say unto you, that there shall be no other name given nor any other way nor means whereby salvation can come unto the children of men, only in and through the name of Christ, the Lord Omnipotent." (Mosiah 3:5–11, 17.)

How well prepared were the hearts of the people for those delicious words of eternal significance! In fact, as their prophet testified of the mighty works Christ would perform, of the terrible temptations, pain, hunger, thirst, and fatigue he would endure, and of his great anguish, which could cause blood to come from every pore, the people of King Benjamin fell "to the earth, for the fear of the Lord had come upon them.

"And they had viewed themselves in their own carnal state, even less than the dust of the earth. And they all cried aloud with one voice, saying: O have mercy, and apply the atoning blood of Christ that we may receive forgiveness of our sins, and our hearts may be purified; for we believe in Jesus Christ, the Son of God, who created heaven and earth, and all things; who shall come down among the children of men." (Mosiah 4:1–2.)

After the people of King Benjamin cried out for mercy, "the

Spirit of the Lord came upon them, and they were filled with joy, having received a remission of their sins, and having peace of conscience, because of the exceeding faith which they had in Jesus Christ who should come, according to the words which king Benjamin had spoken unto them." (Mosiah 4:3.)

They all possessed an abhorrence for sin and wanted "to do good continually" (Mosiah 5:2), and they possessed a desire to share their worldly goods. They also learned that because they now were truly born again, if they desired to maintain that great condition, they must "retain in remembrance, the greatness of God, and your own nothingness, and his goodness and long-suffering towards you, unworthy creatures, and humble yourselves even in the depths of humility, calling on the name of the Lord daily, and standing steadfastly in the faith of that which is to come." (Mosiah 4:11.)

I love the story of King Benjamin. Here we have a whole group of people who came to a marvelous, individual knowledge of the atonement of the Savior and in so doing obtained sufficient faith to become spiritually begotten of Christ. They, having received of the divine nature of Christ, became "his sons and his daughters" (Mosiah 5:7) and enjoyed, not just theoretically, but in a marvelous, real way, the sacred name of their Redeemer, Jesus Christ.

Another great sermon on the spiritual second birth is Nephi's discourse in 2 Nephi 31 and 32. In fact, it is my opinion that these two chapters shed more light on what it means to enjoy the spiritual second birth than any other single sermon in all of holy writ. I recommend strongly that you study carefully and prayerfully these two very illuminating chapters.

Getting through the Gate and onto the Path

When I was baptized and confirmed a member of the Church at the age of eight, I assumed I had entered the gate and obtained the path. Nephi would have disagreed. He indicated that we haven't gone through the gate and obtained the path until we are baptized "by fire and by the Holy Ghost." (2 Nephi 31:17; see also vv. 18–19.) Nephi testified further that if we, after receiving "the baptism of fire and of the Holy Ghost, and can speak with a new tongue, yea, even with the tongue of angels, and after this should deny me, it would have been better for [us] that [we] had not known [him]." (2 Nephi 31:14.)

Nephi made some important observations about "following the example of the Son." (2 Nephi 31:16.) First of all, he explained that we must follow him into the waters of baptism and, like him, be baptized of fire and of the Holy Ghost. Second, we must endure to the end in following Christ's example. In other words, it is one thing to get onto the straight and narrow path and another thing to live out our lives in following Christ's example. This latter requirement is achieved through "feasting upon the word of Christ." (2 Nephi 31:20.)

The efficacy of baptism, like that of all ordinances of the gospel, depends upon our attitude, preparation, and faith in Christ. If we have no hypocrisy and no deception, if we have really repented, and if we are truly willing to take upon ourselves the name of Christ (see 2 Nephi 31:13), then and only then will the baptism of fire and the Holy Ghost occur. We should understand that if, when we were baptized, we did not meet all these qualifications, as soon as we do, our baptism by water and our confirmation will be followed by the baptism of the Spirit.

"Ye shall know them by their fruits." I think the Lord wants us to know exactly where we stand in fulfilling our covenants with him. He doesn't want us to wonder from day to day if we are acceptable to him. That is particularly true of the covenant of baptism. He has told us exactly what he expects of us and further, that if we will take upon ourselves his name, keep all of his commandments, always remember him, bear one another's burdens, stand as a witness of him at all times, and continue to be faithful (see Mosiah 18:9), then we can expect without qualification to be forgiven of our sins, receive the gift and daily guidance of the Holy Ghost, and obtain while yet in the flesh the promise of eternal life.

The Savior said, "Ye shall know them by their fruits." (Matthew 7:16.) We can know by our fruits if we are truly born again. What are the hallmarks of one who is spiritually begotten by

Christ? Nephi discussed five important characteristics we will enjoy if we are really on the straight and narrow path.

Speaking with the tongue of angels. The first thing Nephi said would happen to us if we are baptized of fire and of the Holy Ghost is that we would "speak with the tongue of angels." (2 Nephi 31:13.) He then told us that to do so is to speak under the influence and power of the Holy Ghost. (See 2 Nephi 32:2–3.) It seems so natural, so logical that one who has tasted fully of the transforming power of God would enjoy the privilege of speaking by the power of the Holy Ghost. You and I have acquired our faith in Christ primarily because we have heard the testimonies of others who spoke words charged with the heavenly element of the Holy Ghost. The Lord wants us to be like them, to be instruments in testifying to others of the marvelous truths we have learned. To speak with the tongue of angels is continually to speak words of comfort, encouragement, and love. It is to teach by the Spirit and to reflect in all we say the inspiration and power of the Lord.

I'm sure all of us from time to time have felt the indescribable thrill of saying things that we knew at the time came directly from the Lord—we know the power such words can carry in everything we say.

One example of enjoying the ability to speak with the power of the Spirit was a special teaching moment I had with three daughters aged three, four, and five. I was babysitting while my wife was out. The children seemed to be in an unusually receptive spirit and had even asked if I would tell them gospel stories. I decided to tell them the story of the brother of Jared. We got the eight barges built and solved the air problem, much to the relief of the five-year-old, who said, "It would sure be *stuffy* in there!" Then I told my daughters that the brother of Jared went up on the mountain with sixteen transparent stones so that the Lord might touch them and provide light for the voyage.

I told them that the brother of Jared prayed fervently and that he saw the finger of the Lord. Quietly, I said, "And then, because of the faith of the brother of Jared, the Savior appeared to him and talked with him." At that moment I glanced down and saw our five-year-old looking up at me with tears streaming down her face, and she said, "Oh, Daddy, that's just beautiful, that's just beautiful!" And then with great feeling she continued, "Daddy, some day I've just got to see Jesus, I've just got to see him!" Oh, how that touched my heart. There was no question my precious daughter knew through the Spirit that the story I was telling her was true. At least in part, perhaps that is what speaking with the tongues of angels is all about.

Shouting praises to the Holy One of Israel. Another character-istic we enjoy through the second birth is wanting to "shout praises unto the Holy One of Israel." (2 Nephi 31:13.) Although Nephi does not elaborate on this characteristic, I think it is ob-vious what he is referring to. (See 2 Nephi 25:26.) I would like to believe that one common denominator among all Saints who have tasted of the goodness of Christ and who have felt "to sing the song of redeeming love" (Alma 5:26) is to stand unashamedly as a witness of Christ "at all times and in all things, and in all places" (Mosiah 18:9), not as a casual witness, or one who merely spoke of the Savior in a veiled manner, but rather one who would "shout" by his life, his words, and his deeds, that the Savior is his Redeemer and that through him life has incredible meaning.

We are commanded to hold up the Savior as our light. (See 3 Nephi 18:3.) How natural it is to spontaneously hold him up when indeed he is our light: "A city that is set on an hill cannot be hid." (Matthew 5:14.) It is not possible for a Latter-day Saint filled with the light and power of the Savior to move among the children of men without their knowing that Christ is the source of their light and power.

To shout praises to the Holy One of Israel is to "mention the loving kindness of their Lord, and all that he has bestowed upon them according to his goodness, and according to his loving kindness, forever and ever." (D&C 133:52.) To "shout praises to the Holy One of Israel" is a hallmark of true conversion. The ability to so shout is a gift that comes through the ordinances as a result of mighty faith in Christ. In that shout, the central object is Christ and the central message is that he is our personal Redeemer.

I feel I have a profound responsibility in bearing testimony to those who are not members of the Church so that they clearly understand the relationship between Joseph Smith's divine calling and the position of the Savior in that divine calling. I want every nonmember I have the privilege of speaking to, to know that the reason I love and honor Joseph Smith so much is that Joseph Smith revealed anew the majesty and reality of the living Christ.

Recently I took a trip to Nepal to do some trekking in the unbelievably beautiful Himalayas. I needed some information, so while waiting in the Bangkok airport, I looked around and noticed a Malaysian man who really stood out in the crowded airport. He had an unusually impressive countenance. I walked up to him and asked him my question. He graciously responded with the information I needed. I then said something like the following: "You really look like a happy man; you have such a beautiful countenance. How come you look so happy?" His response was subdued and most reverent, but he spoke with remarkable sincerity, "I have Jesus Christ in my life!" He then complimented me by saying, "I sense that you too have the Lord and Savior Jesus Christ in your life." I replied, "Yes, yes, indeed I do." I then shared with him the marvelous message of the Restoration. I gave him a copy of the Book of Mormon and bore my testimony that he could come to know the Savior more fully as he studied that sacred record and that he would come to know that in the Mormon church, the central reality is Jesus Christ and him crucified.

Doctrine and Covenants 46:9 illustrates a very exciting aspect of what happens when we try to pull down the greater blessings of the gospel. The Lord said that the gifts of the Spirit "are given for the benefit of those who love me and keep all my commandments, and *him that seeketh so to do.*" (Italics added.) In other words, long before we are able to keep all of the commandments and because we "seek so to do," the Lord allows us the privilege of possessing at least some of the gifts of the Spirit.

When we desire deeply to be baptized of fire and of the Holy Ghost and while seeking with all of our hearts to do so, before the greater endowment comes, the Lord in his graciousness allows us to have spiritual experiences along the way that whet our appetites to have such experiences consistently. Long before we enjoy the Spirit regularly in our lives, we have had enough experiences with the Spirit to give us the determination to keep reaching.

The gospel is serious, but we mustn't take ourselves too seriously. We must reach for all we can, even though there is some risk involved. We must strive to grow in the powers of godliness, but we mustn't let our mistakes, our awkwardness, and our slipping from time to time deter us. If we are really trying, rejoicing in our blessings but desiring greater blessings (see Abraham 1:1–3), the Lord will allow us to "see through a glass, darkly" (1 Corinthians 13:12). And if we persist, our vision, our enjoyments, and our blessings will become greater and greater. I repeat that striving for the spiritual second birth, striving to know the Lord and to obtain his blessings and powers, is the most challenging, difficult, and yet exhilarating experience of mortal life.

Possessing a perfect hope. Third, Nephi indicated that once we are on the straight and narrow path, we "must press forward with a steadfastness in Christ, having a perfect brightness of hope, and a love of God and of all men." (2 Nephi 31:20.) I think having a perfect brightness of hope is to enjoy the constant assurance from the Savior through the Spirit that if we will maintain our commitment to him, we will inherit everlasting life. To possess a perfect hope is more than simply to have a lively desire, for hope arises from a righteous heart. Hope is a confidence, born of the Spirit, that we will inherit exaltation. The prophet Mormon said of hope, "And what is it that ye shall hope for? Behold I say unto you that ye shall have hope through the atonement of Christ and the power of his resurrection, to be raised unto life eternal." (Moroni 7:41.) With all due respect to the joy of earth life and its eternal significance, I think it is most natural to hope someday to be carried beyond this vale of sorrow into a far better land of promise. (See Alma 37:45.) Moroni said, "Wherefore, whoso believeth in God might with surety hope for a better world, yea, even a place at the right hand of God, which hope cometh of faith, maketh an anchor to the souls of men, which would make them sure and steadfast, always abounding in good works, being led to glorify God." (Ether 12:4.)

To love God and all men. Fourth, to have been baptized of fire and of the Holy Ghost is to be an heir, or possessor, of charity, the pure love of Christ. All the examples of men and women who are truly born again reflect without exception that marvelous quality. Nephi declared that having obtained the path and being steadfast in Christ, we will have "a love of God and of all men." (2 Nephi 31:20.)

As the Spirit works with us, we are often quite amazed at how strongly we feel about others, how unreservedly we love them, not because we *should* love them but simply because we *do.* I'm sure all of us have been caught off guard, so to speak, with feelings of love for others that have come into our hearts on different occasions, and we have deeply sensed it is because of the Lord and not simply our own doing.

On one such occasion I was driving from Los Angeles to Ridgecrest, California, for a lecture. It was a beautiful spring day, and as I drove across the desert, I noticed up ahead on my right a dirt hill about five hundred feet high. There were a half dozen or so "souped-up" cars maneuvering all over the hill. I decided to stop and watch their antics. As I got out of my car to get a better view and also to enjoy the California sun, I noticed there was a car parked about forty feet behind me, and standing in front of the car were a young man and a young woman. They looked like they were in their late teens and, judging by their overall appearance, I concluded they were way off the path — in fact, I decided they probably didn't even know there was a path!

After watching the cars for a few minutes, I glanced at my watch and knew I must be hurrying on. As I turned to get in the car, I glanced back and noticed the young man was still standing there, watching the cars, but the girl had gotten into the car. Right at that moment I felt strongly impressed to walk back and chat with the young man.

I quickly introduced myself and asked him a couple of questions that I hoped would cause him to ask who I was, which he did. I told him that I taught in the Religion Department at Brigham

Young University, in Provo, Utah. He got a funny look in his eyes and responded, "Oh, you must be a Mormon." I said, "Yes, I am." He paused for a moment and then a little apologetically said, "Well, I am too."

Then I knew why I had been so impressed to introduce myself to him. Immediately I felt such a strong love for that young man. I reached up, put my hand on the back of his neck, pulled him closer to me, rested my forearm on his chest, and quickly shared with him my feelings about the Lord, my gratitude for the Church, and my testimony that my life had been changed because of my relationship with the Savior. The words came easily. I wasn't preachy, but I came on strong, and he was receptive. His eyes glistened with excitement and gratitude as he told me how much he appreciated what I was saying. Knowing I had to hurry, I pulled away, but he caught hold of my hand and kept saying, "Thanks. Thanks so much." How I wanted to put him in the car and take him home and get him back on the path! I couldn't help but acknowledge that I had at least tasted of a love that was a gift—a love that came in spite of my having been judgmental.

Feasting on the words of Christ. The fifth and final characteristic Nephi spoke about is "feasting upon the word of Christ," which really teaches us powerfully why being baptized of fire and of the Holy Ghost is such a marvelous experience. It has to do with what we must do after we are on the straight and narrow path.

Nephi explained what it means to feast upon the word of Christ. He says simply, "the words of Christ will tell you all things what ye should do." (2 Nephi 32:3.)

I wish I could express what a tremendous effect Nephi's teachings about living by the Spirit have had on my life. I know that the same doctrine of living with the constant companionship of the Spirit is spelled out beautifully in the sacrament prayer, that is, if we remember the Lord, his Spirit will be with us always. I know that if the Savior is the exemplar for all of us to follow— and he constantly took his directions from the Father—we, in following his example, will take our directions from the Savior constantly. I have learned that I have the obligation and the responsibility to live my life so that Jesus Christ will, through

112

the Spirit, be my constant companion and will, through the Spirit, show me all the things that I should do. Certainly it's hard to live by the Spirit regularly; certainly it's hard to wrestle and struggle with the decisions we make, hoping to get confirmation that what we have decided is correct. It may seem hard to believe that we can arrive at a point where all the decisions we make are correct, but I believe that to truly follow the example of Christ and to feast upon the words of Christ means that ultimately we need not make mistakes.

Summary of Indicators That We Are Born of the Spirit

Throughout the scriptures we find a number of indicators that help us know if we are born of the Spirit. Here are the major ones, including the five Nephi gave us:

1. We will have experienced a broken heart and have a contrite spirit. (See D&C 20:37.) We can't come to a revealed understanding of the Atonement without sensing profoundly our own inadequacies and sins, without sensing deeply our total dependence on the Lord, without our hearts being broken and our spirits contrite. We will remember the "greatness of God, and [our] own nothingness, and his goodness and long-suffering towards [us], unworthy creatures, and humble [ourselves] even in the depths of humility." (Mosiah 4:11.)

2. We will have an overwhelming daily awareness of Christ and his marvelous atonement. We will root our lives and our labors in the kingdom in the reality of Christ's atoning sacrifice. We will "shout praises unto the Holy One of Israel" (2 Nephi 31:13) and will "stand as witnesses of God at all times and in all things, and in all places" (Mosiah 18:9).

3. We will look upon sin with abhorrence (see Alma 13:12) and have no disposition to do evil (see Mosiah 5:2; 2 Nephi 9:49). Movies (R- and X-rated, and many rated PG!), literature, and television, regardless of how artistically they are done, and all other things that partake of the grossness and sensuality of the world will clearly be repugnant to us.

4. We will have a profound love of God and of all men. We

will sense the infinite worth of each of our Heavenly Father's children and do all in our power to treat everyone in a Christlike way. (See 2 Nephi 31:20; Matthew 25:40.)

5. Our very nature will be changed. With our nature changed, our personality will become more like the Savior's. "Those who have got the forgiveness of their sins have countenances that look bright, and they will shine with the intelligence of heaven." (Brigham Young, in *Times and Seasons,* 6:956.) "When the will, passions, and feelings of a person are perfectly submissive to God and His requirements, that person is sanctified." (Brigham Young, in *Journal of Discourses,* 2:123.)

6. Our great drive in life will be to do all in our power to bring individuals to the Father through Christ. We will be willing to make whatever effort and sacrifice are necessary to encourage people to repent and live the gospel. (See Alma 31:35; Helaman 10:4–5.)

7. We will be free with our temporal goods. (See Mosiah 4:16.) We will pay our tithes, be generous in our fast offerings, and live the spirit of the law of consecration. (See 4 Nephi 1:3.)

8. We will have prophetic views of that which is to come. (See Mosiah 5:3.) We will look forward to the Second Coming. (See D&C 45:39.)

9. We will desire with all our heart to live by the Spirit: "For as many as are led by the Spirit of God, they are the sons of God." (Romans 8:14.)

10. We will speak with the tongue of angels. (See 2 Nephi 32:2.)

11. We will not allow our children to quarrel; rather, we will "teach them to love one another, and to serve one another." (Mosiah 4:14.)

12. We will see in a mighty way the mantle of divine authority resting on the Lord's anointed, and "his word [we] shall receive, as if from [the Lord's] own mouth, in all patience and faith." (D&C 21:5.)

13. We will be "harrowed up by the memory of [our] sins no more." (Alma 36:19.)

14. We will be filled with peace and "a perfect brightness of hope." (2 Nephi 31:20.) We will know our hearts are right and

that we are acceptable to the Lord. Elder Harold B. Lee told of an experience he had with this principle being taught:

"Brother Romney and I were sitting in the office one day and a young missionary came in. He was getting ready to go on a mission, and he had been interviewed in the usual way and had made confessions of certain transgressions of his youth. But he said to us, 'I'm not satisfied by just having confessed. How can I know that I have been forgiven?' In other words, 'How do I know that I am born again?' . . .

"Brother Romney said to him again, 'My son, you wait and pray until you have the peace of conscience because of your faith in Jesus Christ's atonement; and you will know that your sins then have been forgiven.' Except for that, as Elder Romney explained, anyone of us is impoverished; and we are wandering in a fog until we have had that rebirth." (*Instructor*, June 1963, p. 222.)

15. We will see ourselves as "babes in Christ" (1 Corinthians 3:1; see also 1 Peter 2:2); that is, we will realize that having been "quickened in the inner man" (Moses 6:65), we are on the threshold of great spiritual growth and development. But we will be aware that there is much to learn, much yet to do, and much yet to become before we can put on the full stature of Christ. We will also realize that once we are born again, we may yet fall from the grace of God and lose our standing with him. (See D&C 20:31–32.)

Those Who Are Truly Born Again

President David O. McKay, as a young man, was sailing to the Samoan Islands on a Church assignment. A particularly beautiful sunset and a series of ideas and reflections prepared him for a remarkable experience that taught him ever so powerfully of the importance of being born again. He recorded:

"Toward evening, the reflection of the afterglow of a beautiful sunset was most splendid! The sky was tinged with pink, and the clouds lingering around the horizon were fringed with various hues of crimson and orange, while the heavy cloud farther to the west was somber purple and black. These colors cast varying shadows on the peaceful surface of the water. Those from the cloud were long and dark, those from the crimson-tinged sky, clear but rose-tinted and fading into a faint pink that merged into the clear blue of the ocean. Gradually, the shadows became deeper and heavier, and then all merged into a beautiful calm twilight that made the sea look like a great mirror upon which fell the faint light of the crescent moon.

"Pondering still upon this beautiful scene, I lay in my berth at ten o'clock that night and thought to myself: Charming as it is, it doesn't stir my soul with emotion as do the innocent lives of children, and the sublime characters of loved ones and friends. Their beauty, unselfishness, and heroism are after all the most glorious!

"I then fell asleep, and beheld in vision something infinitely sublime. In the distance I beheld a beautiful white city. Though it was far away, yet I seemed to realize that trees with luscious fruit, shrubbery with gorgeously tinted leaves, and flowers in perfect bloom abounded everywhere. The clear sky above seemed to reflect these beautiful shades of color. I then saw a great concourse of people approaching the city. Each one wore a white flowing robe and a white headdress. Instantly my attention seemed centered upon their leader, and though I could see only the profile of his features and his body, I recognized him at once as my Savior! The tint and radiance of his countenance were glorious to behold. There was a peace about him which seemed sublime — it was divine!

"The city, I understood, was his. It was the City Eternal; and the people following him were to abide there in peace and eternal happiness.

"But who were they?

"As if the Savior read my thoughts, he answered by pointing to a semicircle that then appeared above them, and on which was written in gold the worlds:

These Are They Who Have Overcome the World —
Who Have Truly Been Born Again!

"When I awoke, it was breaking day over Apia harbor." (*Cherished Experiences,* pp. 59–60.)

Some thirty-nine years later, President McKay pleaded: "May

God grant that . . . we may instruct our young people, and the members of the Church everywhere, to resist temptations that weaken the body, that destroy the soul, that we may stand truly repentant as we were when we entered the waters of baptism; that we may be renewed in the true sense of the word, that we may be born again; that our souls might bask in the light of the Holy Spirit, and go on as true members of the Church of Jesus Christ until our mission on earth is completed and God receives us and rewards us according to our merits." (In Conference Report, Apr. 1960, p. 29.)

The spiritual second birth is the experience the Lord has ordained to change our lives and prepare us for entrance into the celestial kingdom. If that experience occurs, we will be forgiven of our sins, our nature will be changed, and we will enjoy the daily companionship of the Holy Ghost. Because of the companionship of the Spirit, our love for everyone will be godly, and we will come to know the Lord and Savior Jesus Christ in a marvelous way and dedicate our lives to the building of the kingdom of God.

The following statement by President Ezra Taft Benson points out the need for the second birth and the changes that transpire in our lives when we are truly born again:

"The Lord works from the inside out. The world works from the outside in. The world would take people out of the slums. Christ takes the slums out of the people, and then they take themselves out of the slums. The world would mold men by changing their environment. Christ changes men, who then change their environment. The world would shape human behavior, but Christ can change human nature. . . .

" 'Human nature *can* be changed, here and now,' said President McKay, and then he quoted the following:

" ' "You can change human nature. No man who has felt in him the Spirit of Christ even for half a minute can deny this truth. . . .

" ' "You do change human nature, your own human nature, if you surrender it to Christ. . . . " (Quoting Beverly Nichols, in *Stepping Stones to an Abundant Life*, comp. Llewelyn R. McKay [Salt Lake City: Deseret Book, 1971], pp. 23, 127).'

"Yes, Christ changes men, and changed men can change the world.

"Men changed for Christ will be captained by Christ. Like Paul they will be asking, 'Lord, what wilt thou have me to do?' (Acts 9:6). Peter stated, they will 'follow his steps' (1 Peter 2:21). John said they will 'walk, even as he walked' (1 John 2:6).

"Finally, men captained by Christ will be consumed in Christ." (In Conference Report, Oct. 1985, pp. 5–6.)

Chapter 6

LIVING DAY TO DAY BY THE SPIRIT

We should all seek to be spiritually born of God so that in becoming free from sin and having our nature changed, we might enjoy the marvelous companionship of the Holy Ghost, grow in the knowledge and stature of Christ, and receive the Savior's guidance in our daily lives. When we are born again we are "babes in Christ" (1 Corinthians 3:1), standing as it were at the threshold of unlimited knowledge, capable of becoming in time a man or woman of Christ in the fullest sense of the word. The primary element in our growth toward perfection is the Spirit, and our primary goal should be to live daily by the influence and power of the Holy Ghost.

Years ago a prominent entertainer who was heavily involved in a protestant movement came to Brigham Young University to speak at a devotional assembly in the old Smith Fieldhouse. A tremendous personality, the guest speaker began his address by saying, in effect, "I can't see that you Mormons believe a lot differently from how I do, except you keep talking about the Holy Ghost!" I was high in the upper levels of the Fieldhouse, and it was all I could do to restrain myself from jumping up and yelling, "Hey! That's the whole difference!"

While what I wanted to say was perhaps a bit oversimplified, it really does sum up the main difference between the restored Church and all other churches on earth. That we actually possess the gift and power of the Holy Ghost by the laying on of hands is what makes the restored Church distinctively divine. The gift of the Holy Ghost is what sets us apart. United States President Martin Van Buren once asked the Prophet Joseph Smith wherein Mormonism was different from other religions of the day. The Prophet wrote later that he had told President Van Buren that "we differed in mode of baptism, and the gift of the Holy Ghost by the laying on of hands. We considered that all other considerations were contained in the gift of the Holy Ghost." (*History of the Church*, 4:42.)

The Holy Ghost is the connecting link between God and man, enabling man to possess the powers of heaven. Although we often speak of many different manifestations of the power of God, such as the power of faith, the power of the priesthood, and so forth, in a very real sense essentially all power manifested by God to man is by and through the Holy Ghost.

President Brigham Young taught: "The Holy Ghost takes of the Father, and of the Son, and shows it to the disciples. It shows them things past, present, and to come. It opens the vision of the mind, unlocks the treasures of wisdom, and they begin to understand the things of God. . . . It leads them to drink at the fountain of eternal wisdom, justice, and truth; they grow in grace, and in the knowledge of the truth as it is in Jesus Christ, until they see as they are seen, and know as they are known." (In *Journal of Discourses*, 1:241.)

The Holy Ghost enables us to be patient, long-suffering, gentle, and meek. (See D&C 121:41–42.) The Holy Ghost enables us to be gently persuasive in a Christlike way. The Holy Ghost gives us a sensitivity, a kindness, a patience that nothing else can give us. The Holy Ghost gives us an appreciation of the tremendous value of others. Elder Parley P. Pratt, in the most perfect description of true character development I have ever read, indicated that there is no facet of human character and personality that cannot be brought into full bloom under the workings of the Holy Ghost:

"An intelligent being, in the image of God, possesses every organ, attribute, sense, sympathy, affection that is possessed by God himself.

"But these are possessed by man, in his rudimental state, in a subordinate sense of the word. Or, in other words, these attributes are in embryo and are to be gradually developed. They resemble a bud, a germ, which gradually develops into bloom, and then, by progress, produces the mature fruit after its own kind.

"The gift of the Holy Ghost adapts itself to all these organs or attributes. It quickens all the intellectual faculties, increases, enlarges, expands, and purifies all the natural passions and affections, and adapts them, by the gift of wisdom, to their lawful use. It inspires, develops, cultivates, and matures all the fine-toned sympathies, joys, tastes, kindred feelings, and affections of our nature. It inspires virtue, kindness, goodness, tenderness, gentleness, and charity. It develops beauty of person, form, and features. It tends to health, vigor, animation, and social feeling. It invigorates all the faculties of the physical and intellectual man. It strengthens and gives tone to the nerves. In short, it is, as it were, marrow to the bone, joy to the heart, light to the eyes, music to the ears, and life to the whole being." (*Key to the Science of Theology*, p. 61.)

Surely as we reflect that it is the role and power of the Spirit that bears special witness to those who hear the gospel for the first time to invite them to come into the waters of baptism; that it is the Spirit that enables us to gain control over our bodies; that it is the Spirit that conveys a remission of sins and cleanses and purifies sin-laden souls; that it is the Spirit that distills the very nature of the Redeemer into our beings as we live by faith; that it is the Spirit that endows faithful believers in Christ with charity, the pure love of Christ; that it is the Spirit that seals all ordinances according to the faithfulness of the members so that heavenly assurances of eternal life can be obtained while we are yet in mortality—as we reflect on all of these and many more, surely we will exclaim, "What a privilege, what a blessing to have the gift and power of the Holy Ghost."

Our First Commandment

Although we receive at our confirmation the *gift* of the Holy Ghost, we do not receive the *power* of the Holy Ghost unless we seek mightily for it. Indeed, to stress the point, the first commandment we receive when we are confirmed members of the Church is to "receive the Holy Ghost."

President Brigham Young received such instruction from the Prophet Joseph Smith in a vision several years after the Prophet's death:

"Joseph stepped toward me and looking very earnestly, yet pleasantly, said: Tell the people to be humble and faithful, and be sure to keep the spirit of the Lord and it will lead them right. Be careful and not turn away the small still voice; it will teach them what to do and where to go; it will yield the fruits of the Kingdom. Tell the brethren to keep their hearts open to conviction, so that when the Holy Ghost comes to them their hearts will be ready to receive it. They can tell the spirit of the Lord from all spirits; it will whisper peace and joy to their souls; it will take malice, hatred, strife and all evil from their hearts; and their whole desire will be to do good, bring forth righteousness and build up the kingdom of God. Tell the brethren if they will follow the spirit of the Lord, they will go right. Be sure to tell the people to keep the spirit of the Lord; and if they will, they will find themselves just as they were organized by our Father in Heaven before they came into the world. Our Father in Heaven organized the human family, but they are all disorganized and in great confusion." (Journal History of the Church, 23 Feb. 1847.)

President Wilford Woodruff had a similar experience with Brigham Young after Brigham's death:

"On one occasion, I saw Brother Brigham and Brother Heber ride in a carriage ahead of the carriage in which I rode when I was on my way to attend conference; and they were dressed in the most priestly robes. When we arrived at our destination I asked Prest. Young if he would preach to us. He said, 'No, I have finished my testimony in the flesh I shall not talk to this people any more. But (said he) I have come to see you; I have come to watch over you, and to see what the people are doing. Then (said he) I want you to teach the people—and I want you to follow this counsel yourself—that they must labor and so live as to obtain the Holy Spirit, for without this you cannot build up the kingdom; without the spirit of God you are in danger of walking in the dark, and in danger of failing to accomplish your calling as apostles and as elders in the church and kingdom of God." (In *Journal of Discourses*, 21:318.)

Considering the profound spiritual experiences the prophets Joseph Smith and Brigham Young enjoyed and their grasp, in such an awesome way, of the splendor and magnificence of the theology of the gospel of Christ, I find it tremendously significant that when each one visited with his immediate successor in the kingdom of God, each counseled simply, "Seek for and live by the Spirit!"

When the Son of Man returns in great glory at his second coming, the parable of the ten virgins will be fulfilled. Those who will be caught up to meet him will be those "that are wise and have received the truth, and have taken the Holy Spirit for their guide, and have not been deceived— . . . they shall not be hewn down and cast into the fire, but shall abide the day." (D&C 45:57.)

Often in gospel discussions we hear detailed elaborations of what the Savior really meant when he said, "Therefore I would that ye should be perfect even as I, or your Father who is in heaven is perfect." (3 Nephi 12:48.) Most of the elaborations imply that perfection, in the fullest sense, is an achievement for another world. Could we consider a goal to attain in this life to be that of enjoying, while in mortality, a remission of sins and the constant companionship of the Holy Ghost? The Lord himself promised, "That which is of God is light; and he that receiveth light, and continueth in God, receiveth more light; and that light groweth brighter and brighter until the perfect day." (D&C 50:24.) Further, our beloved Redeemer declared, "And if your eye be single to my glory, your whole bodies shall be filled with light, and there shall be no darkness in you; and that body which is filled with light comprehendeth all things." (D&C 88:67.) What marvelous promises, and they are predicated on our obtaining the Spirit in our lives.

Living by the Spirit, then, should be our food and our drink, our desire and our determination. We should be willing to do anything and everything we have to do to obtain and live by the Spirit. President Brigham Young declared: "I never have cared but for one thing, and that is, simply to know that I am now *right* before my *Father in Heaven.* If I am this *moment,* this *day,* doing the things *God requires* of my *hands,* and precisely where my *Father in Heaven wants me to be,* I care no more about to-morrow than though it never would come." (In *Journal of Discourses,* 1:132.)

The Still Small Voice

It's very important to understand that although there are marvelous, spectacular manifestations of the Spirit, the most common method of revelation — in fact, the very spirit of revelation — is the quiet whispering of the Holy Ghost to the heart of man. (See D&C 8:2–3.)

Elijah learned the lesson that the Lord was not in the wind, in the earthquake, or in the fire; rather, he was in the still small voice. (See 1 Kings 19:11–12.) The Nephites and Lamanites learned the same lesson when, having been exposed to wind, fire, and earthquake, what seemed to have the greatest effect upon them was hearing a voice from heaven: "It was not a harsh voice, neither was it a loud voice; nevertheless, and notwithstanding it being a small voice it did pierce them that did hear to the center, insomuch that there was no part of their frame that it did not cause to quake; yea, it did pierce them to the very soul, and did cause their hearts to burn." (3 Nephi 11:3.) So it is that most of the knowledge we acquire from God comes to us by the quiet workings of the Spirit.

Reasons We Don't Get the Spirit

There are many reasons the Saints don't enjoy the guidance of the Spirit in their lives as they should. Obtaining the Spirit rests upon the broad foundation of keeping the commandments and honoring covenants made with the Lord. President Joseph Fielding Smith noted: "We have a great many members of this Church who have never reached a manifestation through the Holy Ghost. Why? Because they have not made their lives conform to the truth. . . .

"That great gift [of the Holy Ghost] comes to us only through humility and faith and obedience. Therefore, a great many members of the Church do not have that guidance." (*Deseret News*, Church Section, 4 Nov. 1961, p. 14.)

I would suggest some additional and specific things that keep us from enjoying the Spirit in the manner we should.

We don't ask. My experience has taught me that many Saints simply are not aware that they should be seeking for the Spirit in their lives; consequently, they do not seek for it. We should seek for it as the twelve Nephite disciples did: they knelt down and "pray[ed] for that which they most desired; and they desired that the Holy Ghost should be given unto them." (3 Nephi 19:9.)

We go to the Lord only in times of trouble. We need to cling to the iron rod, or the word of God. In a symbolic sense, we should move along the iron rod hand over hand, never removing one hand until the other one has a solid grasp on the iron rod. Often we call upon the Lord and his power only when great difficulties transpire or tragedies strike; when things really get rough, we run to him with great intensity, pleading for help. We ought to strive continually to enjoy his Spirit. We ought to reach for his presence, blessings, and powers when things are going well, when the sun is shining, and when there are no apparent storm clouds or shadows. We need to let the Lord know how much we appreciate all of our blessings while those blessings abound, and then when the storm clouds gather, when the great trials come, we will have the solid assurance that having sought the Lord in our prosperity, we can have him with us in our adversity. We will discover that every trial, indeed, every challenging experience that comes into our lives will be a stepping stone to greater heights and the very means by which we will in time become sanctified.

As recorded in Doctrine and Covenants 101:4–8, the Lord chastised the Saints in Missouri for not acknowledging him in their lives when things were going well — in fact, he chided them for turning to him only when great difficulties came upon them.

Perhaps you remember that at the time this revelation was given, the Saints had been driven from Jackson County because of "envyings, and strifes." (V. 5.) In fact, the Saints had been told that they needed to be "chastened and tried, even as Abraham." (V. 4.)

Let's liken verses 7 and 8 unto ourselves. Perhaps in doing so, we will appreciate more how desperately we need to cling to the Lord at all times: "You were slow to hearken unto the voice of the Lord your God; therefore, the Lord your God is slow to hearken unto your prayers, to answer them in the day of your trouble.

"In the day of your peace you esteemed lightly my counsel; but, in the day of your trouble, of necessity you feel after me."

I'm completely convinced that if we sense our dependency on the Lord and seek mightily for the Spirit, then through sunshine and darkness, we will have the Comforter to be with us.

We are not decisive. So many times as we seek for the mind and will of the Lord in our lives, we seriously limit our ability to obtain the Lord's direction because we are not decisive enough — that is, we don't think through our problems, weigh carefully the various options, select the one we think is right, and then seek in prayer for a confirmation. (See D&C 9:8.) The Lord expects us to do our homework, to make a choice, and to present him with a decision that he can respond to. Too often we are afraid to make the decisions because we don't know what to decide, and it becomes more difficult when despite our earnest prayers, we seemingly receive no explicit direction. But if we will make a decision, using our best judgment, and then ask him for confirmation, he will guide us. President Brigham Young illustrated this principle: "If I do not know the will of my Father, and what He requires of me in a certain transaction, if I ask Him to give me wisdom concerning any requirement in life, or in regard to my own course, or that of my friends, my family, my children, or those that I preside over, and get no answer from Him, and then do the very best that my judgment will teach me, He is bound to own and honor that transaction, and He will do so to all intents and purposes." (In *Journal of Discourses*, 3:205.)

The Lord wants you and me to be decisive, to present our decisions to him so we can learn to understand the whisperings of the Spirit in response to the decisions we make.

We expect too much too soon. Obtaining the constant companionship of the Spirit isn't something that comes at the snap of a finger, simply from desiring it. We discover quickly that it takes time and a great deal of patience to harmonize our desires with those of the Lord, to freely submit our wills to the will of our Father in Heaven, to discipline the thoughts and intents of our hearts and the words spoken by our tongues. We must be careful of the friends we choose and the recreation we engage in. Seeking mightily for the blessings and the directions of the Master can be risky—it seems that we can't seek for the spirit of revelation without at the same time inviting temptation of the adversary. It appears that the degree to which God reveals himself to us is the degree to which he allows Satan to tempt us. We can't genuinely claim a revelation or endowment of power is truly ours until Satan tries to take it from us and we successfully resist his every effort. To grow in the spirit of revelation takes time and patience and perseverance, but if we keep our faces turned heavenward and keep struggling, even though our progress may often seem slow, in time we will reach our goal and enjoy the constant companionship of the Holy Ghost.

Learning to live by the Spirit is a little like learning to fly an airplane. One of my brothers was a pilot in the Air Force, and much to my delight as a young teenager, he frequently flew fighter planes home. What fun it was when he flew over the farmhouse and put on an air show just for the family! Over several years I was given many a thrilling ride—some of the time a little more thrilling that I wanted! At the same time, I developed a real desire to learn to fly a plane. One spring arrangements were made for me to receive flying lessons at the local airport.

The day I went out to have my first lesson was absolutely beautiful. There were a few fluffy clouds in the sky, there was no wind, and it was just perfect for flying. Hoping we would quickly get in the plane and take off, I was very disappointed when the instructor insisted on taking up a lot of valuable time talking about the basic structure of the airplane—I felt I was already familiar with all of that. It seemed so ridiculous to walk around the plane so many times while he went on and on about things that seemed totally irrelevant. I wanted to fly! I didn't want to know how to *make* an airplane! It took all the patience I could muster to keep from blurting out, "Hey, look, when it come to airplanes, I've been around them, in them, and up in them—dozens of them. I already know the things you're telling me. Let's get in the plane and up in the air."

Finally, we climbed aboard, I in the front cockpit and he right behind me. The plane had a tail wheel instead of a nose wheel so the nose was much higher than the tail, pointing the plane at an angle that made it impossible for the pilot to see the runway directly ahead. My instructor told me that the first thing I was to learn was how to taxi down the runway going from one side to the other so I would be able to see if other aircraft were on the runway. That sounded simple enough. The runway looked like it was at least sixty feet wide, the controls seemed easy enough to handle, I was a fair athlete with what I thought was reasonably good muscular coordination, and I just knew that taxiing back and forth per instruction would be a cinch. After receiving what I thought were more than adequate instructions, I started the engine, released the brake, and started down the runway. Immediately I was absolutely astounded at how sensitive the controls were! Having been told to zigzag back and forth across the runway, I had barely begun to zig the runway when I was all the way across, and before I could zag, I had run off the runway and was making tracks in the sagebrush and grass. The instructor yelled at me to get back on the runway, which I quickly did, but only momentarily because I overcorrected and was now off on the other side! The instructor got pretty excited—so excited that I thought he was going to bail out of the plane before it had even taken off.

I was so frustrated, irritated, embarrassed, and disappointed at how hard it was to properly handle the controls that I wanted to tell the instructor to stop what I thought was a very temperamental plane and I would immediately cease my flying lessons for good. But he was patient, and I was somewhat determined;

consequently, I eventually got so I could handle the controls just right, taxiing smoothly while staying all the time on the runway. After I'd practiced a few more times, the big moment finally arrived—we took off, and oh, what a thrill it was to my young heart to be at the controls of the plane, to lift off the ground, to gain adequate altitude, and then to fly around the valley. It was more than worth all the frustration of achieving adequate control.

So it is with trying to live by the Spirit. It is frustrating to try to arrive at a point where we can handle and control our mind, our tongue, our desires, and our passions so that the sensitive, delicate promptings of the Spirit can enable us to thread our way through the sensuality of our day and the clouds of intellectual sophistry that are so prevalent on every side. It takes time and patience to learn to discern the promptings of the Spirit, to learn the boundaries, rules, and regulations for receiving personal revelation. It can be discouraging, but in seeking to live by the Spirit, we are attempting to do the single most important and challenging thing on earth, and we should anticipate a tremendous soul-stretching experience. We must realize that having the Spirit is more than worth the struggle it takes to obtain it.

Further, it is so important to realize that if our hearts are pure and we genuinely desire righteousness and we diligently keep the commandments, honor the prophets, and pray mightily, then the Lord's power, strength, and direction will be ours. We may not enjoy the visions, the dreams, and the open revelations that we desire as soon as we would like them, but we will, without qualification, have peace, and in that peace we will have the sweet assurance that if we endure in righteousness, ultimately everything will be ours.

To be patient in seeking for the Spirit is to be patient in well-doing. (See D&C 64:33.) Thus we will fashion a crown of righteousness by persisting mightily in seeking "to be a greater follower of righteousness, and to possess a greater knowledge." (Abraham 1:2.)

The following personal experiences may help to illustrate the challenge it is to obtain the guidance of the Spirit. It is often one thing to know the Lord is with you and another thing to discern exactly what he is telling you. And often, some of the most important decisions we make stem from an almost imperceptible whisper of the Spirit. I know, however, that if we will persist and not get discouraged, we will grow in the spirit of revelation.

Being Strengthened for Sorrow

To my recollection, the first experience I had with the Spirit (although I didn't understand at the time what was happening) was on 12 February 1939. I was nine years old. My closest childhood friend and I were walking through the neighborhood, chewing gum and chatting as friends do. It had rained the night before, leaving many puddles on the unpaved road. We crossed an alley and walked by an open garage. As I walked past the garage I glanced in, noticing the garage was empty; but, right at that moment, there flooded over me a powerful feeling—I'll never forget it. The feeling imprinted every detail of the moment onto my mind. I didn't know what it meant or what was happening, but I did know that the feeling was real and unique and that something very important was being made known to me.

In time we ended up at my friend's house, went upstairs, and were playing in his bedroom. I heard the phone ring downstairs and, somehow, I immediately knew that it was for me and that my mother had died. Before my friend's sister finished answering the phone, I had grabbed my coat, run downstairs, and rushed toward home. When I met my bereaved father and brothers and sisters, I felt a comfort that I will never forget—a comfort that was such a blessing that day and in the months to come. Perhaps for the first time the role of the Holy Ghost as a "comforter" had interceded in my life.

Go to School

Most of the whisperings of the Spirit that have affected my life in the most dramatic way didn't seem that consequential at the time. For example, most of my growing-up years were spent on a farm, and I learned to love working in the fields. Even before I completed high school, I determined to make farming my life's vocation. Following high school, I attended a year of college at Logan, Utah, after which I served my mission. I remember visiting with elders on different occasions and when the subject of future plans would come up, I emphasized that my college days were over and that after my mission I would return to the farm, get married, and live happily thereafter. Although I enjoyed my experience at Logan, I had no desire or inclination whatsoever to return to college.

I returned from my mission at Christmastime, started preparing the tractor and machinery for the coming spring, and really looked forward to settling down to a life of agriculture. It was great to get back into the swing of farming, and when spring came I was delighted to put my hand to the plow, convinced that that was where it would remain. Much to my surprise, however, I found myself very restless after just a few months of farming. It was hard to pin down my feelings—I enjoyed what I was doing, and yet I had a vague feeling of discontent.

One morning I was walking to the south end of the farm to change the water. I had a shovel over my shoulder and wasn't really thinking of anything in particular when quite unexpectedly (to put it mildly), there came into my mind the idea that I should return to college that fall. There was no big hurry, as long as it was that fall, and it didn't matter where I went to college, as long as it was Brigham Young University! The idea came so forcefully and caught me so totally off guard that I flipped the shovel off my shoulder, stuck it into the mud alongside the road, quickly turned, and ran all the way back to the farmhouse. I excitedly announced to my dad and stepmother that I knew, without question, that I should return to college. Although I didn't know what I should study, I knew I should be in school, and that one idea changed the entire course of my life. Little did I dream that because of that powerful intimation of the Spirit I would be willing to stick with my education until I finally obtained all three degrees.

After my wife and I were married, the children came with clocklike regularity, and of necessity I had to teach constantly for the family to survive economically. There were many moments when I seriously questioned the validity of what I was attempting to do. But always at the moment of greatest discouragement, there would come into my mind that precious experience of walking along a dirt road and learning so fully that the most important thing for me to do then was to return to college. With that remembrance, renewed determination would come that enabled me, finally, to reach my goals.

It's Important Where You Ski

Have you ever ignored the distinct promptings of the Spirit and then suffered from missing an opportunity or a blessing? Let me share with you an experience when that happened to me.

I was particularly close to my brother who was just older than I. We spent long hours together working in the fields, milking the cows, double-dating, playing on the same football team for a year, and other things. Just before my mission, he married his childhood sweetheart, and I was his best man. We corresponded regularly while I was in the mission field, and in that correspondence I learned that he and his wife were very active in a little branch in Oregon. It was at that point in his life that he obtained a personal testimony of the divinity of the Restoration, which was a source of great delight to me.

After returning from my mission, what a special thrill it was for me to have my brother and his family come home for Christmas. I'll not forget how excited I was to see him and embrace him again. I was anxious to share with him the joys of missionary work, but his excitement for his newfound testimony and his desire to share it with me precluded my getting much said.

Several days later we decided to take a skiing trip to Sun Valley, Idaho. Four of my friends had returned home recently from their missions or from the armed forces, and I invited them to come and join us.

After we arrived in Sun Valley, we went skiing on Dollar Mountain, which is a beginner's mountain and isn't terribly challenging, so it wasn't too surprising when my four close friends and I decided it would be more exciting to go over to Baldy Mountain to finish out the day of skiing. When we had made the decision, I skied over to where my brother was and asked him if he would like to go over to Baldy with us. He declined the invitation by saying he wasn't sure he was ready to tackle the more difficult slopes of Mount Baldy, but he encouraged me to go with my friends if I so desired.

At that moment I received an impression quietly but firmly suggesting that I stay on Dollar Mountain and ski with my brother and let my friends go to Baldy. I'm embarrassed to relate my reaction to that impression. In my mind I said: "My goodness, I've been on a mission for two years, and you hounded me constantly there. Can't I have one day of skiing without you telling me where I should ski? Not only that, but what difference could it possibly make where I ski?"

I continued to feel that I shouldn't go with my friends, but I went anyway. While riding on the ski bus from Dollar Mountain to Baldy, I felt terrible—it seemed that the Spirit was really grieved with me for not responding to his promptings. I spent the remainder of the day skiing with my friends, but it wasn't particularly enjoyable. At the end of the day we all piled in the car and returned home. Early the next morning my brother, his wife, and their new son left for Oregon.

The next time I saw my beloved brother was six months later. He was lying in a hospital bed in Oregon stricken with the advanced stages of a terrible cancer. As I quietly stepped into his hospital room and saw him lying there so sick and weak that he could hardly acknowledge me, there came into my mind the scene on Dollar Mountain. I then realized that the Lord, who knows all things, had tried to tell me on Dollar Mountain, "Look, this is the last day you'll be with your brother. Being with your friends is important, but not nearly as important as being with your brother," but I wouldn't listen. How marvelous it would have been to have spent that last day with my brother, skiing with him, pausing and chatting with him, and sharing ideas one with another.

Misreading the Spirit

That summer when my brother was stricken with cancer and eight weeks later died, I learned one of the hardest lessons on personal revelation that I have ever learned. When I first was told that Warren had cancer, I immediately went into a pattern of fasting and prayer. I pleaded night and day that the Lord would spare his life. It seemed to me that Warren had every reason to live. He had finally finished his schooling, he had a good job, he had just been blessed with a beautiful son, he and his wife were happily married. They were preparing to go to the temple to be sealed that fall.

As I wrestled in mighty prayer, fasting each week, there came a great peace into my heart. The calm feeling was one of such intensity that I felt for sure that Warren would be healed. I continued to fast and pray and by the time three weeks had elapsed, I was completely convinced that he would not die and that all would be well. I announced to his wife that I knew he would soon be healed. I announced it to the family and relatives. I announced it boldly and strongly. I wrote it in letters. I was so sure.

Five weeks later, he passed away. I was devastated. It was so hard to understand. Why had I failed to recognize what the Lord was telling me? There was absolutely no question that he had spoken peace to my heart, and how could I have peace unless Warren were to live?

The day of the funeral, I and an older brother who was inactive in the Church were preparing for the services. My heart was already so heavy I could hardly bear it when the casual conversation ended abruptly and my brother, whom I love dearly, criticized me and my foolish faith. "Surely," he said, "the wind has been knocked out of you for being so unwise as to promise everyone our brother would live." He really reprimanded me both for my belief and for my having made such promises.

Obviously, the words cut deeply—what could I say? How could I defend myself, or the concept of healing by faith? After my brother finished speaking, I walked up the stairs and outside. It was a beautiful June day. As I glanced upward, some feelings of rebelliousness and resentment surfaced in my mind and the thought formulated, "Heavenly Father, if you think I will ever try again to understand your mind and your will through the Spirit, you're wrong!" I didn't say it, but I would be less than honest in not admitting that I was deeply hurt, terribly embarrassed, and very confused.

Yet, while sitting in the chapel during the funeral, I felt peace come into my heart. I quickly and vividly recalled the many times the whisperings of the Spirit, the revelations of the Holy Ghost, had come so unmistakably into my heart. I recalled the sureness and intensity of the moment when I learned that Jesus is the Christ, that Joseph Smith is a prophet, and that the Book of Mormon is true. Many beautiful memories of the workings of the Spirit at other times in my life flooded into my mind and heart. Indeed, peace came, and with that peace the thought distilled deeply into my being, "It is one thing to know that my Spirit is upon you, but it is another thing to discern correctly what I am trying to reveal to you." I learned a great deal from that entire experience. I vowed I would try harder to discern the workings of the Spirit and not make such a mistake again.

Often students will ask, "How can I know for sure that I'm being inspired and that it's not simply my own desires surfacing?" I suggest that the only way you can know is through experience. It simply takes experience. The more we make decisions, present them to the Lord, and try to discern his answer, the quicker we will grow in our ability to sort out revelation from our own desires.

There Is No Witness Until . . .

Another challenge that presents itself in trying to live by the Spirit is this: some of the time the Lord seems to insist that we make a decision and implement that decision before we get a confirmation that the decision is correct. It is an interesting but somewhat nerve-racking principle.

One summer day my father and I were irrigating some sugar beets and chatting back and forth. I remember leaning on my shovel and listening intently as he informed me that if I was interested in farming for a livelihood, he would be pleased to will everything to me, which at the time would have been a fairly sizable inheritance. He indicated, however, that if I wasn't interested in agriculture as a lifelong vocation, he would make arrangements to have everything divided equally among all members of the family. I responded by telling him I appreciated his offer and that I would keep it in mind and see how things developed in the next several years.

In time I served my mission and then commenced the pattern of alternating between going to school and farming. After three years, I married. My sweetheart and I hoped we could finish school soon but because of Dad's failing health, we returned to the farm for what we thought would be "one season"; however, we ended up staying there for five years. Shortly after arriving back on the farm, I had received an invitation to teach full-time seminary, which I gladly accepted. Now, five years later, because of both farming and teaching, I found it extremely difficult to finish my bachelor's degree.

One spring morning the telephone rang. It was an administrator in the Church Educational System. He said, "Brother Pace, we are making part-time teaching assignments in Utah Valley for teachers who want to finish their degrees. Would you be interested in accepting one of those assignments?"

I immediately began to tell him all the reasons why it would be very difficult to drop everything and return to school. He said he understood that it would be a challenge, but he didn't call to hear all of that—he simply wanted to know if I wanted to do it. He said, "You make the decision. I'll call back tomorrow morning at 10 to find out what it is."

Both my wife and I felt it was an awfully important decision, and we were both stunned that we had to make the decision before 10:00 A.M. the next day! I felt that if I ever left the farm to go back to school full time, we would never return. It was just a feeling, but nevertheless it was strong and caused me some concern. We immediately prayed with all our hearts, together and separately, about what we should do. That night, we put the little girls (ages four, three, and two) in their bunny rabbit pajamas and carried them up to my parents' home. I told them our plight and asked them what they thought we should do. I remember Dad saying, "I can't make your decision for you, but I will tell you one thing for sure—whatever you decide to do, we will support you one hundred percent." I wanted to say, "Well, thanks, Dad, but won't you make our decision for us?" I had a lot of weaknesses, but one that gave me perhaps the most difficulty was that of indecisiveness. The Lord knew I desperately needed to be placed in a position where the decision had to be made and had to be made now.

After continued discussions and struggling in prayer, we decided we should return to school. I took the decision to the Lord and expected either an immediate confirmation or a stupor of thought. I didn't receive either! I felt more of a fifty-fifty feeling. I returned in prayer and pleaded with the Lord for a clearcut answer. Still, there was no tipping the scales. I reminded the Lord that this was one of the most important decisions of my life. Once again, no stronger feeling came one way or the other. The following morning I indicated to the Lord that I absolutely had to know before 10:00 A.M., but that didn't seem to help at all.

The phone rang at the appointed hour. I boldly answered the expected query with, "Yes, yes, I'm going to come back and finish my degree!" Even as I voiced my decision and showed (finally) some real decisiveness, I found myself glancing upward and thinking in my mind, "Now, Lord, you know without question that I'm serious about my decision. Would you be kind enough to give me a confirmation before I hang up the phone?" But still I couldn't discern even a slightest ripple of a feeling as to what I should do.

All of this occurred early in the spring. We weren't actually going to leave until fall, so I continued to strive in every way I knew how to obtain the coveted confirmation. Again, I felt that this was a crucial decision, one that would affect my entire life, my family, and my loved ones. Throughout the following months I kept struggling for the confirmation, but no confirmation came.

Finally, the big day arrived. We backed a two-ton farm truck up to the little house where we had spent the first five years of our married life. Just the memories of what had occurred during those most important years made the thought of leaving unbelievably hard, let alone knowing that the move would terminate an unusually close association with my father. We started loading the furniture, and as I carried out chairs and tables, in my heart I was again telling the Lord that I had been and that I was now decisive, that I was doing what I felt I should do and what I had said I would do—couldn't I please, now, before actually leaving, know without question that my decision was correct? But still the answer was neither yes nor no. Although Dad was quite severely hampered with arthritis and it was most difficult for him to walk, let alone carry things, he cheerfully assisted us all he could. Still, it was easy to tell it was extremely difficult for him to have us leave.

After the truck was loaded, with a heavy heart I put a little padlock on the door of the house, embraced and kissed my dad and stepmother goodbye, and got in the truck. We drove out of the lane, across the creek that ran not far from the house, and up onto US 30, heading the truck toward Utah. All the while my heartstrings were being pulled harder than at any previous time in my life. The truck had four forward gears, and with the heavy load, it took some time to pick up enough speed, finally, to get it shifted into the fourth gear. After that last shift, with my foot firmly planted on the accelerator, with my mind wondering if I would emotionally survive the feelings that were coming, it happened—the confirmation came! And what a confirmation! The refulgence of the Spirit came with such intensity that if there was ever a perfect knowledge of anything, surely this was it. The peace, the buoyancy, the tingling excitement—I thought I would be lifted right off the seat. I felt like I had a date with destiny, and I knew, I knew, I knew that the decision was correct, acceptable to the Lord, and that he was pleased.

I cried out in my heart, "Oh Lord, why, why did you wait so long to give me my confirmation? Why didn't you give it to me months ago?" There came into my mind with some force the following words: "Ye receive no witness until after the trial of your faith." (Ether 12:6.)

It was true, as I had suspected, that having left the farm, I never returned except for periodic visits. The decision to return to school ended five choice years of teaching seminary but opened the door to the institute program and then in time to an opportunity to serve at the Church university and to enjoy the many privileges and opportunities that come from such positions.

Don't Count the Cost

As we are exposed to more and more experiences of life within the setting of the Church and kingdom of God, we become quite mindful that the way we determine whether or not we should do a particular thing isn't by asking first whether or not we can afford to do it, or whether or not we have the energy, or training, or ability, but rather by finding out what the Lord would have us do and then bending every effort to do it. That's a challenging lesson to learn, but one that continually makes its appearance as we try to live by faith.

One experience that taught me a great lesson in this area and helped me appreciate the blessing of having the companionship of the Spirit is the following. My wife was raised in Portland, Oregon, a city girl through and through, not acquainted at all with the ways of the farmer. It is ironic that a year before we met and married, while traveling through Idaho on her way to Brigham Young University, she had observed to friends in the car, "I can't imagine living in one of those tiny houses out in the middle of nowhere!" Almost before she realized what was happening, she found herself plunked in one of those little farmhouses — out in the middle of nowhere!

Although I convinced her quite often to join me in the barn while I was milking the cows, she never became accustomed to the smell and only rarely would she actually consent to touch a cow. She wondered why it was necessary to milk cows twice a day — what a waste of time and effort, she would say — why not just milk them at noon and let it go at that? Irrigating was another puzzlement to her. It seemed absurd to her to have to irrigate every ten days — why not really flood the place and let that last for a month? It was hard for her to realize that during the summer months, which ordinarily are vacation time, it was next to impossible to make a trip to Portland to see her parents and family. The demands of milking night and morning, constantly irrigating, cultivating, and so forth, plus being on a limited budget, all joined in making even a three- or four-day trip home to visit her folks a herculean effort. Nevertheless, each summer we would make the trip. I might add that the fact that her folks had a motor boat

139

and lived right on the banks of the Willamette River, which facilitated some great water skiing, was somewhat of an enticement for the annual trip in spite of the challenge and sacrifice.

This particular year, early in the summer, I determined that there was simply no way we could make the trip. We were running another farm along with ours, the work load was piling up, and we were broke. Realizing that on several occasions in previous years I had said, "We cannot and will not make the trip!" and then a few days later had given in and changed my mind, I knew that I would have to be firm in announcing my decision. I would have to make the announcement to her with a patriarchal note of finality in my voice. In fact, my wife had already bestowed the dubious title "tower of jelly" upon me, because there had been many times I had boldly announced new plans, programs, and policies that I just knew would enable the family to be translated in six months, and then I'd had to back down after trying them for only three days! Somehow, my firm patriarchal announcements had a tendency to disintegrate whenever I would see even the beginning of a tear form in the eye of my wife, or when one of my daughters would slip her arms around me and tell me what a great guy I was.

Well, after getting myself fully prepared, I marched into the kitchen, stood in front of my Sweetie, and announced with great solemnity that we would not be going to Portland that summer. I then turned and hurried out of the house, hoping to get out fast enough not to hear her laughing.

Several weeks later I was walking out across an alfalfa field, not thinking of anything in particular, when clearly and powerfully the impression came into my heart, "George, I want you to tell your wife to prepare herself and the little girls to go to Portland tomorrow!" I thought I would die! I remember glancing heavenward and mentally saying, "Do you know with what finality I told my wife we would not go to Portland?"

But the feeling persisted so strongly that I spun around, hurried back to the house, marched in, stood in front of Sweetie, and quickly said, "Please get yourself and the children ready for a trip. We are going to Portland in the morning!" I hurried out, hoping I wouldn't hear her laughing, but I wasn't halfway to the door before her laughter reached my ears.

The following morning we left for Portland, arriving in the early evening. As indicated earlier, on previous trips I was able to do a lot of water skiing, and we had also done some sightseeing on occasion. This time, though, we all just stayed in the house and talked and talked. After two days I began to get quite nervous and really wondered why there had seemed to be such an urgency to come. I announced to the family that we should leave early the next morning. After breakfast and family prayer the next day, I loaded the baggage and the three little girls, and then started the car and waited impatiently for Diane to come out and get into the car. Several minutes later she came out with her parents, walking particularly close to her father. As she came to the passenger side of the car, she and her father slipped their arms around one another and shared their deep feelings for one another. As I sat and watched and listened, I thought, "What a beautiful experience. What a great father-daughter relationship they have. How dearly they love one another." At that moment the feeling came into my heart that that was the reason the trip was made. I felt at peace and not so anxious about things.

We then returned to Idaho and carried on with the many things that needed to be done. A few weeks later, we received a long-distance call from Diane's mother. She informed us that Diane's father had passed away very suddenly after a fairly routine operation. Immediately, there came into my mind with great clarity the experience just weeks before of walking across the alfalfa field and the Lord making known to me that I should take my wife home to see her father one last time. It didn't matter that we couldn't afford it, it didn't matter that there was too much work to do. How grateful I was that the Lord in his loving kindness prompted me to make that trip, and it confirmed the idea to "never count the cost," to just find out what the Lord wants and then do it.

One day, I became aware that when I have really significant impressions come to me, the surrounding circumstances — what I was wearing, where I was, the time of day, who I was with, and so on — seem to be indelibly imprinted on my consciousness. I've concluded that that might be one way to know that indeed the Lord is working with us and wants us to acknowledge his role in our lives.

Seek for the Constant Companionship of the Spirit

The sacrament prayers and the scriptures are quite pointed on the idea that we should seek for the constant companionship of the Spirit. The sacrament reminds us that if we remember the Savior always, his Spirit (the Holy Ghost) will be with us always — which, incidentally, is quite often! (See Moroni 4; 5.) And Nephi said that the Holy Ghost will show us all things that we should do. (See 2 Nephi 32:5.) Although many other scriptures could be used to justify such a conclusion, I was deeply moved by the following statement by Elder Marion G. Romney:

"Now, I tell you that you can make every decision in your life correctly if you can learn to follow the guidance of the Holy Spirit. This you can do if you will discipline yourself to yield your own feelings to the promptings of the Spirit. Study your problems and prayerfully make a decision. Then take that decision and say to him, in a simple, honest supplication, 'Father, I want to make the right decision. I want to do the right thing. This is what I think I should do; let me know if it is the right course.' Doing this, you can get the burning in your bosom, if your decision is right. If you do not get the burning, then change your decision and submit a new one. When you learn to walk by the Spirit, you never need to make a mistake. I know what it is to have this burning witness. I know also that there are other manifestations of guidance by the Spirit." (*Improvement Era,* Dec. 1961, p. 947.)

I think we all sense what a difficult challenge it is actually to enjoy the constant companionship of the Spirit, yet it's easy to see that striving for it with all our hearts would invariably increase our receptiveness to personal revelation.

I have wondered if we were to develop sufficient attentiveness to the Spirit such that we are told all things we should do, would we somehow become robots or maybe even lose our free agency or perhaps never develop rugged individualism or self-sufficiency? And then I remembered that the most intelligent of all of God's children, even Christ, became a God by following the very pattern of doing and saying only what was given him of the Father. (See John 5:19–10; 8:28; 12:49.)

"But," you may ask, "what about the passage in the Doctrine and Covenants where the Lord said, 'For behold, it is not meet I should command in all things . . . '?" (D&C 58:26.) My reply would be, "Ah, yes, I have read that section many times. Do you know the circumstances that prompted that great revelation? Are you aware that many Church members were going to Joseph Smith and asking if he would inquire of the Lord on their behalf about what they should do?" Several sections of the Doctrine and Covenants resulted from such inquiries. Finally, the Lord with some force reminded the members of the Church, "Verily I say, men should be anxiously engaged in a good cause, and do many things of their own free will, and bring to pass much righteousness; for the power is in them, wherein they are agents unto themselves." (D&C 58:27–28.)

What is the power the Lord speaks of here? Why, surely it is the Holy Ghost. The Lord expects us to use that power to learn from him all we should be doing and not have to be commanded of a prophet in all things.

Burning in the Bosom—Peace of Mind— Stupor of Thought

On occasion we may expect more of an assurance from the Spirit than the Lord seems desirous to give us. It just might be, for instance, that the "burning in the bosom" promised Oliver Cowdery (see D&C 9:8) might be quite rare for the average member of the Church who is diligently seeking personal revelation.

From my own experience and from visiting with many individuals, I believe that more frequent than the "burning in the bosom" is the great peace that settles in our mind and heart after we have made a decision. (D&C 8:2–3.)

Perhaps a couple of illustrations would help. It was not unusual while I was serving as a branch president in the Missionary

143

Training Center for frustrated young missionaries to come in for an interview and confide that they didn't know for sure if they really had a testimony of the gospel. After visiting for a while, I would say simply, "Elder (or Sister), do you know that I know that God lives, that Jesus is the Christ, that Joseph Smith is a prophet of God?" Each one I asked gave the same answer: yes. I would then say, "If you know that I know the gospel is true, then you also know because it is the Spirit that has told you I know!"

The question I have been asked most often as a teacher is, "Brother Pace, how can I know that the one I'm in love with is the one I should marry?" The most effective answer I have is something like this: "If you will weigh carefully your feelings, and you discover there is a consistent peace in your heart and a satisfaction in your mind about such things as wanting to spend as much time with each other as you can, thinking you just might die when you are separated from each other, wanting to stand tall and become all you can become when you are with that special person, and so on, then make a decision, go to your Heavenly Father in mighty vocal prayer, and tell him of your decision. Then, having made the decision, move in the direction of fulfilling that decision. If in the ensuing days your relationship continues smoothly and you feel peace in your heart, you probably have made the right decision, and the continued natural unfolding of your relationship and the peace you feel will generally be the extent of the Lord's confirmation to you."

Interestingly enough, it seems it is often easier to discern a "stupor of thought" than it is to sense the quiet assurance that your decision is approved of the Lord. I really don't think the Lord will let you make a serious mistake in an important decision if you are trying diligently to discern his will by keeping the commandments and asking with all of your heart. The method he will probably use to tell you no is to cause a heaviness in the pit of your stomach, a restlessness and an uneasiness in your heart, in short, a lack of peace.

As you strive to grow in the spirit of revelation, remember that the beautiful promises and invitations in the scriptures that speak of the marvelous power, endowments, visions, dreams, knowledge, and so on that are available to the Saints are for real. The Lord hasn't given us marvelous promises like the first ten verses of Doctrine and Covenants 76 just to tantalize us. He's given us such promises so that we might realize that we too can hear marvelous things, see marvelous things, and be endowed with his great power. (See 1 Nephi 10:17.)

But remember, it is important to realize that to grow in any area of life takes time, indeed, it is "line upon line, precept upon precept" (D&C 98:12), until—to paraphrase Mormon—it can be said of us that we have waxed stronger and stronger in our humility, firmer and firmer in our faith in Christ, because we have yielded our hearts to God (see Helaman 3:35).

Joseph Smith, more than any man in this dispensation, understood this principle. He summed up the struggle to become like the Father through Christ in the following way: "We consider that God has created man with a mind capable of instruction, and a faculty which may be enlarged in proportion to the heed and diligence given to the light communicated from heaven to the intellect; and that the nearer man approaches perfection, the clearer are his views, and the greater his enjoyments, till he has overcome the evils of his life and lost every desire for sin; and like the ancients, arrives at that point of faith where he is wrapped in the power and glory of his Maker and is caught up to dwell with Him. But we consider that this is a station to which no man ever arrived in a moment: he must have been instructed in the government and laws of that kingdom by proper degrees, until his mind is capable in some measure of comprehending the propriety, justice, equality, and consistency of the same." (*Teachings of the Prophet Joseph Smith*, p. 51.)

Fulfilling the divine purposes of our membership in the Church is inextricably tied to seeking for and obtaining the guidance and direction of the Holy Spirit. It is through the workings of the Spirit that we develop a close relationship with the Father through the Savior. We cannot be moved upon by the Spirit but what we sense the personal presence of the Lord. We cannot receive a confirmation of an important decision but what we sense Christ is our friend. The man or woman who is most alive to the reality of God and Christ and the infinite privilege of earth life is that man or woman who is filled with the Holy Spirit.

Don't let a day go by without pleading with all the faith you possess that you might have the constant guidance and companionship of the Holy Ghost. If you will seek and seek diligently, you will come to know without question that Jesus Christ is your sole source of the light, life, and love you need to become like him.

Chapter 7

A GOD OF POWER

The crop we raised on our farm in Idaho that seemed to require more work than any other was the sugar beet crop. Thinning the beets was a backbreaking job, for it had to be done with a short-handled hoe. Throughout the summer, the weeds continually had to be hoed. In the fall, the beets had to be dug one row at a time and the tops cut off, often in the rain and snow. Finally, they were hauled to the sugar beet dump in wagons pulled by teams of horses. The memories of planting, cultivating, and harvesting sugar beets have left such indelible impressions on my mind that whenever I get discouraged with teaching, I just reminisce for a while about my experiences with sugar beets and I lose all discouragement!

There was, however, one experience related to harvesting sugar beets that has left a bright spot in my memory and from which I learned an important lesson. After my brothers and I topped several rows of beets by hand, my father drove the wagon, pulled by a team of horses, between the rows so we could load the wagon by hand with five to seven tons of beets, a handful of beets at a time. Because it was not uncommon for us to harvest in rain and snow, it frequently became very difficult for the horses to pull the loaded wagon out of the wet, muddy field. Many times I would compliment myself, thinking, "Wow, George, look what you're doing! You are responsible for seeing that seven tons of beets are being pulled out of the field!" It was quite a humbling thought one day to realize that the power that was holding the reins was not the same power that was pulling the load.

So it is with us. I believe that one of the most important lessons for all of us to learn is that it is by the Lord's power and only by his power that we are able to accomplish all that the Lord wants us to do. It is true that we might possess administrative ability, we might enjoy remarkable success in the field of business or other areas, we might have professional training and be highly skilled—we might, as it were, hold the reins in responsible callings in the kingdom; but if the wagon is to be pulled successfully, if we are to be enabled to do all the Lord would have us do, it will be by the Lord's power and not our own. It is a sobering thought to realize that it is our Lord and Savior who points out the path to eternal life to us, who gives us the desire and enables us to get on the path, and who encourages us to walk the path successfully all the way to him! Indeed, Moroni declared that we must rely "alone upon the merits of Christ, who was the author and the finisher of [our] faith." (Moroni 6:4; see also Philippians 2:12–13.) If we want what we do in righteousness to be consecrated to the welfare of our souls, if we want to be successful in our labors in the kingdom to bring people to the Father through Christ, then we absolutely must look to the Savior and obtain his power or all of our labors will be in vain.

A great theme in the first book of the Book of Mormon is how Jehovah enabled Lehi and his colony to escape destruction in Jerusalem and arrive safely in the promised land. Lehi was given a remarkable vision of the doom impending upon Jerusalem. (See 1 Nephi 1:13.) After Nephi and his brothers had exhausted every other means to obtain the brass plates, Laban was miraculously delivered into Nephi's hands and the plates were obtained. (1 Nephi 4:6–24.) The colony received the Liahona to guide them through the desert; without it they never could have found their way. Their meat was made sweet by the Lord so that fire, which perhaps might have attracted roving bandits, would not be necessary. (See 1 Nephi 17:12.) At a time of crisis, Nephi was able to make a bow of sufficient quality to shoot wild animals for desperately needed food. (See 1 Nephi 16:23, 31.) Laman and Lemuel were overpowered by God several times to preserve

Nephi's life. (See, for example, 1 Nephi 18:20–21.) The women were made strong like unto the men so they could better endure their journeyings through the desert. (See 1 Nephi 17:2.) Nephi was able to construct a ship designed by the Lord, and the colony was preserved upon the deep and enabled to land safely on the shores of the promised land–all because the Lord manifested his marvelous power. (See 1 Nephi 18.)

The Lord wanted Nephi to know "that I, the Lord, am God; and that I, the Lord, did deliver you from destruction; yea, that I did bring you out of the land of Jerusalem." (1 Nephi 17:14.) Is it any wonder Nephi declared with great faith, "O Lord, I have trusted in thee, and I will trust in thee forever. I will not put my trust in the arm of flesh; for I know that cursed is he that putteth his trust in the arm of flesh. Yea, cursed is he that putteth his trust in man or maketh flesh his arm." (2 Nephi 4:34.)

I don't think there is a better example, aside from the Lord himself, of a man who understood more fully the role God's power plays in our success than Ammon, one of the missionary sons of Mosiah. He expressed so beautifully his appreciation for the Lord's help. His success as a missionary was phenomenal. He brought thousands of souls to Christ. He displayed an ability to relate to kings and to servants in a manner that quickly won their confidence and trust. He taught the gospel in a way that capitalized on the limited spiritual understanding of the Lamanites. He was a servant's servant, anxious to do anything and everything he could to show forth the Savior's power to his fellow servants. (See Alma 17:29.) The power of God rested upon Ammon and allowed him to accomplish things that were so marvelous that Lamoni was convinced that Ammon was God himself, or the "Great Spirit." (Alma 18:11.)

After their missions were over, Ammon and his brothers began to share their experiences. Ammon recounted his great successes, and even though he ended his report by saying, "Blessed be the name of our God; let us sing to his praise, yea, let us give thanks to his holy name, for he doth work righteousness forever" (Alma 26:8), his brother Aaron rebuked him and accused him of boasting. But Ammon became even more forceful as he gave credit where credit was due:

"I do not boast in my own strength, nor in my own wisdom; but behold, my joy is full, yea, my heart is brim with joy, and I will rejoice in my God.

"Yea, I know that I am nothing; as to my strength I am weak; therefore I will not boast of myself, but I will boast of my God, for in his strength I can do all things; yea, behold, many mighty miracles we have wrought in this land, for which we will praise his name forever.

"Therefore, let us glory, yea, we will glory in the Lord; yea, we will rejoice, for our joy is full; yea, we will praise our God forever. Behold, who can glory too much in the Lord? Yea, who can say too much of his great power, and of his mercy, and of his long-suffering towards the children of men? Behold, I say unto you, I cannot say the smallest part which I feel." (Alma 26:11–12, 16.)

Oh how we, like Ammon, should be most anxious to show forth the mighty works of God. How anxious we should be to bear testimony that the Lord will watch over us and bless us and enable us to accomplish great things through his power.

The prophet Moroni summed up in a remarkable way the promises and blessings that are available to those who really come to know Christ. Moroni leaves no question that the man or woman of Christ will acknowledge fully that his or her achievements in righteousness are because of the Savior's endowment of power: "And again, if ye by the grace of God are perfect in Christ, and deny not his power, then are ye sanctified in Christ by the grace of God." (Moroni 10:32.)

How important it is not to take credit to ourselves. Probably one of the greatest tragedies in every age is the tendency of men and women to arrogate to themselves the credit for the things they have achieved. This tendency extends to every phase of human endeavor. President Brigham Young said, "Every discovery in science and art, that is really true and useful to mankind, has been given by direct revelation from God, though but few acknowledge it." (In *Journal of Discourses*, 9:369.)

President Joseph Fielding Smith confirmed the same idea when he said: "We see a man with extraordinary gifts, or with great intelligence, and he is instrumental in developing some great principle. He and the world ascribe his great genius and wisdom to himself. He attributes his success to his own energies, labor, and mental capacity. He does not acknowledge the hand of the Lord in anything connected with his success, but ignores him altogether and takes the honor to himself. This will apply to almost all the world. In all the great modern discoveries in science, in the arts, in mechanics, and in all the material advancement of the age, the world says, 'We have done it.' The individual says, 'I have done it,' and he gives no honor or credit to the Lord." (In Conference Report, Oct. 1969, p. 110.)

We as members of the Church should be mindful that with all due respect to the abilities and capacities of thousands of Saints in this last dispensation, no individual or set of individuals is responsible for the great work that has been done in the restored kingdom. That work has been done because the Savior poured out his Spirit and power upon his people. Had he not done so, the work would have been impossible. I love the following statement, also by President Joseph Fielding Smith, which explains in a powerful way our dependency on the Savior:

"Remember that it is the gift of God to man, that it is his power and his guiding influence that have accomplished what we see has been accomplished. It has not been done by the wisdom of men. They are instruments in the Lord's hands in accomplishing his purposes, and we should not deny that they are such; we should honor them. But when we undertake to give them the honor for accomplishing this work, and take the honor from the Lord, who qualified the men to do the work, we are doing injustice to our Heavenly Father." (In Conference Report, Oct. 1968, p. 124.) The Lord himself said, "In nothing doth man offend God, or against none is his wrath kindled, save those who confess not his hand in all things, and obey not his commandments." (D&C 59:21.)

God Is a God of Miracles

We can't study the scriptures without recognizing that where there is faith, there are miracles. To believers, miracles are marvelous confirmations of faith and devotion to the Lord. To unbelievers, miracles are simply signs that condemn.

We are invited by the Lord to believe in his miraculous power, to realize that all things are possible to him. We need to recognize that especially between now and the Second Coming, the Saints need to acquire a much greater faith because the only way to survive the economic upheavals, the great persecution, and the calamities that will be poured out is through the miraculous power of the Lord. Indeed, Nephi left no doubt that in the final holocausts that will be poured out on the earth, "He [the Lord] will preserve the righteous by his power, even if it so be that the fulness of his wrath must come, and the righteous be preserved, even unto the destruction of their enemies by fire. Wherefore, the righteous need not fear; for thus saith the prophet, they shall be saved, even if it so be as by fire." (1 Nephi 22:17.)

It has always been difficult for people to believe in the miraculous. Laman and Lemuel just couldn't accept the idea that the Lord was more powerful than Laban and his soldiers. (See 1 Nephi 3:31.) It was so hard for Sarah to believe that she could conceive a child at her age that she laughed out loud. (See Genesis 18:12.) Thousands of Nephites and Lamanites were so stunned when Samuel the Lamanite's prediction of the day, the night, and the day as being one day was fulfilled that they "fell to the earth and became as if they were dead." (3 Nephi 1:16.) In our day, the biblical account of a universal flood, of the earth becoming "like as it was in the days before it was divided" in the days of Peleg (D&C 133:24), of the faithful Saints ultimately seeing eye-to-eye politically, economically, and socially — all of these are simply too much for some Saints to believe.

One of the true tests the Saints face, then, is not whether they believe the Church is true, but whether they will so live their lives that they will come to know that there isn't anything God will ask them to do but what they can obtain his power to do it. (See 1 Nephi 3:7.)

I grew up with a heavy emphasis on the idea that "God helps those who help themselves," that we must "use wisdom in all things," that we need to be very realistic and practical — all of which are great guidelines, but only to a point! The trouble with this outlook is that somehow the idea of miracles — of God's actual intervention in my life — was only a minor part of my faith in

Christ. In time, however, the challenges I faced (which I assume are quite typical) became so great that relying primarily on the rational, practical (humanistic) approach simply wasn't sufficient to meet them. I knew that unless I believed with all my heart that God would be a God of miracles in my life and that unless I diligently sought for that power, I would never accomplish the things I knew I was to accomplish.

It's important to realize that before all the miracles referred to in 1 Nephi—and everywhere else in the scriptures—Nephi and others had to do all in their power to accomplish what the Lord asked them to do in order to pull down the power of God. President Joseph Fielding said, "God . . . does not do for us one thing that we can do for ourselves, but requires of us that we do everything for ourselves that is within our power for our salvation." (*Doctrines of Salvation*, 2:308.) Or, as Nephi put it, "We know that it is by grace that we are saved, after all we can do." (2 Nephi 25:23.)

In fact, it seems to be an integral part of the Lord's plan for the lives of faithful Saints that even though they have planned carefully, worked hard, and used wisely their available energies and talents—all of which needs to be done— invariably they will be confronted with challenges that can only be met and overcome by the Lord's making bare his holy arm. (See Isaiah 52:10.) If we will seek his power—again, having done all we can—we will come to understand by personal experience that just as the Lord sent quails and manna into the camps of the Israelites (see Exodus 16:12–15), he can and will miraculously provide for our needs. We will become aware that there are many forms of modern-day manna as the Lord enables us to meet very practical kinds of challenges, be they emotional, physical, intellectual, or financial, and resolve those challenges by his power. In fact, as we become aware of his help again and again, we will want to shout, "My God, How great thou art!" (*Hymns*, 1985, no. 86.)

Sacrifice and Trials, Keys to the Power of God

How can we obtain the power from the Lord that will increase our abilities far above our own natural capabilities? I suggest that at least two crucial keys are sacrifice and trials.

Sacrifice. It's undoubtedly true that we find most sacrifices tucked away or interwoven in the daily routine of the man or woman of Christ rather than marching blatantly into the crossroads of our lives. Such sacrifices include our giving up activities or things that in and of themselves may not be evil but have little relevance to fulfilling directly our commitment to the Lord. For example, we can turn away from idly watching television or reading inconsequential material to spending that time in serious pursuit of scriptural knowledge; we can learn to pause from pursuing our vocational or professional goals to assist in binding up broken hearts, wiping away tears, and just being a friend to the friendless. The Lord sends forth his power in labors and efforts such as these so that when the more obvious and greater sacrifices are required of us, we will be able to yield our will to his and do whatever he would have us do.

Trials. We know that we all "must needs be chastened and tried, even as Abraham, who was commanded to offer up his only son. For all those who will not endure chastening, but deny me, cannot be sanctified." (D&C 101:4–5.)

I have often felt that when the Lord discovers that we are really serious about going back to the presence of the Father, that we are willing to bear the shame of the world (see Jacob 1:8), that we want with all our hearts to see the Lord while yet in the flesh, that we want to make our calling and election sure, that we desire to have the heavens opened to us and know with a perfect knowledge that the path we are following is ordained of God—in short, when he sees that we are willing to sacrifice anything and everything for him, then his power will grow in our lives.

It is the experience of all Saints, without exception, who determine to climb all the way to the lofty spiritual peaks of their own Mount Sinai to be quite overwhelmed at the trials, the tribulations, the temptations, and the heavy responsibilities that are theirs. But all of those challenges are part of the great purpose of earth life, and if we didn't have them, we wouldn't be able to acquire the faith in Christ we need to be redeemed. For as we take upon ourselves our individual crosses, we will all come to know that the path we must follow is so challenging, the load we must carry so heavy, that the only way we can do it is by obtaining the marvelous sustaining power of the Master in our lives.

Oh, that you and I would realize that in our allowing heavy responsibilities to be laid upon our shoulders, in our joyfully going through trials and tribulations, in our trying to do the impossible, we will come to know that the Lord is a God of power. The power to do what the Lord would have us do is in direct proportion to the assurance and confidence we feel coming from him that we are doing what he wants us to do! In fact, Joseph Smith, in *Lectures on Faith,* emphasized that such an assurance is absolutely a prerequisite to enjoying the power of faith:

"Such was, and always will be, the situation of the saints of God, that unless they have an actual knowledge that the course they are pursuing is according to the will of God they will grow weary in their minds, and faint."(Pp. 67–68.)

Through our sacrifices to be obedient and our perseverance through trials, the power of the Lord will be made manifest to us. In my own life I have had several experiences in which the Lord has made bare his mighty arm. In some instances I didn't see the hand of the Lord until some time afterward; in other instances, the mighty arm of the Lord was unveiled in a most visible, obvious way. But all of the following experiences represent my personal testimony of the Lord's kindness, his love, and especially his great power that are the very delight of earth life.

Handling a Twentieth-Century Handcart

As a young man, I felt disappointed that I hadn't been born a hundred years or so earlier so I could have shown my faith and devotion to the Lord by willingly pushing a handcart across the plains. But since that time, as our lives have unfolded, neither my wife nor I have felt any regret for not being sent to the earth as handcart pioneers. Our challenges, in fact, have seemed akin to the pushing and pulling of a ten-ton handcart!

Early in our married life, we faced three major challenges that seemed destined to tax our faith, our physical stamina, and our finances far beyond their limits. First, there was no question in our minds that we were to have a large family. I had been blessed that I would have "children not a few." Incidentally, for obvious reasons, I thoroughly researched the scriptures to determine the meaning of the word *few* and drew the conclusion that it means at least eight! Peter, speaking of those whose lives were spared in the Flood, said, "Wherein few, that is, eight souls were saved by water." (1 Peter 3:20.) Nephi, speaking of the witnesses to the gold plates, said there would be three who would see them "and there is none other which shall view it, save it be a few according to the will of God." (2 Nephi 27:13.) And as we know, there were eight other witnesses. Thus it seemed to me that the promise I had received of "children not a few" meant more than eight! Both my wife and I hoped our faith would match the promise.

Second, also with the help of many other unmistakable assurances from the Lord, I knew it was required of me to obtain all the education I could. I say "required" because I was not all that excited about higher education, and I had hoped that somehow one year of general agriculture at Utah State Agricultural College would satisfy the Lord's educational plans for me.

Third, we sensed strongly that the Lord would be pleased if I would pursue my livelihood in Church education. Now this was a challenge because economically it was very difficult to have a large family and pursue all three academic degrees on an educator's salary.

Confronting those three challenges, we discovered that we were trying to push a handcart that simply was impossible even to budge unless we obtained the power of the Savior himself. But as those three great challenges of our lives crystallized in our hearts, we gradually felt a boldness in the exercise of our faith that would not have been possible had we not known by the quiet whisperings of the Spirit what the Lord would have us do. In one of the great lessons on priesthood in the Doctrine and Covenants, the Lord said, "Let thy bowels also be full of charity towards all men, and to the household of faith, and let virtue garnish thy thoughts unceasingly; then shall thy confidence wax strong in the presence of God." (D&C 121:45.) It is phenomenal how much faith we can exercise, how strong our confidence will wax in the presence of God if we deeply feel that we know without question what he wants us to do! I'm sure your soul resonates with mine when I say that in knowing his mind and will, we can approach the throne of his grace and in humility and confidence say in effect, "Oh, Lord, I know you want me to do this and this and this, but I cannot unless you bless me with this and this and this!" Oh, what a powerful principle, how important to plead for righteous desires, to seek for the witness that you can do what he has asked you to do, for out of that assurance will come a bold faith to pull down the powers of heaven.

"None but the Women of the Latter-day Saints"

The summer before he died (1973), President Harold B. Lee reiterated at the Hill Cumorah Pageant a prophecy the Prophet Joseph Smith had made. President Lee quoted Sister Lillie Tucket Freeze, who, in speaking at a conference in Box Elder on 10 September 1890, had said: "We should post ourselves regarding the prophecies which have been predicted. I will mention one in particular that was uttered by the Prophet Joseph Smith—he said the time would come when none but the women of the Latter-day Saints would be willing to bear children." (In *Young Woman's Journal,* 2:80–81.)

What a sacred privilege it is to have children, but, oh how careful we must be not to judge others either by how few children they have or by how many they have! The number of children a couple should have is a private matter. One prophet of this dispensation, when asked by a daughter who had several children if she could quit, replied, "Don't ask me. That decision is between you, your husband, and your Father in Heaven. If you two can face him with a good conscience and can say you have done the best you could, that you have really tried, then you may quit. But, that is between you and him." (Quoted in *Ensign*, Aug. 1979, p. 23.)

Okay, but How Many?

My wife and I, long before we met each other, individually decided to honor the counsel of Church leaders "to proceed immediately with their family responsibilities" — to refrain from limiting the size of the family for economic or educational reasons. (Spencer W. Kimball, in Conference Report, Oct. 1952, p. 51.)

More recently President Ezra Taft Benson admonished us: "Young mothers and fathers, with all my heart I counsel you not to postpone having your children, being co-creators with our Father in Heaven.

"Do not use the reasoning of the world, such as, 'We'll wait until we can better afford having children, until we are more secure, until John has completed his education, until he has a better-paying job, until we have a larger home, until we've obtained a few of the material conveniences,' and on and on.

"This is the reasoning of the world, and is not pleasing in the sight of God. Mothers who enjoy good health, have your children and have them early. And, husbands, always be considerate of your wives in the bearing of children.

"Do not curtail the number of your children for personal or selfish reasons. Material possessions, social convenience, and so-called professional advantages are nothing compared to a righteous posterity. In the eternal perspective, children — not possessions, not position, not prestige — are our greatest jewels." (*To the Mothers in Zion* [address to a fireside for parents, 22 Feb. 1987, Salt Lake City, Utah], pp. 3–4.)

In addition, as mentioned earlier, the Lord had also revealed to me clearly that he would be pleased if we would have a large family. Nevertheless, it required a tremendous exercise of faith. I was a twenty-five-year-old college sophomore; my wife and I

had absolutely no money; we had no maternity insurance; and—
what made it doubly hard—we had many well-meaning friends
and loved ones who continually cautioned us about how hard it
would be to have children right away and to have very many.
There was no question in our minds that we needed the sweet
assurance of the Lord that he would bless us in having and taking
care of all the children he wanted us to have.

That assurance came. On one occasion, when we had several
children and were wondering if we would yet have more, the
following experience occurred. As part of family home evening,
we decided to draw the floor plans for our dream home. On a
large sheet of butcher paper on the floor, we commenced sketch-
ing out the plan with advice from each of the children. Finally,
after adding more and more butcher paper for more and more
rooms, I announced that the plan was finished and that I was
ready to count the number of rooms in this palatial dream house.
I was about to give the final tabulation when all of a sudden
Sweetie said, "Wait a minute. What about when the rest of the
children come?" There was a pause while we looked at each
other, and then there quietly descended upon Diane and me (and
I believe upon the children there as well) an assurance that the
Lord would be pleased if we yet had more children. It was a
simple, beautiful distilling of his will to our hearts, and from that
experience came the profound desire, strength, and determination to have more children.

On another occasion, the assurance that the Lord was pleased
we were willing to have another child came after the baby had
arrived. This pregnancy had been unusually hard, and it seemed
the whole family had had to sacrifice more than usual. After the
baby was born and the day arrived to bring my wife and the new
little one home, I felt a special peace and excitement. The timing
was beautiful, for it was the Lord's Day and the children had just
arrived home from church. As I drove up in front of our home,
the children, Grandmother, a brother-in-law, and some close
friends came running out of the house. The excitement they
radiated was really a delight to see. I stood back and watched the
scene as the baby was passed from one to another. After we
entered the front room and the baby was still being held by first

one and then the next, it seemed to me that there were others in the room who were witnessing that marvelous welcome. It was as though unseen visitors were rejoicing that she had arrived safely at her new home, and they especially seemed to rejoice because the baby was so warmly and gratefully welcomed. The many months when Diane wasn't feeling well, the frustration of finding it hard to keep the house in order, the challenge of doing everything we wanted to do for the children—all of these things seemed at that moment completely insignificant.

I got everyone's attention and asked them if we could kneel down and express together our appreciation to the Lord for sending us another of his precious offspring. The experience that day in our living room was a veil-thinning experience. How totally we knew that the Lord had protected, nurtured, and strengthened my wife and the entire family. How totally we knew he was pleased that we had so gratefully welcomed the new baby into our home, and how perfectly we knew there were many unseen loved ones who had come to rejoice in that glorious experience.

All husbands should be most mindful that it is the wife who carries the heavier burden when it comes to having and rearing children, and even though he may do all in his power to help with that burden, unless the wife is strengthened by the Savior, her strength will often not be adequate. The following experience, written by my wife, shows that God will ease the heavy burden of carrying a child by bestowing the needed power and strength to do his will:

"When I was expecting our seventh child, I had an experience which has since given me great strength and a divine power to accomplish whatever the Lord would have me do. We were living in Palo Alto, California, at the time, in a large, two-story home. It was late one night, my husband was gone, and the children had all been tucked in after what I would call 'one of those days.' It seemed that everything had gone wrong! I felt so inadequate, and I was sure I was the worst mother in the whole world.

"As I started up the stairs to my bedroom to retire, I had thoughts and feelings come in upon me that were so vivid I remember them to this day. We knew the Lord wanted us to have a large family, and I recognized our responsibility to have many children. As I prepared for bed, I convinced myself that I must pray in spite of my weariness.

"I am so grateful that I had learned before this experience that I could go to my Heavenly Father at any time, for any reason, and he would hear me and answer my prayers. I had also learned to be very specific and to openly and honestly pour out my heart to One who loves me with a perfect love, who knows me better than I know myself, and who could give me perfect answers.

"I was specific indeed that night; in fact, I complained a bit. My prayer was, in essence, 'Heavenly Father, I know we are supposed to have many children, but I can't do it! I'm so tired! I'm sick to my stomach, my head aches, my back aches, and my feet ache. It's just too hard! I can't do it!'

"That night as I knelt in prayer, the Lord spoke to me in my heart and mind. I did not hear his voice, but the words came as they so often do when he reveals through his Spirit. We know when it comes from him—it changes our lives, and the words are forever written across our hearts. The words that came to me were these: 'My daughter, how can you complain about the small miseries required of you to bring my spirit children into the world and give them birth? If I could just give you a glimpse of the magnificent suffering of your Savior in your behalf that you might have a second birth and come back into my presence.'

"The Lord's words chided me a bit, but at the same moment I felt a power come into my whole soul as I received my own personal witness of the great atoning sacrifice of my Savior for me. I felt his godly love for me and my worth in his eyes as I realized he was willing to suffer for me in spite of my weaknesses and often unworthy condition. The power that came was the assurance that I could do anything the Lord required of me, including having more children. If I needed help to get through just one day at a time, that power would be available if I would pay the price to humble myself and plead for his assistance. It has come in that manner. My pregnancies have not become any easier—in fact, the challenge has been increasingly difficult physically and emotionally with the increasing responsibility of a growing family in numbers and ages, but the help has come. I know it will come to all of us whatever the circumstances, whatever our needs. The power is indeed available as we struggle to discern his mind and will, make every effort to do his mind and will, and seek for his power to accomplish what he would have us do."

Getting married and having all the children the Lord would like you to have, be it a few or many, is not unlike setting off on a challenging mountain-climbing trip. As you and your spouse go to the foot of the mountain and pause to put on your mountain-climbing gear, well-meaning friends and particularly close loved ones pause in their climbing to call back to you about how risky and hard it is to ascend the mountain successfully (that is, to have all the children the Lord would like you to have). Even though you think you're filled with faith and you have taken seriously the counsel of the living prophet, hearing their well-reasoned advice causes you to become quite apprehensive. But breathing deep and feeling a new surge of confidence from the Lord, you start out.

The farther you go in trying to fulfill the Lord's will, the more advice is being shouted to you from those who have elected to stay comfortably on a wide ledge not far up the mountain. Many times you look back at your comfortable advisers and you wonder why you chose such a difficult climb. But the more challenging the terrain becomes, the more you hold on to each other and the more your prayers ascend to God. Many times at what seems to be the last moment, when it appears that surely you will lose your hold and fall onto the rocks below, the Lord reaches down, makes bare his mighty arm, and lifts you onto safer footing. You don't get halfway up the mountain but what you both marvel at the power and love of your Redeemer.

No decision made by a husband and wife is a deeper pledge of their love for each other and of their confidence in the power of a divine Redeemer than the decision to have all the children the Lord would be pleased to send to their union. Many beautiful things have happened in our lives, things that have manifested to us how great God is, but none have shown us the Lord's mercy, his goodness, his power, and his love as has having and taking care of the children he has been pleased to send us.

Struggling by Degrees

There were a lot of reasons why I thoroughly enjoyed my high school days — football, skiing, tumbling, and track, to name a few, as well as a vigorous social life and heavy involvement in student government. Those reasons, incidentally, were the very same reasons why I wasn't very serious about academics! And as if I didn't have enough distractions, there were the twenty cows that needed to be milked every morning and night and the farm work to be done in the spring and fall while school was yet in session. I felt fortunate to have survived academically as well as I did, but part of the price I paid for my extracurricular activities was that I didn't think college was all that important and that perhaps one year of university life would be more than enough for me.

My mission brought into focus a previously ignored injunction in my patriarchal blessing to "obtain all the education you can." Again, an awareness of what the Lord wanted me to do began to crystallize in my heart, and with it came the assurance that in spite of poor study habits and not having the foggiest notion what I should study, it was imperative that I return to school and obtain a college degree.

My classes at Brigham Young University immediately set both my mind and my spirit on fire, and I really became excited about learning. I picked a major but wasn't sure what I would actually do for a livelihood. I did have the assurance that I was at least going the right direction, however. All the while, I prayed a great deal and sought with all my heart for inspiration about what specifically I needed to do to prepare for a profession.

Although I didn't realize the far-reaching implication of what was happening, I did notice that I was immensely more interested and fascinated by what I was learning in my religion classes than in all the other classes I was taking. Also, I had been called to be a Sunday School teacher in what was then Campus Branch, and that one experience gave me a taste for teaching and a desire to teach that became the determiner of my life's work.

Much to the disappointment of my wife and me, after only a brief stay at the Y, it became necessary to interrupt my schooling to return to the farm to help my father whose health was failing him. How hard it was to leave! I so desperately wanted to move vigorously ahead to obtain my degree, and I also felt I needed to take some classes to help me decide what I should do—but that wasn't the game plan. The stage was set effectively, however, to give us the very answers we were seeking. Indeed, we were to learn that "God moves in a mysterious way / His wonders to perform." (*Hymns,* 1985, no. 285.)

We had been home for only a few months when I was invited to teach full-time seminary! I had taught just a few weeks when I knew with all my heart that I wanted to teach in the Church Educational System permanently. Again, the assurance that came to me that my life was unfolding as the Lord would have it unfold brought a sense of purpose and a degree of motivation that I don't think could have come in any other way.

Other assurances that we were doing what the Lord wanted us to do came frequently. One such experience that had a strong effect on me occurred during summer session of school. We had returned to school from the farm and were living in Wyview Village, which was university housing for married couples. The individual houses had at one time been used as housing for military personnel at Mountain Home Air Force Base in Idaho. In my earlier years on the farm, I had watched those very same houses being hauled along US 30 to Brigham Young University, never dreaming that someday I would live in one. Whoever designed the houses probably didn't realize that in the summer they were nothing more than family-size saunas! Oh, they were hot! In fact, in making bread all Diane had to do was prepare the dough, knead it, and leave it on the table to bake! In addition, we were living on a shoestring, Diane was expecting, and, all in all, the circumstances were somewhat challenging.

One day I was in the Joseph Smith Auditorium with several hundred seminary and institute teachers listening to a talk by Elder A. Theodore Tuttle. His talk was on commitment, and while he was speaking, I received the marvelous assurance that the sacrifices my wife and I were making were exactly what the Lord wanted of us. It was really a powerful assurance. When Elder Tuttle finished, I hurried back to the hot little house, ran into the kitchen, and threw my arms around my wife. The spirit I had felt while in the auditorium seemed to return as I shared with her the assurance I had felt. She knew as well as I did that at that point in life we were doing exactly what the Lord wanted us to do and that the sacrifices we were making then were most acceptable.

The hardest challenge in getting a degree came when we decided to launch into a doctoral program at Brigham Young University. At the time we made the decision, we were living in Palo Alto, California, where I was directing the institute of religion near Stanford University. The experience there had been especially enjoyable. We loved the beauty of the entire Bay area, and the intellectual stimulation we found on campus was a delight. Economically, however, it was just impossible! Even though we were as careful as we could be, we were sinking further and further into debt.

I remember that when the idea of applying for sabbatical leave first came into my mind, my greatest concern was financial. I recall telling the Lord that we hadn't been able to live on a full salary, and I wasn't sure how we would live on the reduced, sabbatical salary. As I inquired, I didn't get much comfort, just the strong confirmation that I should do it! I was really concerned because our debts had increased, as had the number of our children (we now had seven), and all of us were so addicted to things like food, clothes, and shelter.

But I made the application, the sabbatical was granted, we moved to Provo, and I commenced work on the doctorate. As the year progressed, I again had a strong assurance that we were right where we should be, and I was doing exactly what I should be doing. Our economic situation continued to worsen so much, however, that I felt there would be no way we could continue under those circumstances another year. Yet, as I prayed mightily to the Lord, I felt an overriding peace that somehow things would work out.

When summer arrived, I readily accepted my first invitation to do Education Weeks in Arizona and Texas, knowing it would supplement the income a little. The money for expenses for the trip — motels, food, and travel — was sent ten days in advance, and

I simply couldn't resist the temptation to use at least part of it to meet current needs.

The day before I was to leave I was feeling extremely anxious about how tight our circumstances were when I went to pick up the mail. There was a letter from a choice couple in another state. I opened it and read in part: "We appreciate deeply what you are doing—we admire your determination to return to school for the doctorate. We feel it's wonderful you are willing to have a large family, and we are grateful you have stayed in Church education. Some time ago, we told the Lord that if he would bless us in a particular investment, we would share with you a portion of the returns on that investment. The Lord has blessed us, and enclosed is a check for the first payment of your portion we promised the Lord we would share with you. Please do not feel obligated to thank us for it. It was the Lord who made it possible."

I quickly thrust my hand back into the envelope and pulled out the enclosed check. I could hardly believe my eyes when I looked at the amount of that blessing. I ran excitedly into the house and found Sweetie talking on the phone to a good friend. As I somewhat enthusiastically did back handsprings and cartwheels, it occurred to her that perhaps I had something important to say. She hung up the phone, and I put my arms around her, showed her the check, and read her the letter.

As we held on to each other tightly and wept a few tears, there came into our hearts a marvelous assurance, a perfect knowledge that the Lord had heard our prayers and opened the way so we could accomplish what we knew we should do. It was still a tremendous struggle to get the doctorate, but in the meantime, we were having the children the Lord wanted us to have, Sweetie did not have to work outside the home, and, through it all, we knew that the Lord had heard our prayers and blessed us with power in ways we never dreamed possible.

Be It Ever So Humble

As I try to view the overall perspective of what's going to happen between now and the Second Coming, I see a challenging picture revealed through the Lord's prophets. Economically, politically, and socially there will yet be great upheavals. It surely will be that in the final analysis what will carry us through is making sure we have built solidly on the rock of Christ—believing he can and will bless us both temporally and spiritually through the troublesome times ahead. We all have different circumstances and different needs and the Lord responds in different ways according to his wisdom and justice, but I believe we can rest assured that he will enable us to do what he has commanded us to do.

It was a terrific challenge, as it is with most couples, to negotiate the buying of our first home. The Lord helped us immeasurably in achieving that goal; his power came through. To help you appreciate more fully how much it meant to us to finally get our own home, it might be helpful to reminisce about our abode while we were on the farm.

When my wife and I left school to help my father on the farm, we moved into a little, three-room house. My use of the term *house* is very loose because the house was so loose. It had been built in 1909 without a foundation. The kitchen floor slanted toward the southwest—which was convenient if we spilled anything on the floor, because we could just go to the corner and mop it up. When we moved in, the house received its first painting and wallpaper. From then on Sweetie referred to it as a cottage, but I still saw it primarily as a shack.

The only running water was in the creek that ran below the house. Our bathroom was totally unmodern, consisting of four walls and a path—or, in other words, an outside toilet, or privy. It did not matter too much if the windows were opened or closed; the velocity of the Idaho wind through the house was about the same, making it virtually impossible to keep the house warm.

We heated the water to do the dishes with an electrical heating unit, which we plugged into an outlet. For our Saturday night bath, we would put some water in an oblong galvanized tub on Thursday, put the heating unit in the water, and usually by Saturday night the water would be at least up to body temperature.

As we struggled and gradually were able to get a hot water heater, replace the hot plate with an electric range, and in time actually build on a little bathroom, we appreciated in a special way each such blessing we received in our lives.

The bedroom situation was crowded but handy. We had our bed, the crib, and bunk beds to accommodate us and our three precious little girls. I say it was handy because when the baby awakened and needed changing we could just reach over and do it without getting up.

Those five years on the farm were challenging, but oh, what beautiful memories. It was the challenges during those "hungry years" that deepened our love for each other and our dependency on the Lord.

Later, after teaching for year and a half at the Y, I received an invitation to join the faculty there, which meant our nomadic wanderings through Idaho, Utah, Colorado, California, and back to Utah were finally over. No more journal entries from which we could have written our own version of *Grapes of Wrath!*

Because it was very difficult to rent a home for a family the size of ours, we looked forward to buying our first home and settling in the Provo, Utah, area. But I, being extremely busy with my graduate program, a heavy teaching load, and a demanding Church calling—I found a ready excuse not to spend much time searching the want ads and tromping the pavement in search of permanent living quarters. In fact, when I did turn myself to the task, it was half-hearted, perhaps for two reasons: one was that I felt strongly that when the right time came, the necessary doors would open to enable us to obtain a home; and second, we had managed to maintain quite consistently a zero balance in our savings account.

To illustrate the idea of the "right time" concept, I remember how excited we were in the fall when a friend offered to sell us a building lot in the north end of the valley at a very fair price. Without specifically clearing the decision with the Lord (isn't it obvious that everyone needs to buy a home?), we successfully obtained a down payment from the credit union and drove to the alumni camp at Aspen Grove to meet our friend and close the transaction.

As my wife and I drove to make the appointment, I felt heavy and negative about what we were doing. It was difficult to sort out my feelings. I knew we desperately needed a home, that the deal we were to make was fair, and that Diane had evidenced great joy at the prospect of having our own home. Yet I felt that indeed we shouldn't close the deal.

We didn't talk much during the thirty-minute drive up the canyon. Much to our surprise, the good brother who was to meet us didn't show up. We waited till quite late and then drove back down the canyon. The heavy, negative feelings persisted. I wanted to stop the car, look my wife right in the eye, and say, "I don't know why, but we are not supposed to buy that lot and build a home there!" but I didn't have the nerve—I thought surely she would be devastated with disappointment.

I spent a restless night, and when I awakened in the morning, it was abundantly clear in my mind that we should forget building a home right then. I awakened my wife, put my arms around her, and told her what I felt we should do. When I did, she squealed with delight and said, "That's exactly how I feel, and I felt that way when we went up the canyon, but I just couldn't bring myself to tell you, because I was afraid you'd be so disappointed!"

The "right time" came the following spring. I had finished giving a final exam, and I was chatting with one of my students from California. Among other things, I told her how excited we were that we would be settling in Provo. She responded, "Why don't you buy Dad's home here in Provo? It's up for sale." I casually asked, "Where is it?" She told me it was on the east bench above the temple. I immediately attempted to conclude the conversation by saying simply, "We really wouldn't be interested in looking at homes in that particular area"—a fairly veiled way of telling her there was no way we could afford a home in that section of the city. But she was persistent: she later brought me a pencil drawing of the floor plan of the house, and she kept insisting that we at least come and look at it.

Several weeks later, somewhat on a lark, and yet feeling impressed to do it, I asked my wife if she would like to ride up and at least look at "that" house. She said she would, and anyway, we did have friends in Idaho who had told us to keep our eyes open for a house they might buy.

I called the realtor and made an appointment for that morning.

When we drove up to the house, we noticed the realtor's Cadillac parked in front of it. Considering the appearance of our car, I wondered if perhaps it wouldn't be appropriate to park some distance down the street.

We were met at the door by a very gracious woman who told us she was the realtor. As we walked into the hallway, I really got excited—I honestly had the feeling something very important was happening. In fact, I felt as though we were coming home and that the house had been made just for us!

About halfway through the tour, while we were in the family room downstairs, the daughter of the owners came bounding in with several friends who were roommates in the house. These roommates had also been in my classes, and they all seemed pleasantly surprised and pleased to see us. The realtor then made the connection between who I was and previous information she'd been given about how the owners felt about me—which, much to my relief, was most positive! In making that connection, the realtor seemed to increase in her zeal to convince me I should buy the home.

Although I felt so much at home in the house and had strong intimations that somehow beautiful things were about to happen, those feelings were offset by remembering that we had no savings for a down payment and that my salary was surely not adequate to handle the kind of payments a house like this would require. In fact, I was convinced that had the realtor known our economic situation, she probably wouldn't have shown us the house.

Still, the excitement in my heart increased as I looked for the right moment to inquire about the price. When she told us, much of the excitement left. We couldn't afford that much, and I said so. She nevertheless encouraged me to make an offer. I hesitated, but she persisted, so finally I did make an offer. The look on her face suggested that I should perhaps make another offer. But then, with a gleam in her eye, she said boldly, "I've done a lot of crazy things—I will call the owner and tell him what you've offered." Amazed at her bravery and very grateful for her willingness to be so bold, I replied that that would be fine.

Sweetie and I went out to the car and started to drive down into the valley. She looked at me, just a little teary eyed, and said quietly, "What do you think?" I replied that as ridiculous as it seemed, I honestly felt the offer would be accepted and the home would be ours.

The next day, the realtor called, and with a great deal of excitement, informed us that the owner had accepted our offer! The following Monday night, we took the children to see the house. While we were there, the daughter called her parents, and by phone we became acquainted with the owners. They seemed pleased that we were going to buy their home. During the conversation, the owners said they would like us to have the couch in the front room as a housewarming gift. We were so pleased and grateful — in fact, my wife and I had concluded that were we to haul our old couch into such a nice home, we would surely be struck by lightning! (We had a family ritual we went through whenever people came to see us: at a given signal, the children would run through the bedrooms gathering blankets and pillows and cover the couch totally so that the arriving guests who sat on the couch would not be mortally wounded.)

After graciously giving us the couch, the owners indicated they didn't want to haul the furniture back to California and would we be interested in buying all or part of it? (Every room of the five-bedroom house was totally furnished, and there were two television sets, a lovely stereo, and a Ping-Pong table.) We excitedly told them we would be most interested.

Then there was the challenge of obtaining what to us was an immense down payment. Again, the Lord intervened, and the down payment was miraculously provided.

In the early summer, the owners came to Provo to close the deal. They generously took us to dinner, and as the evening ended, the owner asked if we had decided what furniture we wanted to buy and how much we would be willing to pay for it. I told him we wanted essentially all of it but hadn't decided on what we could pay. He asked if we would make an offer by the following morning.

We struggled that evening with that decision — we didn't want to be unfair, and yet we still didn't have any money. The following morning when we met the owners in the home, they handed us a large card that said, "God bless our mortgaged furniture." They laughed as they handed us the card. It was hard for us to laugh with them. I screwed up my courage and said, "We will be happy to pay you $1,000 for the furniture, if we can have two years to pay it off." They started laughing again, which, to say the least, was a bit perplexing. Then the owners said, "You'll do no such thing—$350 is plenty for the furniture."

Even now, many years later, both my wife and I are still quite overwhelmed at the way the Lord provided an opportunity for us to buy such a home and furniture at a price we could afford. Many times when I have hurried home for lunch, as I entered the house there would come such a wave of appreciation over me for just having a lovely home that I would grab Diane by the hand, we would kneel, and together we would express deeply our appreciation for our home and for all the blessings the Lord has given us.

Be it getting our home, obtaining the degrees, or having and raising the children the Lord has sent us—in all things the Savior's power has been made manifest in our lives in a marvelous way.

Doctrine and Covenants 133 expresses beautifully the feelings of gratitude I have for the goodness of the Lord. When the Savior descends in glory at his second coming, "his voice shall be heard: I have trodden the wine-press alone, and have brought judgment upon all people; and none were with me; and I have trampled them in my fury, and I did tread upon them in mine anger, and their blood have I sprinkled upon my garments." (Vv. 50–51.) But then he will speak to those who are redeemed by him—those who have their garments washed white in the blood of the Lamb—and he will say, "And now the year of my redeemed is come; and they shall mention the loving kindness of their Lord, and all that he has bestowed upon them according to his goodness, and according to his loving kindness, forever and ever." (V. 52.) The one thought that will be in our minds and hearts when the triumphant Christ returns to the earth in great glory will be our gratitude for his many kindnesses to us.

The import of this idea came very powerfully to my wife and me one sabbath evening in the summertime. Our meetings were over, and the children seemed to be occupied in worthwhile activities, so I took Diane by the hand and invited her to walk up the mouth of Rock Canyon with me. We came to a huge rectangular boulder and decided to climb up on it and together watch the sun go down. As we sat there close together, quite thrilled with the beauty of our surroundings, our conversation turned to the Lord. We spontaneously talked about experience after experience in which he had bestowed upon us in such a marvelous way blessing after blessing. I don't know that I had ever felt more deeply the reality of his blessings in our lives. We were both deeply moved and so anxious to do all in our power to honor him.

The Lord is God! He is a God of great love and mighty miracles. He does want to reveal to us his mind and will. He does want to give each one of us the power we need to accomplish his mind and will in our lives.

Chapter 8

HIS LIVING PROPHETS

Prophets are sent to gather us to Christ, and unless we respond to them in obedience, we cannot be gathered. A few days before the Savior's atoning sacrifice, there occurred an extremely touching event in his life that teaches us of the Spirit and the manner in which Christ would like to persuade us to come to him. As the Savior stood in the holy city of Jerusalem, a city he loved so much, he began to weep, saying: "O Jerusalem! Jerusalem! Ye who will kill the prophets, and will stone them who are sent unto you; how often would I have gathered your children together, even as a hen gathers her chickens under her wings, and ye would not." (JST, Matthew 23:37.)

One of the sweetest experiences I had as a young boy on the farm was watching how a mother hen would gather her chicks at the end of the day. Just a little while before sundown, the mother hen would start clucking in a special way. It was not the clucking she used to greet the rising sun, not the clucking she used when she had laid an egg, and not the clucking she used when she and the other hens would have their midmorning chat. Her clucking just before sundown was special; she was inviting her chicks to come together, to come to bed, as it were.

As she clucked, she wouldn't run around to all her little chicks to nudge them to a protected place, such as a special nest, but she would stay in one place and invite them, in chicken language, to come to her. Almost without exception, as soon as she clucked her invitation, they would come. Oh, it's true that on occasion one or two little furry chicks would ignore her request and continue to scratch the ground and peck around. Nevertheless, the mother hen did not cease clucking until all the chicks had come all the way to her. As her little ones came to her, she would spread her wings and fluff up her feathers, and the chicks would gather themselves under her wings, close to her body for both warmth and protection.

The Savior raises up and sends mighty prophets to invite us to come home to Christ, to come to him for the peace and protection only he can afford. From Adam to the present prophet, the call has been extended again and again and "with all the feeling of a tender parent." (1 Nephi 8:37.) And oh, the tragedy that has occurred again and again when those prophets have been stoned and killed. No wonder the Savior wept!

Prophets do not invite themselves to be prophets. They are called by the Lord (see John 15:16), and without exception they are called and given the priesthood in the same manner as was Aaron (see Exodus 28:1; Hebrews 5:4). Prophets are qualified to testify as special witnesses of the Savior by their personal knowledge of him and their experience with him. Adam remembered what God was like after the Fall and during his mortal life had the privilege of a marvelous association with Jehovah. Enoch walked and talked with the Lord. (See Moses 7:4.) Abraham had extended conversations with the premortal Christ and received marvelous promises from him. (See Abraham 2:6–12.) Moses, before he was called to lead the children of Israel out of bondage, saw and conversed with Jehovah. (See Moses 1.) Solomon, both before and during the construction of the temple, saw Christ. (See 1 Kings 3.) Lehi, before leading the beginning of a mighty nation to the American continent, saw and was instructed of the Lord, as was the case with Nephi. (See 1 Nephi 1:5–9; 2 Nephi 11:2–3.) The brother of Jared beheld one of the greatest visions from the Lord ever given to man before he led the Jaredites to the American continent. (See Ether 3.) How natural, then, that before Joseph Smith could perform the work of the Restoration, he too would see, converse with, and be commissioned of Christ to restore again the fulness of the gospel.

A prophet who will head a new dispensation is given the marvelous opportunity of being introduced to the Savior by seeing and conversing with him face to face. This introduction is invariably made by God the Father himself. In every dispensation, there is always one who knows the members of the Godhead and Satan. (See James E. Talmage, *Jesus the Christ,* p. 36.) After the prophet receives a perfect knowledge that Jesus is the Christ, the step that usually follows is the visitation of angelic beings who reveal more fully the mind and will of the Savior to him. In the course of these angelic manifestations, not only is instruction given but the holy priesthood is bestowed, the necessary ordinances are performed, and the prophet receives all the priesthood keys and powers he needs to enable him to invite others of God's children to come to Christ. (See Moroni 7:25–32.) The ordained and endowed prophet then moves among as many people as he can, testifying in the power and spirit of the Holy Ghost of what he has seen, heard, and received. As he does so, those who hear and who love truth will allow the Holy Ghost to have place in their hearts, and they will accept the words of the prophet and embrace the heaven-sent message. In time, through their faithfulness, they, like the prophets, may come to a perfect knowledge of Christ by seeing and conversing with him.

When Joseph Smith's experience in the Sacred Grove was over, he returned to his home, " 'leaned up to the fireplace,' " and with fixed determination and marvelous power, planted in his mother's heart the seeds for a redemptive faith as he declared, " 'I have learned for myself that Presbyterianism is not true!'. . .

" . . . His testimony, seasoned by the power of the Holy Ghost, rang in her ears. 'Mother, I have learned for myself!' Nor did he say, 'I believe,' or 'I think,' but with emphasis, 'I have learned for myself!' " (Carter Eldredge Grant, *The Kingdom of God Restored,* p. 28.) With that witness imbued in her heart, the Prophet's mother, like countless others, grew in the testimony, knowledge, and power of Christ.

Speaking of the necessity of a restoration of the gospel and the inadequacy of modern-day Christianity to instill a saving faith in the hearts of its followers, someone once said, "The living faith of the dead has become the dead faith of the living." Even though in our day the Christian world has access to the Bible and has had and does have tens of thousands of well-read and well-meaning teachers who have taught the scriptures to the best of their ability to offer the hope of redemption through Christ, it requires the opening of the heavens, the visitation of God himself, and angelic ministrants to restore the priesthood if "the living faith of the dead is going to become the living faith of the living."

The Doctrine and Covenants indicates that Moses was a type of the ancient prophets and that Joseph Smith, as well as each succeeding prophet, is to us as Moses was to the children of Israel. (See D&C 28:2.) Let's consider that relationship in a little more detail.

The Lord made a remarkable promise to Moses: "Thou shalt be made stronger than many waters; for they shall obey thy command as if thou wert God." (Moses 1:25.) On another occasion, the Lord told Moses that as he fulfilled his calling and used Aaron as his mouthpiece, he, Moses, would be as God to Aaron. (See Exodus 4:16.) What a remarkable position for Moses to hold!

Similarly, in our day, we have received the word of the Lord through Joseph Smith and through his divinely appointed successors. (See D&C 5:10.) The Lord tells us his prophet, seer, and revelator to the Church is to "preside over the whole church, and to be like unto Moses." (D&C 107:91; see also D&C 28:2.)

President Brigham Young said of Joseph Smith: "No man or woman in this dispensation will ever enter into the celestial kingdom of God without the consent of Joseph Smith. From the day that the Priesthood was taken from the earth to the winding-up scene of all things, every man and woman must have the certificate of Joseph Smith, junior, as a passport to their entrance into the mansion where God and Christ are—I with you and you with me. I cannot go there without his consent. He holds the keys of that kingdom for the last dispensation." (In *Journal of Discourses,* 7:289.)

In another address, President Young shared his feelings about the Prophet Joseph Smith, which I believe reflect a confidence and faith in God's prophets that should be emulated by all the Saints: "Though I admitted in my feelings and knew all the time that Joseph was a human being and subject to err, still it was none of my business to look after his faults.

" . . . It was not for me to question whether Joseph was dictated by the Lord at all times and under all circumstances or not. I never had the feeling for one moment, to believe that any man or set of men or beings upon the face of the whole earth had anything to do with him, for he was superior to them all, and held the keys of salvation over them. Had I not thoroughly understood this and believed it, I much doubt whether I should ever have embraced what is called 'Mormonism.' He was called of God; God dictated [to] him, and if He had a mind to leave him to himself and let him commit an error, that was no business of mine. . . .

"It was not my prerogative to call him in question with regard to any act of his life. He was God's servant, and not mine. He did not belong to the people but to the Lord, and was doing the work of the Lord, and if He should suffer him to lead the people astray, it would be because they ought to be led astray. If He should suffer them to be chastised, and some of them destroyed, it would be because they deserved it, or to accomplish some righteous purpose. That was my faith, and it is my faith still." (In *Journal of Discourses*, 4:297–98.)

There should be no question how the Lord views the prophets of our dispensation and what he expects of us in accepting them as his mouthpiece. Even as Christ is the manifestation of the mind and will of God, so are his chosen holy prophets the manifestation of the Lord's mind and will.

Watersheds

The term *watershed* is used in geography to describe a whole region from which a river receives its supply of water. When it rains on the Continental Divide of the Rocky Mountains, the rain that falls on the western slopes will end up in an entirely different river system than the rain that falls on the eastern slopes. The same term is also used in philosophy to describe a dividing point, or juncture, in an area of philosophical thought.

There are also great issues in the Church that can be seen as religious watersheds. How we view the living prophet is perhaps one of the greatest. Both in and out of the Church, it is a comparatively easy thing to profess faith in Christ and a willing-ness to do what he wants us to do. But to accept the Savior on his terms as revealed clearly through his prophets is an entirely different matter, and for many a most difficult one. That accep-tance of the Lord and his anointed can indeed be said to be a dividing line between true believers and nonbelievers.

Somehow, most people of the Christian world love dead prophets much more than they do living prophets. There are many on earth today who "do not desire that the Lord their God, who hath created them, should rule and reign over them." (He-laman 12:6.) I have often wondered why people are so resistant to the concept of living prophets, and I have concluded that per-haps one of the reasons is that, first of all, living prophets have a marvelous way of removing the mystery that surrounds God, Christ, and the gospel. That to many people is unbelievably dis-quieting, for it leaves them no excuse about what is expected of them. Another reason seems to be that living prophets invariably speak clearly and forcefully on current contemporary issues, be they political, social, economic, or spiritual, and what they have to say is often the opposite of what those who love the world are saying. In addition, it is much, much easier to misquote or mis-construe what dead prophets have said—and at least temporarily get away with it—than it is to misquote or misconstrue what living prophets are saying.

Several watersheds seem to cause a struggle for some Saints. Three of the most common are these:

Does the prophet have the right to give directions to the Saints on any subject, be it social, economic, political, or religious?

Is it within the realm of possibility for the Lord through his prophet to give a command that contradicts an earlier command?

Is it possible, if we are totally obedient to the revelations of the current prophet, to become completely united and be as one in every phase of political, economic, social, and religious life?

The answers we give to these questions are most important in determining whether we really sustain the Lord's prophets.

No dividing line between the spiritual and the temporal. Few things cause some Saints to be more upset than the prophet's giving direction in the temporal aspects of life, especially as that direction relates to the social issues of our day. Whether it concerns prohibition, right to work, what kind of people to vote for, the welfare state, or the Equal Rights Amendment, invariably there is an upsurge of criticism. Such has probably always been the case. President Brigham Young observed:

"Some of the leading men in Kirtland were much opposed to Joseph the Prophet, meddling with temporal affairs, they did not believe that he was capable, of dictating to the people upon temporal matters, thinking that his duty embraced spiritual things alone, and that the people should be left to attend to their temporal affairs, without any interference whatever from Prophets or Apostles. Men in authority there, would contend with Joseph on this point, not openly, but in their little Councils. After a while the matter culminated into a public question; it became so public that it was in the mouth of almost every one. In a public meeting of the Saints, I said 'Ye Elders of Israel, Father Smith is present, the Prophet is present, and here are his counsellors, here are also High Priests and Elders of Israel, now, will some of you draw the line of demarcation, between the spiritual and the temporal in the Kingdom of God, so that I may understand it?' Not one of them could do it. When I saw a man stand in the path before the Prophet to dictate [to] him, I felt like hurling him out the way, and branding him as a fool. . . .

"I defy any man on earth to point out the path a Prophet of God should walk in, or point out his duty, and just how far he must go, in dictating temporal or spiritual things. Temporal and spiritual things are inseparably connected, and ever will be." (In *Journal of Discourses*, 10:363–64.)

We would think that almost everyone who has reflected seriously on the subject would draw the conclusion that in and of ourselves we are simply incapable of solving the perilous problems confronting us. We have witnessed millions of people lose their freedom to totalitarian governments. We are aware that the brightest economists in the world cannot solve even the most basic economic problems of their countries. I think we all marvel that the supreme legal powers in the United States have somehow succeeded in giving more concern and protection to the rights of the criminal than to those of the victim. And we are astounded that the government of the United States seemingly can see no relationship between the current welfare state and the imminent bankruptcy of the nation. Our dilemma reminds me of the following words of the Prophet Joseph Smith: "Other attempts to promote universal peace and happiness in the human family have proved abortive; every effort has failed; every plan and design has fallen to the ground; it needs the wisdom of God, the intelligence of God, and the power of God to accomplish this." (*History of the Church,* 5:64.)

There is, then, a solution to the problems facing us, but it is an unpopular solution and one, we may think, that is too slow and ponderous. That solution is to recognize that only as we heed the mind and will of the Savior as revealed to his living prophets will we be redeemed temporally as well as spiritually.

"Whatever Jehovah commands is right." The second watershed for some Saints is the possibility that the Lord, through his prophet, may give a command that contradicts an earlier command. We speak of Abrahamic tests in the Church, of being asked, as was Abraham, to do things that appear inconsistent with previous commandments — to do things that may seem illogical and unreasonable. Often it is hard to understand why the Lord would give such commandments. But can a person's faith truly be tested without such challenging commands? To walk by faith is to walk not by sight but by revelation. To be obedient to God in Abrahamic tests is to be obedient, not because we can understand what he wants us to do, not because it makes sense, but because we know God has asked us to do it!

Perhaps the greatest and possibly the hardest lesson for Joseph Smith to learn was that God can "command and revoke, as it seemeth me good" (D&C 56:4), as was the case when the Lord commanded that Jackson County should be built up and then revoked that command. On one occasion, the Prophet summed up that principle by saying, "Whatever God requires is right, no matter what it is, although we may not see the reason thereof till long after the events transpire." (*History of the Church,* 5:135.)

The Prophet further stated: "A man would command his son to dig potatoes and saddle his horse, but before he had done either he would tell him to do something else. This is all considered right; but as soon as the Lord gives a commandment and revokes that decree and commands something else, then the Prophet is considered fallen." (*History of the Church*, 4:478.)

I've watched with interest many an Arab potter in Israel fashion vessels according to his desire. The potter knows the vessel he wants to create, he knows how to do it, and he knows the kind of clay he needs to accomplish his task. On occasion, the clay he uses will not yield to the gentle pressure of his fingers, and without a pause, he removes it from the wheel and casts it into a nearby basket. In time the potter returns to the basket of clay, and by adding different components and working with the clay, he makes it responsive to his every wish so that he can fashion it into the vessel he desires it to be.

We must be like clay in the Potter's hand. The Savior wants to make us a holy vessel. He knows how to do it—he knows how willing we must be to yield our hearts to his will as manifested through his prophets. He also knows that if we aren't willing to do anything and everything he wants us to do, we cannot be fashioned into the vessel he wants us to be.

When a person has a revealed testimony that this work is the work of God, then whatever is required of that person—be it to accept the ordination of seventies as high priests or the conferral of the priesthood on all worthy males or whatever it might be—it is of no consequence. The only important things are that we know that God is at the helm of his church, that his mind and will are being made known through the prophet and the First Presidency, and that we are obedient to whatever he commands.

"If ye are not one ye are not mine." The third watershed for some Saints is becoming completely united on every phase of political, economic, social, and religious life by being obedient to the revelations of the living prophet.

The intercessory prayer uttered by the Savior just hours before his crucifixion had as its great theme the oneness of the

Father and the Son and the hope that those who believe in the Son would be one with them. (See John 17:21, 23.) In a revelation given in our day, the Savior stated, "I say unto you, be one; and if ye are not one ye are not mine." (D&C 38:27.) I believe with all my heart that if the Savior really dwells in us as individuals, if we are each really filled with the Holy Ghost, then we will be one politically, socially, economically, and spiritually. I believe that we will be one with the prophet in all respects, as the counselors in the First Presidency, the Twelve Apostles, and all the other General Authorities are one with the prophet in every aspect of building the kingdom. Perhaps one of the greatest examples of the oneness that can occur when a group of people is really converted is found in the Book of Mormon in 4 Nephi.

There are those who feel that if the Brethren were to tell us everything we should do, it would rob us of our free agency. What foolishness! When the Father constantly informed the Son of his will, did it rob Christ of his free agency? No!

The Lord wants to free us from sin and ignorance, from spiritual and temporal bondage. The message of the gospel of Jesus Christ is to change men's hearts and minds so completely that as a group of faithful Saints we are one with God and Christ under the direction of the prophets. Only in that oneness will we eradicate all evil and enjoy a perfect society.

Pride and Sin: Roots of Criticism

One of the delights of our homestead in Idaho was a beautiful creek that flowed through the entire length of the farm. Most of the water originated right in the acreage from pure, cold, bubbling springs. Often on hot summer days Dad, my brothers, and I would drop our hoes, pitchforks, or shovels and go down to the creek for a drink. The land bordering the creek was used as a pasture for horses and cows, so we would always go directly to a spring to drink rather than to the main channel of the creek itself, for we knew the water from the spring had not been contaminated. How refreshing it was to pause at the spring and not only quench our thirst but cool ourselves off by immersing our hands and faces again and again in the clear water.

So it is with the Saints of God. We have a veritable stream of pure, clean, living water that is flowing through our midst, but that beautiful stream of living water flows through the impure pasture land of the sophistry of the world, the false traditions of past ages of apostasy that are deeply riveted on the hearts of mankind, and the terrible sensuality that matches that of the days of Sodom and Gomorrah. Oh, how we should rejoice that living water is once again upon the earth and that the Lord has raised up living prophets to dispense that living water *at its source* to all who honestly seek for its life-giving strength.

One great pollution that keeps us from enjoying pure water from the stream of living water is criticism of the Lord's anointed. The source of this criticism is pride that comes from intellectual attainments.

Let me share an insight that came to me years ago while I was acting as an institute director. The most startling difference between teaching on the high school level and teaching on the college level was that on the university level some of the Saints were much more open in their criticism of the prophets. It was quite an eye-opener for me to become aware that some of the Brethren were continually criticized and even openly rejected by Saints associated with the local academic community who seemed extremely proud of their academic achievement.

The critics of whom I speak were basically good people, and all of them were active in the Church. At first I assumed that the difference between critics of the Brethren and those who accepted the Brethren was mostly a matter of semantics and that if we kept a dialogue open long enough, we would come to realize that our faith and confidence in the prophets was really much the same. But such was not the case. The differences were real; things were viewed from two wholly different perspectives.

Nephi, seeing and describing the religious condition of our times, spoke strongly against the corruptions and abominations which he saw, including a tendency of some Saints to teach the precepts of men instead of the gospel. He said, "They have all gone astray save it be a few, who are the humble followers of Christ; nevertheless, they are led, that in many instances *they do err because they are taught by the precepts of men."* (2 Nephi 28:14; italics added.)

All of the prophets of this dispensation have warned of this problem that confronts the Church. The following two statements from Elder Harold B. Lee represent many that are available: "We have gone through another — or are going through — a period of what we might call sophistication. (I do not know what that word means either, but it generally means that there are so many confounded smart people that they are not willing to listen to the humble prophets of the Lord.) And we have suffered from that. And it is rather a severe test through which we are passing." (*"Sweet Are the Uses of Adversity,"* Brigham Young University Speeches of the Year [Provo, Utah, 7 Feb. 1962], p. 3.)

Elder Harold B. Lee also said: "One of the greatest threats to the work of the Lord today comes from false educational ideas. There is a growing tendency of teachers within and without the Church to make academic interpretations of gospel teachings — to read, as a prophet-leader has said, 'by the lamp of their own conceit.' Unfortunately, much in the sciences, the arts, politics, and the entertainment field, as has been well said by an eminent scholar, is 'all dominated by this humanistic approach which ignores God and his word as revealed through the prophets.' " (In Conference Report, Oct. 1968, p. 59.)

Higher education can be, and most of the time is, a blessing to the Saints. And yet when some Saints take great pride in having a doctoral-level understanding in their field of learning but have only an elementary understanding of the gospel, it is invariably a challenge for them to view life and their profession through the lens of revelations of the prophets, instead of viewing the revelations of the prophets through the lens of their academic training.

While there are undoubtedly many roots of criticism besides intellectual pride, few things fuel a tendency toward deep and devastating criticism as does sin. Korihor, one of the anti-Christs in the Book of Mormon, was surely steeped in immorality, for he was successful in "leading away many women, and also men, to commit whoredoms." (Alma 30:18.) He also was a sign seeker, which, according to the Savior, is one of the characteristics of "a wicked and adulterous generation." (Matthew 16:4.)

Elder Harold B. Lee observed: "There are some who look upon the leaders of this Church and God's anointed as men who are possessed of selfish motives. By them the words of our leaders are always twisted to try to bring a snare to the work of the Lord. Mark well those who speak evil of the Lord's anointed for they speak from impure hearts. Only the 'pure in heart' see the 'God' or the divine in man and accept our leaders and accept them as prophets of the Living God." (In Conference Report, Oct. 1947, p. 67.)

One experience might illustrate what I'm attempting to say. A particularly bright young man in an institute class I taught gave me a bad time incessantly about almost everything I said. I had put forth some effort to persuade him to take the class in the first place; however, because of his attitude and its negative effect on the class, I began wondering if I shouldn't persuade him to drop the class.

One beautiful spring day after the students were dismissed, I asked the contentious one if he would stay for a while so we could talk alone. We sat out by a fountain, and as I tried to persuade him to be more accepting of the doctrine of the Church, he continued to argue with sophistication against everything I said. I could easily have wrung his neck! His arguments were well thought out and reflected powerfully the wisdom of men, but they were simply wrong.

All of a sudden it was made known to me that the young man was immoral. The impression came so suddenly and with such force that before I realized what was happening, I blurted out, "Young man, are you sexually immoral?"

His mouth dropped open, his eyes widened, and with a stunned look he said, "Yes, very immoral, and I have been for some time."

I was so relieved to discover that his antagonism and persuasive argument stemmed from a determination to justify his sins that I'm afraid I almost squealed with delight. I told him strongly that I now knew his bold arguments came from a heart aching from a stricken conscience. I pleaded with him to forsake his sins and to go to his bishop and confess. He very humbly acknowledged that he would, and he did! Some months later, he married a nonmember, and what a thrill it was to me to learn that in less than two years, due to the completeness of his repentance, his wife became converted, and in time they were married in the temple.

Members of the Church who are critical of the Lord's anointed are generally suffering from pride or from individual sin, both of which keep us from enjoying the Spirit, without which we cannot build up the kingdom and obtain for ourselves the promise of eternal life.

Knowing by Direct Light

One of the indications that we've actually experienced that most important event, being born again, is our willingness to fully sustain the Lord's anointed. President Harold B. Lee confirmed this idea when he declared: "Now I want to impress this upon you. Someone has said it this way, 'That person is not truly converted until he sees the power of God resting upon the leaders of this church, and until it goes down into his heart like fire.' Until the members of this church have that conviction that they are being led in the right way, and they have a conviction that these men of God are men who are inspired and have been properly appointed by the hand of God, they are not truly converted." (In Conference Report, Apr. 1972, p. 118.)

In effect, our willingness to accept and sustain the Lord's anointed is in direct proportion to the influence and power of the Spirit in our lives. We simply cannot and will not see the mantle of divine authority resting on the Lord's anointed unless we are filled with the same spirit of prophecy that they have. Another way to put it is that it takes a prophet to know a prophet! Surely that is what Moses hoped and prayed for when he said, "Would God that all the Lord's people were prophets, and that the Lord would put his spirit upon them!" (Numbers 11:29.)

What I'm referring to is much more than receiving a witness that the leaders of the Church are prophets; but rather, it is enjoying the consistent, regular companionship of the Holy Ghost that empowers us to accept, understand, and do the bidding of the prophets. The Church has consistently urged the Saints to live on direct light, to know for themselves that they are being led by a prophet. President Brigham Young pleaded with the Saints:

"I am more afraid that this people have so much confidence in their leaders that they will not inquire for themselves of God whether they are led by Him. I am fearful they settle down in a state of blind self-security, trusting their eternal destiny in the hands of their leaders with a reckless confidence that in itself would thwart the purposes of God in their salvation, and weaken that influence they could give to their leaders, did they know for themselves, by the revelations of Jesus, that they are led in the right way. Let every man and woman know, by the whispering of the Spirit of God to themselves, whether their leaders are walking in the path the Lord dictates, or not. This has been my exhortation continually." (In *Journal of Discourses*, 9:150.)

A classic example of the principle Brigham Young was referring to is found in the reaction of Lehi's sons to his revelations and admonitions. All of them heard what was surely a powerful testimony of what their father had seen and heard. In my judgment, all four of Lehi's sons knew in their hearts that their father's words were true. But of the four, Nephi was the only one who really wanted to know more fully about what his father had said — indeed, he wanted to "see, and hear, and know" without question, so he went off by himself and inquired of the Lord in mighty prayer. (See 1 Nephi 10:17.) His heart was softened, and he knew by direct experience that his father was inspired of the Lord. Having seen the same vision enjoyed by his father, Nephi put his hand to the plow and with power constantly sustained his father and fulfilled all the commandments of the Lord.

The Name Is Written in Heaven

One of the most beautiful experiences I've read that shows the blessing of sustaining all the words of the Lord's anointed is an experience of Heber C. Kimball's. It was the spring of 1839; Joseph Smith was in jail; the persecution was terrible. On 6 April Heber C. Kimball wrote:

"My family having been gone about two months, during which time I heard nothing from them; our brethren being in prison; death and destruction following us everywhere we went; I felt very sorrowful and lonely. The following words came to my mind, and the Spirit said unto me, 'write,' which I did by taking a piece of paper and writing on my knee as follows: . . .

"Verily I say unto my servant Heber, thou art my son, in whom I am well pleased; for thou art careful to hearken to my words, and not transgress my law, nor rebel against my servant Joseph Smith, *for thou hast a respect to the words of mine anointed*, even from the least to the greatest of them; *therefore thy name is written in heaven, no more to be blotted out for ever, because of these things.*" (Quoted in Orson F. Whitney, *Life of Heber C. Kimball*, p. 241; italics added.)

May we sense deeply the tremendous importance of living prophets. May we come to know that our very salvation depends upon our honoring and sustaining the Lord's anointed, and that if we will fully and completely accept the Lord's anointed, he, the Lord, will fully and completely accept us. Particularly may we come to realize that faith in Jesus Christ demands faith without exception in those he sends and that a desire and hope to know Christ are inextricably tied to accepting the Lord's anointed.

Chapter 9

A LOVING FATHER

My dad was a very warm, loving man. Often as a child when I heard his car drive up, I would run excitedly out of the house and leap off the stairs into his arms. Invariably, he would hold me for a few moments, give me a big hug and a squeeze, and make some positive comments about me, so that by the time he set me down there was no question in my mind that my dad really loved me.

After my first quarter of college at Logan, Utah (which was the first time I had been away from home for any length of time), my reunion with my father was really something. When I drove into the farmyard, he came running out of the house, and as we came together we didn't shake hands or even exchange greetings—neither of us could speak! We simply threw our arms around one another, embraced, and kissed.

Throughout my life, the love my father and I have shared has been one of the greatest blessings I have known. Would we expect any less of a meaningful relationship with our Heavenly Father and with our Elder Brother? Would we imagine them to be less warm and affectionate, less concerned and loving, than an earthly father? Obviously not. I'm convinced that as members of the Church, we can arrive at a point where the Savior's love for us and our love for him will be the greatest source of joy in our life.

Unconditional Love

Perhaps you would not argue with me when I say that one of the greatest visions from God that has ever been recorded is

Lehi's vision of the tree of life and Nephi's interpretation of that vision. The central object of that dream is the tree of life; the central experience of that dream is the partaking of the fruit of the tree of life. Perhaps not so immediately obvious is that the tree of life is Jesus Christ, and Lehi, in partaking of the fruit, tasted, or experienced, the majesty of the Savior's atonement.

Nephi's already intense appetite for the things of the Spirit increased as his father unfolded the vision. Nephi then "was desirous also that I might see, and hear, and know of these things, by the power of the Holy Ghost, which is the gift of God unto all those who diligently seek him." (1 Nephi 10:17.) Nephi was shown the tree, and he immediately declared that the "beauty thereof was far beyond, yea, exceeding of all beauty; and the whiteness thereof did exceed the whiteness of the driven snow." (1 Nephi 11:8.)

Having seen the tree and knowing that the tree represented the love of God, Nephi wanted to grasp more fully what his father had experienced. He inquired further and was shown Mary, "a virgin, most beautiful and fair above all virgins." (1 Nephi 11:15.) He saw that Mary was carried away in the Spirit for a period of time, reappearing to Nephi's view holding the Christ child in her arms.

As the vision continued, Nephi saw the Savior's life, mission, and atonement. He saw the Savior teaching, healing, sorrowing. He saw people spitting on him and trampling him under their feet. He saw the world judging the Savior "to be a thing of naught." (1 Nephi 19:9.) In short, Nephi *experienced* the awful greatness of the Savior's atonement. He came to know, as did his father, that the greatest manifestation of God's love is the redemptive gift of his Son. The only way we can fully partake of that love is, first, by attaining the straight and narrow path which, as we all know, is to become members of the restored Church, and, second, by clinging to the iron rod, or the word of God — that is, by manifesting our obedience to "every word that proceedeth forth from the mouth of God." (D&C 84:44.)

Lehi and Nephi, like all the prophets, soon became aware that the undergirding, overarching, all-pervasive attribute of the Father and the Son — in fact, the mainspring of the Atonement —

is their unconditional love for us. I am convinced that no man or woman of any dispensation can be instructed by the Spirit about the Atonement without tasting of that same love, and it will become the greatest motivating power of their life. I believe with all my heart that we, like Nephi, can stand by the power of the Spirit, as it were, in Gethsemane and Golgotha and be a personal witness to the Savior's pain, sorrow, suffering, and death. Because of such an experience, we will receive a godly love of such intensity that we, like Nephi, will want to exclaim, "He hath filled me with his love, even unto the consuming of my flesh." (2 Nephi 4:21.)

Unconditional Blessings

At least one other distinct revelation about the love of God is embedded in the vision of the tree of life. Because of the Atonement, a marvelous portion of the love of God is unconditionally shed abroad in the hearts of all men. (See 1 Nephi 11:22.)

Let me suggest some ways in which the love of God is unconditionally shed abroad in the hearts of all people. Through the Atonement (the love of God), all mankind has the promise of immortality through the resurrection and all mankind is blessed with the marvelous light of Christ. I would like to focus particularly on this light of Christ and its relationship to our inherent ability to love others.

I doubt that any of us has yet grasped what the light of Christ can do to endow people with love. For example, there seems to be sufficient love planted in the hearts of all people that the Savior knew he would be on safe ground to command everyone to love their neighbor as they love themselves. (See Matthew 19:19.) A further illustration: all of us are exposed almost daily through the news media to acts of remarkable selflessness on the part of Christians and non-Christians alike that cause us to marvel at the love people across the broad spectrum of humanity can enjoy and manifest to those in need.

I came away from reading the book and seeing the movie *The Hiding Place,* by Corrie Ten Boom, inspired and thrilled with the risks and dangers people in Holland were willing to go through to preserve the lives of Jews persecuted by the Nazis. I have read accounts of the labors of Mother Theresa in behalf of the downtrodden in India and have concluded that her service is surely a product of the love of God, which, according to our theology, is inspired by the light of Christ. I, like millions of others, was deeply moved by the heroic actions of the man who gave his life in saving victims of an airplane crash from an icy death in the Potomac River. I, like you, am pleased with the efforts and contributions of tens of thousands of people to aid the starving millions of Ethiopia. We have all met couples and families outside the restored kingdom of God who have a loving relationship with each other. And we all know couples who have been inactive in the Church all their lives and yet treat each other in a very loving, Christlike way.

Now the question I have to pose is this: if men and women can have such a remarkable love because of their willingness to respond to the Light of Christ without getting on the straight and narrow path, without the aid and assistance of the iron rod, or the word of God, without the cleansing and sanctifying influence of the Holy Ghost, without partaking directly and fully of the majesty of the Savior and his marvelous gospel, then can we begin to imagine what power of love is available when we, under the tutelage of the Spirit, become cleansed by the blood of the Lamb and become filled with the same love that enables us to become, in the fullest sense of the word, the very sons and daughters of Jesus Christ? This greater love, compared to what's available outside the fulness of the gospel, is as different from it as the brightness of the sun is different from the brightness of the moon. We need to realize that through the Restoration a much greater love is available to all mankind, a love that is in a sense conditional, for it is available only through obedience to the fulness of the restored gospel.

A New Commandment

To better understand the contrast between the unconditional love available to all and the greater love the fulness of the gospel has to offer, we could view the unconditional love as the love Moses spoke of when he declared, "Thou shalt love thy neighbor as thyself." (Leviticus 19:18.) There are at least six statements in the New Testament with the same wording. I have been intrigued that so often members of the Church encourage one another with the reminder to love our neighbor as ourselves instead of encouraging others to reach for the greater love.

On the evening before the Crucifixion and just after the events of the Last Supper, the washing of feet, and Judas' leaving to betray his Lord, the Savior said, in what I'm sure was a very touching way: "Little children, yet a little while I am with you. Ye shall seek me: and as I said unto the Jews, Whither I go, ye cannot come; so now I say to you. A new commandment I give unto you, That ye love one another; as I have loved you, that ye also love one another." (John 13:34.)

At once this new commandment bursts the limiting bonds of loving others only as we love ourselves and unveils the unlimited potential of our capacity to love even as God loves us. It is difficult to believe that we mere mortals can actually receive into our very being the love that prompted the Father to send his Son to the earth and that caused the Savior to descend below all things (see D&C 122:8; Moroni 7:48), to "suffer temptations, and pain of body, hunger, thirst, and fatigue, even more than man can suffer, except it be unto death; for behold, blood cometh from every pore" (Mosiah 3:7).

Elder Bruce R. McConkie observed that this was a new commandment "and an old commandment too; a commandment both old and new, a commandment that commences now and yet is everlasting; a commandment that is new each time it is revealed, but is old because it has always been in force." (*Doctrinal New Testament Commentary*, 1:726.)

I believe that this commandment is the standard by which we should guide our lives and the standard by which we as Latter-day Saints will be judged. We simply have no greater responsibility than to love others as Christ has loved us, and only Christ can enable us to reach such a coveted goal.

Charity: The Greatest Endowment

What is this remarkable love that enables us to love others even as God and Christ loves us? It is charity, which is the pure love of Christ. Elder Bruce R. McConkie observed: "Charity is more than love, far more; it is everlasting love, perfect love, the pure love of Christ which endureth forever. It is love so centered in righteousness that the possessor has no aim or desire except for the eternal welfare of his own soul and for the soul of those around him." (*Mormon Doctrine*, p. 121.)

Paul the apostle stressed that charity is a gift of the Spirit. In 1 Corinthians 12, he spoke of nine gifts of the Spirit and their tremendous importance, even likening these gifts to different parts of the human body; but then in summary, he said, "And yet shew I unto you a more excellent way." (1 Corinthians 12:31.) The next thing Paul wrote was, "Though I speak with the tongues of men and of angels, and have not charity, I am become as sounding brass, or a tinkling cymbal." (1 Corinthians 13:1.) We then learn further that even though we might have the gift of prophecy, or the gift of faith, though we might have all knowledge, or have given all we have to the poor, if we have not charity, we are nothing. (See 1 Corinthians 13:2–3.)

Mormon made a great contribution to our knowledge of what charity actually is when he testified, "But charity is the pure love of Christ, and it endureth forever; and whoso is found possessed of it at the last day, it shall be well with him." (Moroni 7:47.)

It is my understanding that charity is a gift of the Spirit, an actual endowment from the Lord that enables us to love others even as God and Christ love us. Mormon testified that this marvelous gift is "bestowed upon all who are true followers of his Son, Jesus Christ; that ye may become the sons of God; that when he shall appear we shall be like him." (Moroni 7:48.)

If your mind works the way mine works, as soon as you find out that charity is a gift of the Spirit, that it is the greatest endowment that the Lord can bestow on us this side of eternal life, that it is a gift reserved for those "who are true followers of his Son, Jesus Christ" (Moroni 7:48), and, further, that the Prophet Joseph Smith declared, "When we have a testimony that our names are sealed in the Lamb's book of life we have perfect love" (*Teachings of the Prophet Joseph Smith*, p. 9), then you will desire that gift above all else.

The Key to Obtaining Charity

The question that then follows is, "How do I acquire such a magnificent endowment?" Mormon answered that question with great clarity: "Wherefore, my beloved brethren, pray unto the Father with all the energy of heart, that ye may be filled with this love." (Moroni 7:48.)

Recognizing that "it is by grace that we are saved, after all we can do" (2 Nephi 25:23), and recognizing that it is important to use our own determination, our own resolves, and our own will to acquire any blessing from God, we must conclude that, while all of our own effort is necessary, *it is not sufficient.* We need to approach our Heavenly Father with "a broken heart and a contrite spirit" (2 Nephi 2:7) and plead with all our energy for this divine endowment of love. If we keep the commandments, if we serve others with an eye single to the glory of God, and if we ask, ask, ask, there will one day come into our souls a divine love, which will first focus on our God and his Christ, then on our spouse and our children, then on our parents and our brothers and sisters. Then that love will reach out with indescribable intensity for all of our Heavenly Father's children.

But again, the key is prayer, not just the casual prayer that so often is uttered, not just the intensified prayer occasioned by mishap or tragedy, but the fervent, daily, persistent, mighty prayer of one who hungers and thirsts for righteousness more than for food, drink, or public acclaim.

To illustrate the blessings that come by persisting in prayer for charity, I would like to share with you the following experience. But first, I would like to emphasize that before I had this experience, I had been diligent in searching the scriptures and the writings of the Brethren for an understanding of what charity is; I had tried to be very serious about magnifying my callings; and I had prayed with all my heart for the endowment of charity.

I was teaching institute classes on campus at Stanford University while the institute building was being constructed. This particular day of which I speak had been about as perfect as any day I could remember. Each class had gone well, the discussions had been lively, and the Spirit had been present.

In the evening I taught a class from 8 until 10 o'clock. After the class there was informal chatting and some counseling so that it was quite late by the time I walked over to the house my family and I were living in. As I approached the house, I noticed all the lights were out, and upon entering and checking the bedrooms, I found that my wife and children were in bed and sound asleep.

Because the day had gone so well, my spirit seemed unusually alive. The last thing I wanted to do was go to bed, so I went into the front room and sat on the edge of the couch. Immediately, I found myself mentally counting my blessings. I thought to myself, What a privilege it is to be alive, to have health and strength, to know who the Lord is, and to have tasted so deeply of his goodness; what an honor to have the priesthood and the gift of the Holy Ghost. There also came into my heart an almost overwhelming sense of gratitude for my precious wife and for our many children. As I continued to reflect on the Lord's graciousness to me, the gratitude I felt grew until it seemed every cell of my body was alive with the Spirit. Maybe the best way to put it is to say my cup was full and even running over.

After twenty minutes or so, I quietly went into the bedroom where my wife was asleep. Without touching her or the bed, I knelt down close to her and in silent but mighty prayer, I told the Lord how grateful I was for her and how especially appreciative I was for her willingness to go, as it were, into the valley of the shadow of death to bring so many of Heavenly Father's offspring along the frail path from his presence to mortality. I continued for some time to pray that the Lord would bless my wife with the Spirit, that her body would be renewed, and that she might have the health and strength she desperately needed to carry the heavy responsibilities that were hers.

I then knelt beside the sleeping form of my oldest daughter and expressed profound appreciation for her, remembering her concerns and anxieties. I did the same for each of my children. By the time I was through, it was quite late, and my feelings of gratitude had increased immeasurably.

I returned to the front room, and still feeling no desire whatsoever to retire, I thought I would conclude the day with vocal prayer. I prayed for an extended period of time, but finally starting to feel tired, I wondered if perhaps I should go to bed. At that moment, a strong impression came to me that I should not retire, but rather that I should continue in prayer, which I did.

When my wife and I were married in the Salt Lake Temple, I really felt that I knew what love was all about. But over the years that love had continued to grow and develop to where I honestly wondered if it could be any greater. That night, however, as I persisted in prayer, there came an endowment of love that transcended anything I had tasted of or felt previously in my life. Before that evening was over, I sensed, at least in a measure, what Nephi must have meant when he said, "He hath filled me with his love, even unto the consuming of my flesh." (2 Nephi 4:21.)

And what intensified feelings of love came first for the Lord, then for my wife and children, and then for my parents and my brothers and sisters and their families; then it seemed to reach out for everyone and knew no bounds.

The endowment of charity is a literal, tangible bestowal of a dimension of love from the Savior that is beyond our capability of describing. If we have the gift of charity, we will see that the majesty of the Atonement, the power to keep the commandments, and the realization of the infinite worth of the souls of all of God's children will cause a joy that is almost more than a mortal body can bear!

Mighty prayer is the key to obtaining charity. We need to ask explicitly with all the energy of our souls that we might receive that endowment of love. As time goes on, we are effective in prayer for others because we have come to love them so dearly. I would counsel you to memorize Moroni 7:48 and not let a day go by without remembering Mormon's admonition and praying with all of your heart for that great endowment.

The greatest manifestation of the Father's love and of Christ's love is seen in their service in our behalf. It is natural, therefore, to anticipate that charity will come to us as we sacrifice to build up the kingdom of God. If we lose ourselves in service in building up the kingdom, we will find ourselves wrapped up in the glory and love of the Savior. We all desire to return home to our Heavenly Father and to be warmly welcomed back into his presence. We will have that privilege if we obtain charity, the pure love of Christ, and are found still possessing that heavenly love when he comes in his glory. The one quality that enables us to become like Christ and heirs of celestial glory is charity, the pure love of Christ. Charity is the capstone of a Christlike character, and by possessing it we will be prepared to return to and abide in the presence of our Heavenly Father. President Brigham Young described in a beautiful way what it will be like when we return to our Father in Heaven: "If we could see our Father who dwells in the heavens, we should learn that we are as well acquainted with him as we are with our earthly father; and he would be as familiar to us in the expression of his countenance, and we should be ready to embrace him and fall upon his neck and kiss him, if we had the privilege." (In *Journal of Discourses*, 8:30.)

Reaching for Others

You will then have a great desire and ability to bring people to the Father through Christ—this effort will be directed by charity-filled members both to other Church members and to nonmembers. For example, Enos, after receiving a remission of sins, "began to feel a desire for the welfare of my brethren, the Nephites; wherefore, I did pour out my whole soul unto God for them." (Enos 1:9.) After receiving an assurance from the Lord that his brethren would be blessed on certain conditions, he then turned toward the Lamanites for whom he labored with many long strugglings in prayer.

Lehi, after partaking of the tree of life, immediately desired to have his family come and partake. (See 1 Nephi 8:15–16.) It pulls at my heartstrings to read of Lehi's realization that Laman and Lemuel would not come and partake, in spite of the fact that "he did exhort them with all the feeling of a tender parent, that they would hearken unto his words." (1 Nephi 8:37.)

Through their mighty missionary labors, the sons of Mosiah changed the history of the Lamanites. It all came about because, having been born again and filled with love of God, "they were desirous that salvation should be declared to every creature, for they could not bear that any human soul should perish." (Mosiah 28:3.)

Charity, the pure love of Christ, causes us to reach out to everyone we come in contact with—we sense the worth of everyone. President Brigham Young said, "The least, the most inferior spirit now upon the earth, in our capacity, is worth worlds." (In *Journal of Discourses,* 9:124.)

George F. Richards, then President of the Quorum of the Twelve Apostles, related the following experience in the October general conference of 1946, just one year after the end of World War II: "I dreamed that I and a group of my own associates found ourselves in a courtyard where, around the outer edge of it, were German soldiers—and Führer Adolph Hitler was there with his group, and they seemed to be sharpening their swords and cleaning their guns, and making preparations for a slaughter of some kind, or an execution. We knew not what, but, evidently we were the objects. But presently a circle was formed and this Führer and his men were all within the circle, and my group and I were circled on the outside, and he was sitting on the inside of the circle with his back to the outside, and when we walked around and I got directly opposite to him, I stepped inside the circle and walked across to where he was sitting, and spoke to him in a manner something like this:

" 'I am your brother. You are my brother. In our heavenly home we lived together in love and peace. Why can we not so live here on the earth?'

"And it seemed to me that I felt in myself, welling up in my soul, a love for that man, and I could feel that he was having the same experience, and presently he arose, and we embraced each other and kissed each other, a kiss of affection. . . .

"I think the Lord gave me that dream. Why should I dream of this man, one of the greatest enemies of mankind, and one of the wickedest, but that the Lord should teach me that I must love my enemies, and I must love the wicked as well as the good?

"Now, who is there in this wide world that I could not love under those conditions, if I could only continue to feel as I felt then? I have tried to maintain this feeling and, thank the Lord, I have no enmity toward any person in this world; I can forgive all men, so far as I am concerned, and I am happy in doing so and in the love which I have for my fellow men." (In Conference Report, Oct. 1946, p. 140.)

Another experience that related to Christlike conduct between Church members was given to us by Elder Bruce R. McConkie: "My grandmother, Emma Somerville McConkie, was a ward Relief Society president in Moab, Utah, many years ago. At the time of this experience, she was a widow.

"My father writes this:

" 'Mother was president of the Moab Relief Society. J _____ B _____ [a nonmember who opposed the Church] had married a Mormon girl. They had several children; now they had a new baby. They were very poor and Mother was going day by day to care for the child and to take them baskets of food, etc. Mother herself was ill, and more than once was hardly able to get home after doing the work at the J _____ B _____ home.

" 'One day she returned home especially tired and weary. She slept in her chair. She dreamed she was bathing a baby which she discovered was the Christ Child. She thought, Oh, what a great honor to thus serve the very Christ! As she held the baby in her lap, she was all but overcome. She thought, who else has actually held the Christ Child? Unspeakable joy filled her whole being. She was aflame with the glory of the Lord. It seemed that the very marrow in her bones would melt. Her joy was so great it awakened her. As she awoke, these words were spoken to her, "Inasmuch as ye have done it unto one of the least of these my brethren, ye have done it unto me." ' " ("Charity Which Never Faileth," *Relief Society Magazine*, Mar. 1970, p. 169.)

Charity and Service

I know a man who enjoyed several very beautiful experiences that led him to a marvelous understanding of the Atonement. Because of a special invitation to speak to a group of Saints on the Atonement, he approached his Heavenly Father in prayer that he might understand even more fully the majesty of that event. He indicated that shortly after he inquired of the Lord there came into his mind a half dozen or so experiences in which others had really gone out of their way to help him. He said each experience returned with such vividness that it was as though he relived each of those experiences and had a total return of the combined feelings of gratitude that had occurred each time.

While this was happening, he wondered what it had to do with the Atonement, when suddenly the experience changed. He found himself remembering many experiences when he had tried with all of his heart to lift, bless, and comfort others, and again the vividness of each memory came with a force that seemed indescribably real. The tremendous feelings of concern, anxiety, and overpowering love that had motivated him to do all he could to help others returned, and he testified that it was almost more than he could bear. He said it took some time for him to appreciate what had happened. He had knelt and asked for a greater understanding of the Atonement, and the Father in effect had impressed his heart with the following: "The whole point and purpose of the gospel is to cleanse the lives of men and women and to fill them with my love. They then will be Christlike with everyone they come in contact with, and by that love, they might successfully entice people to come to the Father through Christ."

This experience reminds us of Isaiah's statement of what the Savior would do when he came to the earth: "The Spirit of the Lord God is upon me; because the Lord hath anointed me to preach good tidings unto the meek; he hath sent me to bind up the brokenhearted, to proclaim liberty to the captives, and the opening of the prison to them that are bound." (Isaiah 61:1.)

We are the only people on earth who have been divinely

commissioned and empowered to bring people to the Father through the sacred principles and ordinances of the restored gospel of Jesus Christ. If we don't do it, no one else will, because no one else can.

Charity and the Power to Forgive

The following story told by a converted Indian, Chief Sam Blue of the Catawba Indian Nation, illustrates dramatically what the love of Christ can do in blessing us with the ability to forgive:

"One day my eleven-year-old son went hunting with six other Indians. They were hunting squirrels. A squirrel darted up a pine tree and my son climbed up the tree to scare him out on a limb. Finally the squirrel ran out where he could be seen. My boy called to the hunters to hold their fire until he could get down out of the tree. One of these Indians in the hunting party had always been jealous of me and my position as chief. He and his son both shot deliberately at my boy. He was filled with buckshot from his knees to his head. One blast was aimed at his groin and the other hit him squarely in the face. The Indians carried my boy toward our home and found a cool spot along the trail under a pine tree. There they laid him down and ran for a doctor.

"A friend came to me in Rock Hill where I had gone to buy goods and said, 'Sam, run home at once, your boy has been shot.' I thought it was one of my married sons. I ran all the way home and found that it was my little boy near death. The doctor was there. He had put the boy to sleep with morphine so he wouldn't be in so much pain. He said my boy could not live. He was right; the boy died in a few minutes.

"The man and his son who had done the shooting were out in my front yard visiting with members of the crowd that had gathered. They did not appear to be upset at their deed. My heart filled with revenge and hatred. . . . Something seemed to whisper to me, 'If you don't take down your gun and kill that man who murdered your son, Sam Blue, you are a coward.'

"Now I had been a Mormon ever since I was a young lad, and I knew it would not be right to take revenge. I decided to pray to the Lord about it. I left the house and walked to my secret place out in the timber where I always have gone to pray alone when I have a special problem, and there I prayed to the Lord to take revenge out of my heart. I soon felt better and I started back to the house. When I approached the house I heard something inside of me whisper, 'Sam Blue, if you don't kill that Indian who shot your boy, you are a coward!' I turned around and went back to my place of prayer and prayed again until I felt better. Then on my way back to the house, at the same spot along the path I heard the voice say again, 'Sam Blue, you are a coward.' I turned again and went back to pray. This time I told the Lord he must help me or I would be a killer. I asked him to take revenge out of my heart and keep it out. I felt good when I got up from praying. I went back to the house the third time and when I reached the house I went out and shook hands with the Indian who killed my boy—there was no hatred or desire for revenge in my heart." (Quoted in Marion G. Romney, *The Power of God unto Salvation*, Brigham Young University Speeches of the Year [Provo, Utah, 3 Feb. 1960], pp. 6–7.)

Almost every day I meet people who have been deeply wronged or profoundly hurt by others. I'm convinced that only by possessing the pure love of Christ as an endowment of the Spirit can we obtain the ability to forgive others completely and love them with a perfect love. Our efforts in proclaiming the majesty of the Restoration, the reality of the appearance of the Father and the Son, and the absolute necessity of repentance and cleansing in the waters of baptism will be rewarded with phenomenal success only when we reflect in all our teaching and in all our conduct the marvelous, marvelous, pure love of Christ.

President Brigham Young said: "If brethren and sisters are overtaken in fault, your hearts should be filled with kindness— with brotherly, angelic feeling to overlook their faults as far as possible." (In *Journal of Discourses*, 8:128.) On another occasion he declared, "The doctrine we have embraced takes away the stoney hearts." (In *Journal of Discourses*, 3:19.) The Prophet Joseph Smith wrote: "Love is one of the chief characteristics of Deity, and ought to be manifested by those who aspire to be the sons of God. A man filled with the love of God, is not content with blessing his family alone, but ranges through the whole world, anxious to bless the whole human race." (*History of the Church,* 4:227.)

Charity and Lifting the Poor

There is a second godly characteristic that will always manifest itself through the lives of Saints filled with charity: an effort to do everything possible to help the poor.

King Benjamin masterfully explained this characteristic: "And now, for the sake of these things which I have spoken unto you — that is, for the sake of retaining a remission of your sins from day to day, that ye may walk guiltless before God—I would that ye should impart of your substance to the poor, every man according to that which he hath, such as feeding the hungry, clothing the naked, visiting the sick and administering to their relief, both spiritually and temporally, according to their wants." (Mosiah 4:26.)

If we are to retain a remission of our sins, we must be engaged in constant, consistent, heartfelt, charitable service to our fellowmen—temporally and spiritually. Amulek strongly admonished us: "And now behold, my beloved brethren, I say unto you, do not suppose that this is all; for after ye have done all these things [faith, repentance, prayer], if ye turn away the needy, and the naked, and visit not the sick and afflicted, and impart of your substance, if ye have, to those who stand in need—I say unto you, if ye do not any of these things, behold, your prayer is vain, and availeth you nothing, and ye are as hypocrites who do deny the faith." (Alma 34:28.)

Amulek continued: "If ye do not remember to be charitable, ye are as dross, which the refiners do cast out, (it being of no worth) and is trodden under foot of men." (Alma 34:29.)

Dross is the film of impurities that rises to the surface of iron ore during smelting, which is skimmed off and thrown away. The Master Refiner will regard as dross and skim from the workmanship of his creation those who disregard the poor, turn away the needy, and fail to recognize the relationship between charity and the Atonement.

Obviously, in many respects, it is somewhat easier to clothe the naked and feed the hungry than it is to declare repentance to a sin-sick world. Nevertheless, charity embraces and makes possible the accomplishment of both with a heavensent system that can relieve the burden of poverty from the poor. In the process "the poor shall be exalted, in that the rich are made low." (D&C 104:16.)

I, like you, love the theology of the kingdom. I am fascinated with how vast it is and recognize that we all will require an extended period of time in the next life before we will know all we must know to inherit a fulness of God's glory. After all the scriptures have been read and digested, and after all the meetings have been held, the Lord's final approval of us will be determined by our one-on-one relationship with his children who stand in need.

In my classes, I have often asked my students what they think will be the bottom line at Judgment Day for entrance into God's presence. The responses have been interesting but often disappointing. It seems that the idea has been most prevalent that what we know, and not what we are, is of paramount importance. It is possible to know a great deal of truth and yet not truly be Christlike. If what we know has caused us to be more like the Savior, then so much the better—but how can we tell? How do we as Latter-day Saints know for sure that our exhaustive efforts to search the scriptures, our many labors to acquire all knowledge, our energy spent in building the kingdom, will really be translated into a celestial character that will enable us to enter into our rest?

Matthew 25:31–46 illustrates my point. We have all read these verses many times and should be familiar with the great message of the Judgment Day given to us by the Savior himself. I want to interpret those verses in my own words, still maintaining, I believe, the basic message contained therein:

In this parable of the sheep and the goats, all of mankind's labors have been performed, be they good or evil. All nations stand before the Lord. Those individuals who have accepted the

Lord and have worshiped the Father in his name, those whose garments have been made white by the blood of the Lamb, are on his right hand and are referred to as sheep. Those who have "not desire[d] that the Lord their God, who hath created them, should rule and reign over them" (Helaman 12:6) are on the Lord's left hand and are referred to as goats.

The Lord then points to those on his right hand, "Come, ye blessed of my Father, inherit the kingdom prepared for you from the foundation of the world." (Matthew 25:34.) The Lord then tells the righteous why they are there, why they are his. Then he translates the width and breadth of an eternal gospel, an eternal priesthood, and a divine church into acts of selfless service by telling the faithful: "For I was an hungred, and ye gave me meat: I was thirsty, and ye gave me drink: I was a stranger, and ye took me in: naked, and ye clothed me: I was sick, and ye visited me: I was in prison, and ye came unto me." (Matthew 25:35–36.)

This statement, taken literally, is a profound article of faith for all the faithful in Christ and is a summary statement about the kind of service that will be most natural to be performed by those who are filled with charity, the pure love of Christ. In the parable, however, the righteous seem puzzled by what the Lord says and want to know when they performed such acts of kindness for him. The righteous are so unassuming, so truly humble, and quite overwhelmed about why they are on his right hand. Then the Lord answers, "Inasmuch as ye have done it unto one of the least of these my brethren, ye have done it unto me." (Matthew 25:40.)

Paul the apostle had much to say about the effects of the Savior's love on him and he said it so well! "For I am persuaded, that neither death, nor life, nor angels, nor principalities, nor powers, nor things present, nor things to come, nor height, nor depth, nor any other creature, shall be able to separate us from the love of God, which is in Christ Jesus our Lord." (Romans 8:38–39.)

Who can say enough about charity, the pure love of Christ? Who can explain adequately that to possess charity is to possess the greatest quality it is possible for God to bestow on his children?

Charity is without question the quality that enabled the converted Nephites and Lamanites to achieve two hundred years of utopian peace: "there was no contention in the land, because of the love of God which did dwell in the hearts of the people." (4 Nephi 1:15.)

There is no question in my mind that our Heavenly Father and his Son love all of us with an unqualified love—we all are of infinite worth in the eyes of God. (See D&C 18:10–11.) Although it is true he has blessed and will continue to bless all of his children in innumerable ways, it is of extreme importance to realize that to receive a fulness of his blessings—such as the endowment of the gifts of the Spirit, the bestowal of charity, the pure love of Christ, and the marvelous promise of eternal life— we must meet certain conditions. The Lord cannot bestow such blessings upon us unless we are obedient to him and keep, with all of our hearts, his divine commandments, as they have been revealed through his prophets of the restored kingdom.

We all must recognize that as followers of Christ, we have a sacred responsibility to acquire from him that greater love so that we might give our lives in service to others. In so doing we entice others to come to the Father through Christ. There is a great power in God's love, which is charity. When we have charity, we have a desire and an ability to keep the commandments. We have a profound motivation to lift, bless, and comfort everyone who is in need. We have a compelling determination to bear witness of the Lord, "to stand as witnesses of God at all times and in all things, and in all places that ye may be in, even until death." (Mosiah 18:9.)

I know our Heavenly Father lives, that Jesus is the Christ, and that we have embraced the only system on the earth that can bring ourselves and others to a possession of the fulness of God's love and his ultimate promise of eternal life.

Chapter 10

To See His Face

In this last chapter, I would like to share some of my ideas, feelings, and suggestions about the importance of striving to see the Lord while we are yet in mortality. Even to entertain such an idea, let alone actually to experience it, seems so remote, so unattainable, so far beyond the realm of possibility that I initially (perhaps like many other Saints) simply dismissed the idea as impossible, seemingly unnecessary, and probably bordering on sign-seeking.

Yet, there are at least three reasons why we simply cannot dismiss or ignore the importance of trying with all our hearts to see the Lord. First, as we come to know the Savior through the quiet workings of the Spirit, there develops an indescribable and irresistible magnetism that draws us to him—a magnetism that seems unrelenting and increases as we learn more of him, a magnetism so powerful that countless people through the ages have been willing to give up everything they have—including their lives, if need be—to obey his mind and his will and to come to a perfect knowledge of him, which is to see him face to face. (See Ether 3:20.)

Second, there is a set, unmovable pattern that whenever God has raised up a prophet to usher in a dispensation of light and truth, that prophet is visited by the Savior himself. There seems to have been no exception. Unless the Savior appears, the prophet cannot obtain sufficient faith or disseminate adequate faith to bring about the redemption of God's children. In addition, in every dispensation, because of the testimony of the prophet, many,

many people in time have the privilege also of coming to a perfect knowledge of the Savior and of seeing him.

Third, there are in the scriptures, in the writings of Joseph Smith, and in the recorded testimonies of many of the prophets since Joseph Smith, innumerable, clear, powerful invitations to all members of the Church to seek to see the face of the Lord.

President David O. McKay expressed his feelings about the marvelous drawing power of the Savior: "It was the divine character of Jesus that drew the women of Palestine to him, that drew as a magnet the little children to Him. It was that divine personality which attracted men, honest men, pure men. . . .

"In the realm of personality, and in the kingdom of character, Christ was supreme. . . .

" . . . Each one's personality may be compared to the Savior's personality only as one little sunbeam to the mighty sun itself." (In Conference Report, Oct. 1968, p. 143.)

How grateful humanity is for the truly influential individuals who have changed the course of history and lifted nations of men and women to greater heights. Yet the lifting power centered in the Son of God, a power capable of transforming this earth and millions like it into planets of transcendent glory, a power capable of exalting all of us to the ranks of godhood, causes all of us to fall to the earth in worshipful adoration.

The Savior draws people away from sin and into a new pattern of life, away from ignorance and into correct ways of thinking, away from selfishness and into a willingness to live for him and for others, and, finally—the great and grand purpose of the gospel—the Savior draws us fully and totally to him.

When I think of the personal magnetism, or the lifting power, of the Savior, I think of a wealthy, elderly tax collector scampering up a sycamore tree so he could see Jesus as he passed along a street in Jericho. We can only imagine the excitement in Zacchaeus's heart as the Savior stopped, looked up at him, and said: "Zacchaeus, make haste, and come down; for to day I must abide at thy house." (Luke 19:5.)

Peter, the chief apostle, also comes into my mind as one who couldn't resist showing unusual excitement whenever he had an opportunity to be with the Savior. In John 21 is an account of such a demonstration. The resurrected Christ had already appeared to the Twelve on two different occasions. Peter had gone fishing with Thomas, Nathanael, and other apostles. They had fished all night without success. As the sun rose the apostles became aware of a stranger on the shore. Suddenly the stranger asked if they had any meat. They replied they didn't. The stranger then invited the fishermen to cast their net on the right side of the ship, and as soon as they did, the net was filled with fish.

John was the first to realize that the stranger was in reality the Lord. Peter, upon the same realization, simply couldn't wait for the boat to reach the shore, so he plunged into the cold waters of the Galilee and soon found himself again in company with his Lord.

Another who strongly felt the compelling urge to be with the Savior was the apostle Paul. Oh, how he loved his Lord and Redeemer! Near the end of his mortal ministry he testified to the Philippians: "For I am in a strait betwixt two, having a desire to depart, and to be with Christ; which is far better: nevertheless to abide in the flesh is more needful for you." (Philippians 1:23–24.)

The Nephites and Lamanites basked in the presence of the resurrected Christ for a day, hearing his voice and feeling his love. When he informed them that he was leaving, "the people were in tears, and did look steadfastly upon him as if they would ask him to tarry a little longer with them." (3 Nephi 17:5.)

It is a natural desire to want to be with the Savior, to want to see him face to face, to converse with him while we are yet in the flesh. It is natural to want to learn from his lips that he is pleased with our lives and that he accepts our sacrifices and efforts in his behalf.

In fact, in my opinion, no faithful Latter-day Saint can receive a remission of sins, feel a change of nature, and increase in the spirit of revelation without there being born in his heart an intense desire to see the Savior. This desire, which is of God, will grow and increase until it influences every thought and every action and becomes the driving force to harmonize his own life totally with the Savior's mind and will.

For They Have Seen Him

Aside from the scriptures, I have obtained about as much understanding about faith in Christ from *Lectures on Faith* than from any other book or combination of books. From the third lecture we learn that three things are necessary in order to exercise faith in God unto life and salvation: first, the idea that God exists; second, a correct idea of his character, perfections, and attributes; and third, an actual knowledge that the course of life an individual is pursuing is according to the Lord's will. (See *Lectures on Faith*, p. 38.)

Our great forefather Adam knew God existed, because in the Garden of Eden he was in the presence of God and "God conversed with him face to face. In his presence he was permitted to stand, and from his own mouth he was permitted to receive instruction. He heard his voice, walked before him and gazed upon his glory." (*Lectures on Faith*, p. 13.) When Adam and Eve were cast out of the Garden of Eden, their knowledge of God was not lost and, just as important, God did not cease to manifest his will to them.

Adam's experience with God is the great prototype of the pattern the Lord uses to enable men and women both to acquire and to disseminate faith to others. Both Adam and Eve could gather their children to themselves and bear testimony in great power that God lives, for they had walked and talked with him. They knew that God has a body of flesh and bones and is a loving Heavenly Father.

It appears that every prophet of every dispensation has been privileged to see and converse with God (Jehovah) and maintain communication with him. Because of that reality, "the Lord God prepareth the way that the residue of men [you and me] may have faith in Christ, that the Holy Ghost may have place in [our] hearts." (Moroni 7:32.)

Enoch "saw the Lord, and he walked with him, and was before his face continually; and he walked with God three hundred and sixty-five years, making him four hundred and thirty years old when he was translated." (D&C 107:49.) The great patriarch Abraham saw the Savior on many different occasions. One appearance is recorded as follows: "I, Abraham, talked with the

Lord, face to face, as one man talketh with another; and he told me of the works which his hands had made." (Abraham 3:11.)

The Old Testament and latter-day scripture portray the prophet Moses as having seen the Lord again and again. "And the Lord spake unto Moses face to face, as a man speaketh unto his friend." (Exodus 33:11.) "Moses was caught up into an exceedingly high mountain, and he saw God face to face, and he talked with him, and the glory of God was upon Moses; therefore Moses could endure his presence." (Moses 1:1–2.)

The Book of Mormon is one continual account of prophets and Saints who saw the Lord Jesus Christ. The second page of that sacred book of scripture records Lehi seeing "One [Christ] descending out of the midst of heaven, and he beheld that his luster was above that of the sun at noon-day." (1 Nephi 1:9.)

Lehi's son Nephi indicated that the reason he quoted at some length the writings of Isaiah was "he verily saw my Redeemer, even as I have seen him. And my brother, Jacob, also has seen him as I have seen him." (2 Nephi 11:2–3.)

When the resurrected Christ appeared on the American continent, he first manifested himself to twenty-five hundred souls, and he said to them: "Arise and come forth unto me, that ye may thrust your hands into my side, and also that ye may feel the prints of the nails in my hands and in my feet, that ye may know that I am the God of Israel, and the God of the whole earth, and have been slain for the sins of the world." (3 Nephi 11:14.)

We can only imagine how many Nephites and Lamanites saw him on the succeeding two days, for when he left after the first day, "yea, an exceedingly great number, did labor exceedingly all that night, that they might be on the morrow in the place where Jesus should show himself unto the multitude." (3 Nephi 19:3.)

Mormon, when he was but fifteen years old, was visited of the Lord and tasted of his goodness. (See Mormon 1:15.)

Moroni gave us perhaps one of the most powerful and beautiful invitations to see the Savior when he spoke of meeting us at the judgment seat of Christ: "And then shall ye know that I have seen Jesus, and that he hath talked with me face to face, and that he told me in plain humility, even as a man telleth another in mine own language, concerning these things. . . . And now, I would commend you to seek this Jesus of whom the prophets and apostles have written, that the grace of God the Father, and also the Lord Jesus Christ, and the Holy Ghost, which beareth record of them, may be and abide in you forever. Amen." (Ether 12:39, 41.)

Seek to See the Face of the Lord

One day shortly after my mission, while I was irrigating sugar beets, I took out of my pocket and read the following experience related by Allie Young Pond, a granddaughter of Lorenzo Snow:

"One evening when I was visiting Grandpa Snow in his room in the Salt Lake Temple, I remained until the doorkeepers had gone and the night-watchman had not yet come in, so Grandpa said he would take me to the main, front entrance and let me out that way. He got his bunch of keys from his dresser.

"After we left his room and while we were still in the large corridor, leading into the celestial room, I was walking several steps ahead of Grandpa when he stopped me, saying: 'Wait a moment, Allie. I want to tell you something. It was right here that the Lord Jesus appeared to me at the time of the death of President Woodruff. . . . '

"Then Grandpa came a step nearer and held out his left hand and said: 'He stood right here, about three feet above the floor. It looked as though he stood on a plate of solid gold.'

"Grandpa told me what a glorious personage the Savior is and described his hands, feet, countenance, and beautiful white robes, all of which were of such a glory of whiteness and brightness that he could hardly gaze upon him.

"Then Grandpa came another step nearer me and put his right hand on my head and said: 'Now, granddaughter, I want you to remember that this is the testimony of your grandfather, that he told you with his own lips that he actually saw the Savior here in the temple and talked with him face to face.' " (Quoted in Lewis J. Harmer, *Revelation*, pp. 119–20.)

How fully I felt the witness on that occasion that Lorenzo Snow had actually seen the Savior in the Salt Lake Temple! The feelings that came into my heart were intense, and I felt a great sense of appreciation for President Snow's marvelous experience.

214

Another experience that has continued to give me great impetus in living a better life is the following experience of Melvin J. Ballard:

"Away on the Fort Peck Reservation where I was doing missionary work with some of our brethren, laboring among the Indians, seeking the Lord for light to decide certain matters pertaining to our work there, and receiving a witness from him that we were doing things according to his will, I found myself one evening in the dreams of the night in that sacred building, the temple. After a season of prayer and rejoicing I was informed that I should have the privilege of entering into one of those rooms, to meet a glorious Personage, and, as I entered the door, I saw, seated on a raised platform, the most glorious Being my eyes have ever beheld or that I ever conceived existed in all the eternal worlds. As I approached to be introduced, he arose and stepped towards me with extended arms, and he smiled as he softly spoke my name. If I shall live to be a million years old, I shall never forget that smile. He took me into his arms and kissed me, pressed me to his bosom, and blessed me, until the marrow of my bones seemed to melt! When he had finished, I fell at his feet, and, as I bathed them with my tears and kisses, I saw the prints of the nails in the feet of the Redeemer of the world. The feeling that I had in the presence of him who hath all things in his hands, to have his love, his affection, and his blessings was such that if I ever can receive that of which I had but a foretaste, I would give all that I am, all that I ever hope to be, to feel what I then felt!" (In Bryant S. Hinckley, *Sermons and Missionary Services of Melvin Joseph Ballard*, p. 156.)

The feelings that come into my heart every time I read that experience seem to form into questions: Who wouldn't desire to taste so fully of the love of Christ that it would seem the very marrow in his bones would melt? Who wouldn't give all they have or ever hope to have to obtain the privilege of dwelling in Christ's presence forever?

Perhaps because we rarely hear of instances of men and women seeing Christ today, I was particularly encouraged to read the following statement of President Harold B. Lee: "I know that this is the Lord's work, I know that Jesus Christ lives and that he's closer to this Church and appears more often in Holy places than any of us realize excepting sometimes to those to whom he makes personal appearance." (Unpublished address, delivered at MIA Conference, 29 June 1969.)

A prophet who has had a great influence in my life was Joseph Fielding Smith. The following quotation from that beloved prophet is choice because it is not only an invitation to see the Savior from one who knew Christ so well but also a beautiful explanation of what needs to be done to accomplish that goal: "Now, what does the Lord expect of us when he says, 'Search diligently?' I think he wants us to seek His face, to call upon Him while He is near, to turn our hearts to Him. He wants us to seek righteousness, to seek an inheritance in His kingdom, to desire the association of clean, upright people both now and forever." (*Deseret News,* Church Section, 3 July 1971, p. 11.)

All of these testimonies should add to our desire to strive with all our hearts to see the Lord. Without question, though, the greatest fire that has entered my heart to testify to me that his servants have seen him and that you and I, too, can see him, has come when his anointed servants have testified that they know Jesus is the Christ. While listening to their testimonies, the Holy Ghost has confirmed to my heart that they have seen him and that you and I, too, can have the same privilege. I marvel at the graciousness of the Lord in teaching us that what they are saying goes far above and beyond the simple words they are speaking. I can't express adequately my appreciation for those in leadership positions in the Church who have paid the price to learn so fully who the Savior is and then, in bearing their witness, extend such a marvelous invitation to all of us to know the Lord as well as they do.

It is important for us to realize that we can desire to see Christ and seek with all our hearts to do so without being a sign-seeker. It is my understanding that we are not sign-seekers if we have been pleased to believe in Christ and keep his commandments solely on the evidence of the workings of the Holy Ghost — in other words, we seek to see him, not so we will believe that he is, for we already have that witness, but we seek to see him so that we might know we are acceptable to him and have become like him.

Then Shall Ye Know That I Am

There are many beautiful invitations in the scriptures for us to seek to see Christ, but the most powerful invitation of all is found in Doctrine and Covenants 93:1: "Verily, thus saith the Lord: It shall come to pass that every soul who forsaketh his sins and cometh unto me, and calleth on my name, and obeyeth my voice, and keepeth my commandments, shall see my face and know that I am."

Surely this scripture is one of the most comprehensive scriptures in all of holy writ. If we will come to know through a powerful witness of the Spirit that these words come from the Savior himself, and if we will keep them in our minds and hearts, then they will transform our lives more than the words of any other single verse of scripture.

"Every soul . . . " The Lord commences his invitation by saying, "Verily, thus saith the Lord: It shall come to pass that *every* soul . . . " (D&C 93:1; italics added.) The Lord is speaking to you, and to me, and to everyone! Black and white, yellow and brown, men and women—everyone can qualify to see the Lord. It isn't a matter of rank or high position in the Church. The invitation transcends all boundaries. One of the greatest challenges we all have is to become convinced that the Lord has invited all of us to see him. Often even those who have been faithful all their lives have a most difficult time accepting the idea that the Lord is serious when he says that everyone can see him. He wouldn't make the promise if it weren't possible to see him—he is speaking literally! The promise is true.

" . . . who forsaketh his sins . . . " Obtaining the ability to forsake our sins is a gift from the Savior. He pricks our hearts and causes us to sense that our lives are not right. He invites us to draw close to him. In our being willing to do so, he teaches us

the stark seriousness of sin and promises us the power to forsake our sins if we will believe in him.

As we forsake our sins, we will be aware that the greatest and most common sins are sins of moral indiscretion. We will be tutored by the Spirit to know that if we will keep our hearts pure by forsaking, among other things, sensual music, movies, television, and literature, we have taken an invaluable step in maturing the body and becoming pure in heart.

Confession will play an important role in our forsaking our sins, and if we seek the Lord's help, He will give us the courage to confess all of our sins to Him and the courage to confess to the bishop whatever sins we should confess to him.

In following explicitly all the steps of repentance, we will realize that we cannot be forgiven unless our hearts are broken and our spirits are contrite. Repentance is a gift of the Spirit and a necessary element in growing in the stature of Christ.

"... who ... cometh unto me ... " The Savior said, "Behold, I stand at the door, and knock: if any man hear my voice, and open the door, I will come in to him, and will sup with him, and he with me." (Revelation 3:20.) The Lord is available to us. Are we available to him? Are we really willing to open the door and invite him fully and totally into our lives? Are we keeping our eyes on Christ as we involve ourselves in the work of the Church, or are we so mechanical in what we do that our church activity is not transforming us or anyone else in the image of Christ? As we get our academic degrees and our professional training and learning, are we judging all things by and through the Savior?

We must keep our eyes riveted on the Savior if we ever expect his ordinances, principles, and programs to transform our lives. We need to realize that accomplishing what we need to accomplish will be predicated more on our allowing the Savior to use us rather than on our using the Savior. He wants us to use our minds, our hearts, and our bodies as tools in his hands to work a mighty work, and if we don't come fully to him, he cannot do so. To come unto Christ is to yield our hearts and whole souls to him that he might dwell in us and we in him, that we might become one and manifest his power, his purpose, and his love in all we do. (See John 17:21–23; Omni 1:26.)

"... who ... calleth on my name ... " King Benjamin added to our understanding of what it means to call upon the name of Christ by telling us "there shall be no other name given nor any other way nor means whereby salvation can come unto the children of men, only in and through the name of Christ, the Lord Omnipotent." (Mosiah 3:17.) Being so constantly battered with substitute names and substitute powers that promise relief from the evils of our day, it is refreshing to be reminded that the Savior and the Savior alone can offer us the way and the means by which we can be delivered fully from all sin, ignorance, and death. Unfortunately, many people tend to give lip service to the name of Christ, but they actually seek for solutions to their personal problems and for development of their character from the reservoir of men's wisdom. Until we center our lives in the Savior and believe that only by and through him can we become all we were created to become, we will enjoy nothing better than a terrestrial level of existence.

To call upon his name is to recognize the importance of mighty prayer, understanding that it is through Christ that our prayers are answered. (See Bruce R. McConkie, *Promised Messiah*, p. 335.) It is to make contact with the Savior and to know he is blessing us and changing our lives. It is also to specifically and pointedly ask for the privilege of seeing him.

Long before we rend the veil and see the face of Christ, our prayers can be as one person conversing with another. (See *Teachings of the Prophet Joseph Smith*, p. 345; Ether 12:39.) Long before we see our blessed Redeemer, it is possible through prayer to have felt of his Spirit and power so strongly that we will wonder if we could know him much better by seeing him than we already know him. There isn't anything that will do more to unlock the doors of heaven and allow the Savior to come totally into our lives than keeping the commandments, serving others, and fervently, faithfully praying to the Father in the name of our Savior, Jesus Christ.

"... *obeyeth my voice, and keepeth my commandments* ..."
It's marvelous to receive a witness that the Church is restored,
that there are living prophets, that the mind and will of the Lord
is being received, that God's commandments to all of his children
are so readily available to all who will yield their hearts to him.

We rejoice and praise God for the veritable flood of knowledge
and intelligence that has come and is coming to bless the lives
of millions. We acknowledge the sanctity of ancient and modern
scriptures and the foundation they represent for personal righteousness. We profoundly appreciate living prophets, who unlock
the great truths of the scriptures. Last, but not least, we recognize
that for ancient and modern scriptures to affect us, for living
prophets to fulfill their divine role, it is imperative that the Saints
individually enjoy personal revelation, that the scriptures and the
living prophets become the very voice of God to us, that the
scriptures and the words of living prophets become as binding
upon our hearts as if Christ himself were speaking, "whether by
mine own voice or by the voice of my servants, it is the same."
(D&C 1:38.)

I see in the scriptures that the great meaning of obeying the
voice of the Lord is our arriving at the point where we, under
the influence of the Spirit, have the voice of the Lord come to
us personally and individually: to obey the voice of the Lord is
to live by the Spirit, to teach by the Spirit, to keep the commandments in the fullest sense of the word. Indeed, it is only by
our hearing the voice of the Lord through personal revelation
that the Savior becomes our Master Potter and is able to fashion,
mold, and shape us as living clay into vessels of glory. (See Isaiah
64:8.)

How else, except through his voice, can our Redeemer become our Good Shepherd and lead us beside the still waters and
restore our souls? (See Psalm 23:2–3.) By our hearing and responding to his voice, Christ becomes our advocate with the
Father by pleading with the Father in our behalf, "Father, spare
these my brethren that believe on my name, that they may come
unto me and have everlasting life." (D&C 45:5.)

What more thrilling invitation than to be asked to drink deeply
at the well of living water and to realize the Savior is knocking

every day at the door of our heart, hoping we will invite him into our lives that he might sup with us and we with him. (See Revelation 3:20–21.)

"... shall see my face and know that I am ... " Those who have seen the Savior and have felt to share their feelings give us a glimpse of the majesty of that experience. Brother John Murdock, who boarded with the Prophet Joseph Smith in Kirtland, Ohio, during the winter of 1832–33, recorded the following in his journal:

"In one of [the prayer meetings] the Prophet told us if we would humble ourselves before God, and exercise strong faith, we should see the face of the Lord, and about midday the visions of my mind were opened and the eyes of my understanding were enlightened, and I saw the form of a man, most lovely; the visage of His face was round and fair as the sun; His hair a bright silver grey, curled in a most majestic form; His eyes a keen penetrating blue; and the skin of His neck a most beautiful white. He was covered from the neck to the feet with a loose garment of pure white—whiter than any garment I had ever before seen. His countenance was most penetrating, and yet most lovely. And while I was endeavoring to comprehend the whole personage from head to feet it slipped from me, and the vision was closed up. But it left to my mind the impression of love, for months, that I never before felt to that degree." (Quoted in *Utah Genealogical and Historical Magazine,* Apr. 1937, p. 61.)

Although we can know the Savior in a remarkable way through the witness and nurturing power of the Holy Ghost, when we see him, we will have a perfect knowledge of him. In that perfect knowledge comes a peace, comfort, strength, and intensity of love that categorizes the experience of seeing him as the single greatest experience mortal man can have. This idea was powerfully expressed by George F. Richards, President of the Quorum of the Twelve Apostles, who spoke of a dream "which I am sure was from the Lord. In this dream I was in the presence of my Savior as He stood in mid-air. He spoke no word to me, but my love for Him was such that I have not words to explain.

I know no mortal man can love the Lord as I experienced that love for the Savior unless God reveals it to him. . . .

"As a result of that dream, I had this feeling that no matter what might be required at my hands, what the Gospel might entail unto me, I would do what I should be asked to do even to the laying down of my life. . . .

"If only I can be with my Savior and have that same sense of love that I had in that dream, it will be the goal of my existence, the desire of my life." (Quoted in Ivan J. Barrett, "He Lives! For We Saw Him," *Ensign*, Aug. 1975, p. 21.)

I know that there are great reasons why we are invited to "seek the face of the Lord." I know that should we concentrate particularly on forsaking our sins, coming to the Savior, calling on his name, obeying his voice, and keeping his commandments. (See D&C 93:1.) And if we do that with determination and fervor and yet we don't see the Lord before we die, that striving to see him will have changed our lives and set us firmly on the path of salvation — the effort to see him will be its own reward.

I know there have been — and will undoubtedly yet be — many faithful, dedicated Saints who have built up the kingdom in a marvelous way, who haven't had the privilege of obtaining a perfect knowledge of the Lord by seeing his face. Yet, because of their faithfulness, they will be among those of whom it is said: "And they shall be mine, saith the Lord of hosts, in that day when I make up my jewels; and I will spare them, as a man spareth his own son that serveth him." (Malachi 3:17.) The really important thing is that we have set a course in our lives of keeping the commandments, of doing all in our power to build up the kingdom. If we follow that course, keeping our eyes upon the Son of God and acknowledging him as the source of redemption, then our lives will be rich and rewarding.

In the great discourse recorded in 2 Nephi 31 and 32, after Nephi stressed the importance of being baptized of fire and of the Holy Ghost, of pressing forward with a "steadfastness in Christ," of keeping the commandments, of having the Holy Ghost tell you all the things you should do, of enduring to the end, then he says: "Behold, this is the doctrine of Christ, and there will be no more doctrine given until *he shall manifest himself unto you in the flesh."* (2 Nephi 32:6; italics added.)

In other words, Nephi's emphasis (and I believe it should be our emphasis) is to concentrate on keeping the commandments — losing your life in doing all the Master would have you do — and then if it's his will and your desire, he will personally minister to you.

I have wondered on occasion if I would know the prophet Nephi any better when I see him than I know him now. I have noticed it's even more so with our experiences and feelings with the Savior. Long before we see him, we will be able to say, "I don't think I'll know him any better when I see him than I know him now!"

The following testimonies sum up my feeling on the importance of seeking to see the Lord. President Marion G. Romney shared this experience:

"I don't know that I'm any more certain in my convictions that it is true now than I was fifty years ago — I never remember having a doubt about the gospel being true — but there is something that's different. After three-quarters of a century, I'm beginning to get to the place where *I can reach out and take hold of the power* more than I could in my earlier years. It wouldn't be difficult to see through the veil — to see the Lord. I've heard His voice many times. . . . I shall not know any better, with more certainty, when I stand before the Savior in the not-too-distant future and see Him — and even if I feel the prints in His hands and in His side — than I know now; that the gospel is true. These things I've told you and referred to tonight are true! They're real!" (My personal notes taken during a talk given by President Romney in the Westday Ward Chapel, Santa Monica Stake, 5 Mar. 1972.)

Elder Bruce R. McConkie wrote: "Now this Lord, whose face has been seen by hosts of the righteous and whose face will yet be seen by multitudes that cannot be numbered, is in our midst from time to time, and we as a people do not see him nearly as often as we should. We are not speaking of him being in our midst in the spiritual sense that he is here by the power of his

223

Spirit. We are speaking of his personal literal presence." (*Promised Messiah*, p. 611.)

President Spencer W. Kimball bore his testimony of the promise of seeing God: "I have learned that where there is a prayerful heart, a hungering after righteousness, a forsaking of sins, and obedience to the commandments of God, the Lord pours out more and more light until there is finally power to pierce the heavenly veil and to know more than man knows. A person of such righteousness has the priceless promise that one day he shall see the Lord's face and know that he is (see D&C 93:1)." ("Give the Lord Your Loyalty," *Ensign*, Mar. 1980, p. 4.)

My own testimony is that Jesus is the Christ, the Son of the living God. I know that the Father and the Son appeared to the Prophet Joseph Smith and that through that mighty prophet they revealed anew the fulness of the gospel of Jesus Christ and restored the Savior's true church to the earth for the last time. I know that we have living prophets upon the earth today, through whom the Lord guides and directs his kingdom.

I testify of the goodness of God in sending his Only Begotten Son to suffer, die, and rise again that we all might obtain the hope of eternal life.

The centrality of the Savior is paramount in all scriptures, and especially is this true of the Book of Mormon. If we will apply in our lives what we learn from the scriptures and from living prophets, I know we can come to know the Savior better than we know anyone else and that his influence on our lives can be greater than the combined influences of everyone else. Centering our life in Christ, as we apply the gospel in everything we do, really does change us. The Lord really can change human nature; he can soften our hearts and give us an abhorrence for sin. He, even Christ, can enable us to sense the infinite worth of all of God's children and endow us with the love we need to be Christ-like to everyone we come in contact with. May he bless us to grow in the knowledge and stature of the Son of God.

BIBLIOGRAPHY

Black, Susan Easton. *Finding Christ through the Book of Mormon.* Salt Lake City, Utah: Deseret Book Co., 1987.

Charge to Religious Educators. 2d ed. Salt Lake City, Utah: The Church of Jesus Christ of Latter-day Saints, 1982.

Ehat, Andrew F., and Lyndon Cook, comps. *The Words of Joseph Smith.* Provo, Utah: Brigham Young University, 1980.

Grant, Carter Eldredge. *The Kingdom of God Restored.* Salt Lake City, Utah: Deseret Book Co., 1955.

Harmer, Lewis J. *Revelation.* Salt Lake City, Utah: Bookcraft, 1957.

Hinckley, Bryant S. *Faith of Our Pioneer Fathers.* Salt Lake City, Utah: Bookcraft, 1956.

———. *Sermons and Missionary Services of Melvin Joseph Ballard.* Salt Lake City, Utah: Deseret Book Co., 1949.

Hymns of The Church of Jesus Christ of Latter-day Saints. Salt Lake City, Utah: The Church of Jesus Christ of Latter-day Saints, 1985.

Journal of Discourses. 26 vols. London: Latter-day Saints' Book Depot, 1854–86.

Kimball, Spencer W. *Faith Precedes the Miracle.* Salt Lake City, Utah: Deseret Book Co., 1972.

———. *The Miracle of Forgiveness.* Salt Lake City, Utah: Bookcraft, 1969.

McConkie, Bruce R. *Doctrinal New Testament Commentary.* 3 vols. Salt Lake City, Utah: Bookcraft, 1965–73.

————. *Mormon Doctrine.* 2d ed. Salt Lake City, Utah: Bookcraft, 1966.

————. *The Promised Messiah.* Salt Lake City, Utah: Deseret Book Co., 1978.

McKay, David O. *Cherished Experiences.* Salt Lake City, Utah: Deseret Book Co., 1976.

————. *Gospel Ideals.* Salt Lake City, Utah: Improvement Era, 1953.

Pratt, Parley P. *Key to the Science of Theology.* Classics in Mormon Literature Series. Salt Lake City, Utah: Deseret Book Co., 1978.

Smith, Joseph. *History of The Church of Jesus Christ of Latter-day Saints.* 7 vols. 2d rev. ed. Edited by B. H. Roberts. Salt Lake City, Utah: The Church of Jesus Christ of Latter-day Saints, 1932–51.

————. *Lectures on Faith.* Salt Lake City, Utah: Deseret Book Co., 1985.

————. *Teachings of the Prophet Joseph Smith.* Selected by Joseph Fielding Smith. Salt Lake City, Utah: Deseret Book Co., 1976.

Smith, Joseph F. *Gospel Doctrine.* Classics in Mormon Literature Series. Salt Lake City, Utah: Deseret Book Co., 1986.

Smith, Joseph Fielding. *Doctrines of Salvation.* 3 vols. Compiled by Bruce R. McConkie. Salt Lake City, Utah: Bookcraft, 1954–56.

————. *Man: His Origin and Destiny.* Salt Lake City, Utah: Deseret Book Co., 1954.

Snow, Eliza R., comp. *Biography and Family Record of Lorenzo Snow.* Salt Lake City, Utah: Deseret Book Co., 1884.

Sperry, Sidney B. *Answers to Book of Mormon Questions.* Salt Lake City, Utah: Bookcraft, 1964.

Talmage, James E. *Jesus the Christ.* Classics in Mormon Literature Series. Salt Lake City, Utah: Deseret Book Co., 1982.

Taylor, John. *The Mediation and Atonement.* Salt Lake City, Utah: Deseret News Co., 1882. Reprint. Salt Lake City, 1964.

Whitney, Orson F. *Life of Heber C. Kimball.* 2d ed. Salt Lake City, Utah: Stevens and Wallis, 1945.

INDEX